Anthropology in North East India

Anthropology in North East India

Edited by

Sarthak Sengupta

GYAN

First Published, 2018

Published by

Gyan Publishing House
5, Ansari Road
Daryaganj, New Delhi-110002
Phone: 9811692060
E-mail: books@gyanbooks.com

Printed at: G. Print Process, Delhi.

Cataloging in Publication Data—DK
Courtesy: D.K. Agencies (P) Ltd. <docinfo@dkagencies.com>

Sengupta, Sarthak, 1955- **author.**
Anthropology in North East India / Sarthak Sengupta.
pages cm
Includes bibliographical references.
ISBN 9788121214247 (HB)

1. Ethnology—India, Northeastern. 2. Tribes—India, Northeastern. I. Title.

LCC GN635.I4S46 2018 | DDC 305.8009541 23

Dedicated
in memory of my teacher
Prof. Dr. Tarun Chandra Sharma
whose hallowed life has been a source of inspiration to my professional and academic quest

Contents

Foreword

With her endless splendours and bounties provided by the nature, North-East India, primarily because of her extremely vibrant disposition, earned the distinction of being one of the major hot-spots within the entire sub-continent. As a physiographic space, her lush green hills, pleasantly gentle undulations as well as the tenderly nurtured floodplains, presents an extraordinarily enchanting treat. Her mighty rivers, many among whom having perennial navigational adroitness offer a rare experience of delight.

Multiple expressions of her human composition and inherent dynamics toward the cultivation of a harmonic balance do not seem to have many parallels. Evident diversities of the cultural kaleidoscope and social formations in North-East India, with hitherto several un-interpreted puzzles and riddles, nevertheless, throw a mighty challenge, particularly to the anthropologists to resolve. Pressure from unending waves of immigrants over centuries together makes the comprehension of the entire socio-political dynamics of North-East India rather a daunting task.

Such challenges and undoubtedly much more had attracted the fairly close attention of innumerable scholars and researchers who contributed substantially toward the generation of valuable empirical information on the land and the people of this region. Beside contributions of the British administrators which are quite rich in ethnographic details, there are at least several others that endeavoured to highlight fairly comprehensive narratives of the land and people of North-East India. Such praiseworthy initiatives notwithstanding with every additional information on record, make us aware of the increasing volume of what still remains to be duly charted. Nevertheless, when such initiatives have often been primarily toward the generation of original empirical information, their adequate analysis and interpretation have remained mostly unachieved. *Anthropology in North East India* is a bold initiative toward confronting the inadequacies.

In terms of its academic coverage, the compendium edited by Prof. Sarthak Sengupta, incorporating eight essays in cultural/social anthropology, five essays in biological anthropology, three dealing with both cultural/

social anthropology as well as biological anthropology, and other two primarily concentrating on palaeoanthropology is a sufficiently comprehensive one. Altogether 29 scholars subscribed to its academic contents, 20 among whom belong to North-East India. This very fact added an extra flavour to the endeavour.

The bulk of the essays in the volume represent Assam, followed by Meghalaya, Arunachal Pradesh, Manipur, Sikkim, and Mizoram in order. Thus, despite being not totally representative of all the States of North-East India in terms of both space and proportions, the bold initiative of Prof. Sengupta and his associates to confront the knowledge gaps deserve encouragement.

Ajit K. Danda

Former Professor, Asiatic Society, Kolkata; &
Former Director,
Anthropological Survey of India

20th December 2017

Preface

North East region of India consists of eight sister states like Arunachal Pradesh, Assam, Manipur, Meghalaya, Mizoram, Nagaland, Sikkim, and Tripura. The inhabitants of the region are mostly tribes, and the non-tribals are mostly formed by the caste-Hindus, Scheduled Castes, Other Backward Classes and the Muslims. In recent years, a large number of immigrants from neighbouring countries have also entered into North East India.

North East India fascinated the anthropologists from different parts of the globe for its uniqueness with its diverse ethnic groups. During the colonial era, pioneering research in anthropology was initiated by the British administrators during the first decades of the twentieth century and ethnographic monographs were prepared on peoples like Meiteis of Manipur; Garo and Khasi of Meghalaya; Mikir (Karbi), Kachari of Assam; Lushai and Lakher of Mizoram; Angami, Sema, Rengma, Lotha, Ao and Zemi Naga of Nagaland. However, the first monograph by a trained anthropologist was on Apatanis of Arunachal Pradesh. Later several population groups of North East India like Purums (Chothe) of Manipur; Garo and Khasi of Meghalaya, Padam-Miniyong of Arunachal Pradesh and many others were studied by professionally qualified Indian scholars.

The British administrators also initiated inventive archaeological research into prehistoric past of the region and report the evidence of Stone Age tools during the latter half of the nineteenth century; however, most of these reports lack reference of any systematic explorations and excavations. Later on, findings on Paleolithic tool traditions, Microlithic industry, Neolithic sites; living megalithism and ethnoarchaeology of the region were also reported by many scholars of repute.

The physical anthropological research was also first introduced in the region at the turn of the twentieth century and since then studies are mostly concerned to assess existing biological variation amongst the population groups of the region. However, at present several anthropologists have turned their attention to investigate population affinities on the basis of globin gene traits, tetrameric STR loci, mitochondrial DNA, and Y chromosome markers.

The genesis of Anthropology as a body of knowledge in the North East Indian context is far earlier than its establishment as an academic discipline. The establishment of Anthropology as a distinct academic discipline in North East India started in 1948 with the establishment of the Department of Anthropology at Gauhati University. The Post Graduate teaching programme, however, started in 1957 only. The Department of Anthropology at Dibrugarh University, Assam started functioning in the year 1966 to impart Post-Graduate teaching and doctoral research. In North Eastern Hill University, Shillong initially the Department of Cultural Anthropology was established in 1980, which was later on renamed as Department of Anthropology in 1983. The Post-Graduate Department of Anthropology was established at Manipur University in 1984. Post Graduate course in Anthropology at Cotton College (now known as Cotton University) was introduced in 1991. In Arunachal Pradesh, the Post Graduate programme in Anthropology was started in 2001 under the aegis of Arunachal Institute of Tribal Studies (AITS), and a separate Department of Anthropology started since June 2012 in Rajiv Gandhi University (formerly known as Arunachal University) of Arunachal Pradesh. In June 2010, one more Department of Anthropology carrying out Post-Graduate teaching and doctoral research was established at Assam University's Diphu Campus. In 2012, a Department of Anthropology started functioning at Nagaland University's Lumami Campus. Department of Social System and Anthropology opened up at Sikkim University in 2013. Apart from the above-mentioned University Departments, the D.M.College of Science under Manipur University has provisions for teaching Anthropology at the Post-Graduate level. Very recently a Post Graduate teaching Department in Anthropology also started at Apex Professional University (a state Private University established in 2013) at Pasighat, Arunachal Pradesh. A good number of affiliated colleges offering anthropology at undergraduate level have also established in the region.

The research personnel attached to North East Regional Centre of Anthropological Survey of India, Shillong (established in 1953); Directorate of Research Arunachal Pradesh, Itanagar (formerly NEFA; established in 1956); the Tribal Research Institute in Shillong, Meghalaya (established in 1963 at Mawlai, Shillong for erstwhile undivided Assam); Tripura (established in 1971); Mizoram (established in 1974); Assam (created in 1977 which later on renamed as Assam Institute of Research for Scheduled Tribes and Scheduled Castes, Guwahati, Assam (established in 1990); Manipur (established in 1987); are also conducting rigorous field-based anthropological research in the region.

Although anthropological research activities in North Eastern India started long back, whatever sketchy, sporadic research work that has been done so far is not adequate enough compared to its vast expanse and numerous unexplored areas. Policymakers of the country often ignored the anthropological research findings.

The field of anthropological research in North East India is enormous and un-researched areas are numerous. Therefore the unrelenting and well-planned strategy of anthropological research and publication of research findings thereof is need of the day.

The present volume is a compilation of research articles. Contributors of the present treatise include some of the bright emerging scholars of their generation, as well as a number of celebrated anthropologists. A few articles included in the compilation are investigative in nature and to a great extent fluctuate in terms of overall attributes, but all of them are quite informative as far as the data are concerned. There is also a great need for the precise documentation of the vast body of anthropological data for the furtherance of the subject both in the national and international scenario. The volume, however, in no way can claim to have detailed coverage of the ongoing anthropological research activities on the people of the region within this inadequate space wrapping the entire aspects, but a good cross-section on emerging issues relating to man, society, and culture of the region is here reflected.

This compilation is dedicated to the memory of my teacher Late Professor Tarun Chandra Sharma, a renowned pre-historic archaeologist of our country who was born in 11 April 1929 in Dakshingaon village in Nalbari district, Assam. He received his early education from Nalbari Gurdon High School, Assam; pursued his graduation with Honours in Anthropology from Cotton College, Gauhati (1951); completed post-graduation in Anthropology from Gauhati University in 1958 and was awarded Ph.D. in Archaeology by University of London (1966). He was the recipient of the 'Gordon Childe Memorial Prize' by the University of London in 1966 and elected Fellow, Royal Asiatic Society of Great Britain (1965). Prof. Sharma after superannuation from Gauhati University in 1989 also served as Visiting Professor at North Eastern Hill University, Kohima Campus (1990-1994) and Nagaland University (1995-1997).

Prof. Sharma participated in excavations at Nevasa, Maharastra (1960-1961); excavations of Neolithic site at Daojali Hading, N.C.Hills (1961-1963); British Museum Excavation at High Lodge, Suffok, UK (1965), and Cambridge University Excavations at Norman Castle Site, Northampton, U.K (1965); Selbalgiri in the Northwest Garo Hills and Ambari in Guwahati city (1969-1971, 1996-1997); Ganol and Simsang Valleys, Meghalaya (1974-1976); exploration on the Quaternary history of Meghalaya and Assam (1977-1978); and prehistoric archaeology of the Garo Hills, Meghalaya (1983-1984); archaeological explorations and excavations in the North Cachar Hills, Assam and the Garo Hills, Meghalaya (1985-86). He also studied museum collections at British Museum, London (1963-64); Museum of Archaeology and Ethnology, University of Cambridge, U.K., (1964); Pitt Rivers Museum; Oxford University, (1964); Mus de L'Homme, Paris, (1965); Muse Von Volke Kunde, Leiden University, Netherlands (1966).

He successfully supervised five Ph.D. dissertations, written three books and more than 135 research papers and popular articles on different aspects of Anthropology and Archaeology in several national and international journals. He attended the 'International Conference on Asian Archaeology', Colombo (1969); 'International Congress of Anthropological and Ethnological Sciences', Chicago (1973); 'Congress of the Indo-Pacific Prehistory Association', Pune (1978); and 'International Congress of South Asian Archaeology of the SAARC Countries', New Delhi (1985). He was elected President of 'Indian Society for Prehistory and Quaternary Studies', Pune (1984); delivered the 'Panchanan Mitra Memorial Lectures' at Asiatic Society, Calcutta (1987) and the 'Platinum Jubilee Lecture', Indian Science Congress (1995). Professor Sharma left for his heavenly abode in 17 November 2011.

The effort expended in compiling this volume will be rewarded if this treatise proves to be informative, stimulus and of use to anthropologists besides other social scientists; administrators, planners, policymakers, academicians and scholars who have a keen interest on the land, environment, and inhabitants of North East India.

25th December 2017 **Sarthak Sengupta**

Acknowledgements

I wish to extend my personal profound gratitude to all the distinguished individual contributors and everyone who had encouraged and unremittingly assisted me in presenting this treatise. I owe a deep debt of gratitude for their academic cooperation, and moral support towards the idea of such a publication.

I am deeply beholden to Prof. A. K. Danda, Former Professor, Asiatic Society, Kolkata and President INCAA, West Bengal, who have so kindly contributed the Foreword for this volume. I would like especially to thank Dr. Arifur Zaman of Department of Anthropology, Dibrugarh University for arranging photographs for the jacket. I also express my sincere thanks to Dr. Sukanya Sharma, Indian Institute of Technology, Guwahati for her academic support.

My heartfelt thanks to all the enthusiastic and diligent staff of Gyan Publishing House, New Delhi both those I have dealt with in person or through e-mail and many others behind the sight, for undertaking the responsibility of publishing the book and bringing it out within the stipulated time.

Last but not the least; I convey my special thanks to my wife Kaveeta for her care, companionship, and support. Thanks to Sushrut, Samrat, Surovee, and Shinjinee for all the smiles which make it all worthwhile.

25th December 2017 **Sarthak Sengupta**

List of Contributors

Dipak K. Adak, Anthropological Survey of India, 27 Jawaharlal Nehru Road, Kolkata, West Bengal, 700016.

R. P. Athparia, North Eastern Social Research Centre, Jagriti, GMCH Road, Christian Basti, Guwahati, Assam, 781005.

Tiluttama Barua, Anthropology Department, Cotton University, Panbazar, Guwahati, Assam, 700001.

Gulrukh Begum, Department of Anthropology, Gauhati University, Bordoloi Nagar, Guwahati, Assam, 781014.

Premananda Bharati, Anthropology Unit, Indian Statistical Institute, 203, Barrackpore Trunk Road, Kolkata, West Bengal, 700108.

Juri Borah, Department of Anthropology, Dibrugarh University, Dibrugarh, Assam, 786004.

Sumitabha Chakraborty, Anthropological Survey of India, Eastern Regional Centre, Kolkata, West Bengal, 700064.

P. Chetry, Anthropology Department, Cotton University, Panbazar, Guwahati, Assam, 700001.

Rajat Kanti Das, Department of Anthropology, Vidyasagar University, Midnapore, West Bengal, 721102.

Pynshailang Dohling Department of Anthropology, North Eastern Hill University, Umsning, Shillong, Meghalaya, 793022.

Dali Dutta, Department of Anthropology, Dibrugarh University, Dibrugarh, Assam, 786004.

Munmi Gogoi, Department of Anthropology, North Lakhimpur College, Khelmari, Lakhimpur, Assam, 787031.

P. Kashyap, Anthropology Department, Cotton University, Panbazar, Guwahati, Assam, 700001.

Namgyal Lepcha, Passingdang, Upper Dzongu, Mangan, North Sikkim, 737116.

H. C. Mahanta, Dibrugarh University, Dibrugarh, Assam, 786004.

Mayanglambam ManiBabu, Department of Anthropology, Manipur University, Chanchipur, Imphal, 795 003

Barun Mukhopadhaya, Biological Anthropology Unit, Indian Statistical Institute203 Barrackpore Trunk Road, Kolkata, West Bengal, 700108.

Evelyn Ngaithianven, Department of Anthropology, Panjab University, Chandigarh, 160014.

R.K.Pathak, Department of Anthropology, Panjab University, Chandigarh, 160014.

J. Phukan, Anthropology Department, Cotton University, Panbazar, Guwahati, Assam, 700001.

Geetika Ranjan Department of Anthropology, North Eastern Hill University, Umsning, Shillong, Meghalaya, 793022.

Shovanjan Sarkar Department of Anthropology.Vidyasagar University, Midnapore, West Bengal, Midnapore, 721102.

Chandana Sarmah, Department of Anthropology, Gauhati University, Gopinath Bordoloi Nagar, Jalukbari, Guwahati, Assam, 781014.

Sarthak Sengupta, Department of Anthropology, Dibrugarh University, Dibrugarh, Assam, 786004.

Chandra Jyoti Sonowal, Centre for Study of Social Inclusion and Inclusive Policies, Tata Institute of Social Sciences, Deonar Mumbai, 400088.

Ratna Tayeng, Department of Anthropology, Rajiv Gandhi University, Rono Hills, Itanagar, Arunachal Pradesh, 791111.

Haobijam Vokendro S. Department of Anthropology, Rajiv Gandhi University, Rono Hills, Itanagar, Arunachal Pradesh, 791111.

Arifur Zaman, Department of Anthropology, Dibrugarh University, Dibrugarh, Assam, 786004.

Lucy T. V. Zehol, Department of Anthropology, North Eastern Hill University, Umsning, Shillong, Meghalaya, 793022.

List of Tables

Chapter - 1

Prehistoric Archaeological Research in Northeast India: A Critical Review

—H. C. Mahanta

Introduction

Geographically, Northeast India, through which India touches the high Asia, is destined to play the most crucial role in shaping the Indian nation in the eastern part of the country. This region of India could rightly be equated with former Northwest India, through which India was linked with Western and Central Asia. Earlier the whole of Northeast India was known as Assam. Prehistoric archaeological research from this vast and one of the most strategic regions of India is still so inadequate that any attempt to trace the course of the unrecorded past human history becomes a difficult task.

Since 1839, when Jame's Princep deciphered the Brahmi Script and put ancient India on a well-founded chronological base, and in 1861, when Cunningham carried on the first systematic archaeological exploration in the country, archaeology in India achieved a commendable success in undertaking the lost and buried human civilisation of India. Unfortunately, this wave of archaeological research hardly permeates into Northeast India. Consequently, Northeast India was not receiving any attention of archaeologists and researchers of repute in the pre-independent period. Even in the post-independent period, it was not that way considered as it was done in other parts of India.

Northeast India can be considered as a corridor for connecting the Indian subcontinent to the Eastern world. The region lying at the junction of East Asia, South Asia and Southeast Asian countries have played an important role in early human migration and hence, cultural affinities can be traced throughout the time leading to rich cultural heritage in this part of the country. Northeast India lays between 22° and 29°18′ north latitude and 89° 40′

and 97°22′ east longitude covering eight Indian states of Assam, Arunachal Pradesh, Manipur, Meghalaya, Mizoram, Nagaland, Tripura and Sikkim, surrounded by international boundaries of Nepal, Bhutan, China, Myanmar and Bangladesh. The region can be divided into two geological settings *viz*; the plain regions covering the districts located in the Brahmaputra and Barak basins of Assam and Tripura, the remaining states are hilly and forested geological settings.

The present status of prehistoric archaeological research is very poor and it can still be considered as *terra incognita* compared to other parts of India. In this regard, mention can be made about the statement by Mills in the 1930s the spade, *'the chief tool of archaeologists had hardly been used in research in Assam'* which is still valid in the present context too.

Archaeologists, all over the world are of the opinion that the knowledge of the archaeology of Northeast India is very important and essential to understanding the world archaeology. This is because of the fact that, this region is known to have played an important role in the domestication of a number of edible plants essential for man including rice. Archaeologists dealing with the global archaeological problem are very much interested in the archaeological potentialities of Northeast India, as evident from the writing of Glover. He quoted "India is the centre of greatest diversity of domesticated rice with over 20,000 (out of 50,000) identified species and Northeast India is the most favourable single area of the origin of domesticated rice" (Glover, 1985: 266). Further its location in the border of the mainland Southeast Asia in one hand and the India on the other also considered to be a strategic one.

Realising the importance of Northeast India in archaeological research, the Indo-Pacific Prehistory Association, Canberra, in its Pune Congress, December 1978 fostered the following resolution:

> *"In view of the importance of prehistory of Northeast India confirmed by the papers presented at the conference of Indo-Pacific Prehistory Association in Pune, as (i) a potential area for the domestication of a number of important plants, and (ii) a physical and cultural bridge between the body of India and Southeast Asia. The General body of the IPPA recommends the desirability of an intensified archaeological research programme in Northeast India to realise the potentiality of the area"* (Wissowa, 1980: 2-5).

Paddayya (2002-2003: 291-301) has highlighted the prehistoric archaeological potentialities of Northeast India in his article on the status of archaeological research of India rightly stated in his own words

"Northeast India, which has in recent years yielded Pre-Neolithic Cultural assemblages, offer excellent scope for investigating diversity in human adaptations. Forming as it does a halfway house between Indian mainland and Southeast Asia, this area probably enabled early societies to develop individual identities of their own."

Despite the prehistoric efficacious, this region could draw only marginal attention in academic arena due to several drawbacks such as less academic departments/research institute, relying on age-old approach, lack of adequate technological knowledge and multidisciplinary approach, infrastructure etc. These are some of the factors in limiting problem-oriented research with recent development in the discipline. In the archaeological map of India, this region is left blank. The reason behind the blank space is due to a limited number of explored and excavated sites with stratigraphic cultural sequence corroborated with absolute chronology. Apart from the above drawbacks, there are several physical problems in prehistoric archaeological research in this area. Some of the main problems are as under:

1. Lack of reliable Pleistocene Stratigraphy, if otherwise existed might have been covered by the present Holocene deposits;
2. The luxuriant vegetation coverage in the hilly areas of Northeast India does not allow for prospecting archaeological materials on the surface;
3. The region falls under the Tropical Rainforest zone. The long duration of rainy season becomes unfavourable for archaeological exploration and excavation;
4. Most of the areas are at present inaccessible due to insurgency problem;
5. Erosion of surface soil cover due to Shifting cultivation cultivation in hilly areas resulting displacement of the context of the archaeological materials and deposits;
6. Poor preservation of archaeological and organic materials in this region due to the humidity of the climate and nature of acidic soil.

Further, it is very sad to say that, after being established a potential area for archaeological research till date, not single collaborative archaeological research have initiated in Northeast India. So Northeast India in spite of its great potentialities would perhaps remain as an archaeologically unknown area. Despite so many constraints and shortcomings, some prehistoric archaeological researches have been done in this region and in the present chapter, an attempt has been made to critically highlight some of the important issues for further research in this region.

Evidence of Human Occupation in Northeast India

Few attempts have been made to establish the earliest human occupation in Northeast India. In recent years, it is observed that establishing the earliest human occupation is one of the major research issues in Prehistoric Archaeology that is evident from various attempts made by different scholars in different parts of the world. A good number of researches on Prehistoric Archaeology have been done in recent years; however, there are hardly any attempts to trace out the deposits for early human occupation in Northeast India. This is perhaps due to lack of datable evidence in the archaeological context. On circumstantial evidence, Northeast India as it connects Indian Subcontinent with East and Southeast Asian landmass may have acted as a possible mid-way from Africa to Southeast Asia through South Asia for the Eastward dispersal of early hominids. Many early Palaeolithic sites are found in neighbouring Southern China dated to early Pleistocene geological period. If Northeast India has acted as a corridor for these dispersals, great possibilities occur to have many unexplored sites dated to the early Pleistocene period.

The earliest signs of human occupancy in the Northeast region are generally believed to have occurred during the Neolithic period or at the earliest, mid-palaeolithic times. The wide spread occurrence of Palaeolithic tools, Mesolithic tools, Neolithic tools and Megaliths in the region suggests a continuation of human culture since early Pleistocene period. Whether these very early settlers evolved into successive generations of pre and protohistoric human societies is difficult to answer at this moment. The present distribution of different racial and linguistic groups leads one to believe that the earliest occupancy of this region were the Mongoloid people. On the basis of linguistic evidence, three distinct groups occupying the region can be identified. The Mongoloid people, speaking Tibeto-Burman language, were perhaps the first group to arrive from Tibet or adjacent areas followed by people of peripheral mountains, including the Nagas who spilled over from the Burmese highland. The Austric or Austro-Asiatic groups represented by the Khasis-Syntengs were one of the early settlers, in Northeast India, who settled the hilly areas away from the Brahmaputra valley. The next important group that arrived in Northeast India, though remained confined to Brahmaputra valley, were the Indo-Aryans who brought with them an Indo-Aryan language and culture. Regarding the migration of Tibeto- Burman language family. Driem (1998:67-102) stated that "*the proto homeland of Tibeto-Burman language family in Szechwan Yunnan, which is the present geographical centre of these languages. The first migration within the language family out of this area was the migration of the Western Tibeto-Burman to the fluvial plains of the Brahmaputra and the surrounding hill tracks. Neolithic implements found in this area represent artefacts of the Eastern Indian Neolithic, for which neither calibrated nor stratigraphic dates are available".* Worman (1949:181-200) of the Washington Academy of Science in his essay on *The Neolithic Problem in the Prehistory of India* paid special attention to the Neolithic cultures of Assam with a view to supporting his theory of Eastern Asiatic origin of Neolithic Celt making tradition in India. Later Dani (1960), who classified the Neolithic tools found in various parts of Northeast India into 6 (six) zones viz. Cachar Hills Zone, Sadiya Frontier Zone, Naga Hills Zone, Khasi Hills Zone, Garo Hills Zone and Brahmaputra Valley Zone demonstrated the similarity of stone tools and pottery tradition with various parts of Southeast Asia and East Asia. Based on the characteristic tools viz. ground flat celts and shouldered celts, and cord-marked pottery and the assumptions put forth by Worman (1949), Dani (1960) and Driem (1998) we may try to make inferences that the Eastern Indian Neolithic was connected to Western Tibeto-Burman linguistic group. Bellwood (Paddayya and Bellwood, 2002: 328) believe that the two language families of Neolithic Southeast Asia were probably Austronesian and Austro-Asiatic. The time period for migrations of the Austro-Asiatic speakers to Northeast India has not been dated until now, but it is assumed to be earlier than the Tibeto-Burman speakers. Geldern (1945:138) formulated an elaborate migration theory that associated certain styles of stone implements with prehistoric population movements. He identified Eastern Indian Neolithic with the ancient Austro-Asiatic forebears of the Munda, whereby he presumed that the Austro-Asiatic spreads into India from Southeast Asia.

Palaeolithic Evidence in Northeast India

Northeast India is left blank in the Palaeolithic map of India. In the post-Independent period, several attempts have been made by many scholars to trace out the palaeolithic history of Northeast India. As a result, a good number of Palaeolithic tools have been unearthed from many areas of Northeast India. On the basis of tool typology and tool technology, these were studied by many scholars and classified them and placed them in different phases of Palaeolithic periods. One of the main problems with these Paleolithic materials is that most of them are found on the surface with Neolithic stone tools and potteries in mixed up condition. Garo Hills of Meghalaya provide the largest amount of Palaeolithic stone tools, but the chrono-stratigraphic context of the materials is still not well established. The prehistoric tools from Garo Hills are studied by various scholars like Goswami and Bhagabati (1959a, 1959b), Sharma (1967), Medhi (1980), Sonowal (1987), Mahanta (1995). Sharma (1972) has divided the prehistoric cultures into the Palaeolithic, Mesolithic and Neolithic culture. In 1969, Sankalia visited Garo Hills and was convinced that some of the sites discovered earlier yielded palaeoliths. He incorporated some of these materials in his book *Prehistory and Proto-history of India and Pakistan* (Sankalia, 1974: 41-43). However, Ghosh (1978:6-25) has strongly contradicted the occurrence of Palaeolithic artefacts in Garo Hills and he referred to the tools as "Neolithic debitage" and he further argues that the climate was not favourable for the early man and they failed in adopting in the Garo Hill. After realising the problems of archaeological research in Northeast India, Sundara (1985:39-57) writes " In view of the many practical difficulties confronting archaeologists in Assam, a national study team of scientists and archaeologists should be sent for carrying out the systematic survey and large-scale excavations". Rajaguru (1977-78) carried out an extensive survey on the quaternary formations in Garo Hills with a view to preparing a background of quaternary geology for the Stone Age cultures reported earlier. Sharma (1972), Medhi (1980) while studying the quaternary formations in Garo Hills observes that the Palaeolithic materials occur in sub-recent terraces and weathered rock surfaces of the late Quaternary period. They term these artefacts as 'Pre-Neolithic'. On the basis of further research on the stone artefacts and their context in Garo Hills, they further point out that the tools are not found in stratified context, and the chipped stone artefacts are not simply 'Neolithic debitage' as expressed by Ghosh; but purposefully knapped artefacts.

Arunachal Pradesh is the easternmost state of India. It touches Bhutan, Tibet, China and Burma. Through the mountain passes of the Arunachal Hills India maintained contact with the above countries throughout the ages. The Eastern Himalayan States, therefore, holds the key to study the East-West cultural contacts that are known to have persisted since the prehistoric times. Researches into the prehistoric archaeology of the state were initiated by the British Administrators. After Anderson (1871) and Banerjee (1924), the fascinating discoveries were made in the post-independent period. Bopardikar (1972:1-8), of Archaeological Survey of India with a multidisciplinary team, explored the Daphabhum area of Lohit district of Arunachal Pradesh brought to light evidence of Palaeolithic tools but without stratigraphic context. Singh (1993) also claimed to have been unearthed some palaeolithic tools from Manipur but failed so far in establishing an undisputed chronology for the prehistoric cultures prior to the Neolithic.

Tripura the southeastern-most border state of Northeast India is found to have occupied a crucial position in respect of prehistoric cultures of the region. The prehistoric cultural materials of the state were brought to light by the Geologists B.C. Poddar and N.R. Ramesh of the Geological Survey of India (Poddar and Ramesh, 1983:1-4). They discovered several Stone Age sites in parts of Haora and Khowai river valleys around Agartala. The implements were found exposed on eroded surfaces of river terraces, which have been dated by the C-14 method to Late Pleistocene (T_1) 35,690 ±3,050 B.P. Further, Ramesh opined that "—— this date has enabled us to establish firmly for the first time the chronology of the palaeolithic period of Northeast India" (Ramesh, 1987: 321). This has to help set aside all the doubt expressed by some scholars about the palaeolithic man and their culture in Northeast India.

Early-Holocene Evidence in Northeast India

The Mesolithic cultural evidence from Northeast India has been discovered from Garo Hills of Meghalaya and from Manipur. The Mesolithic of Northeast India is unique development so far its tool traditions are concerned and the period represented two distinct tool traditions: the Microliths and the Hoabinhian (Sharma, 1985:91). The microliths unearthed from Garo Hills were from the sites Bibragre, Nagalbibra, and Selbalgre-II. The excavation at Selbalgre–II represents a distinct Mesolithic horizon consists of microliths and hoabinhian (sumatraliths) tools (Mahanta, 1995). The Hoabinhian from Garo Hills was first reported by Sharma (1979) from a terrace site at Rongram. Singh (1983: 1-26) discovered two Stone Age sites in Manipur viz. Napachik and Nongpok Keithelmanbi. Singh has classified the cultural materials of Napachik into two phases:

(i) Edge ground knife of the Hoabinhian characters;
(ii) The fully ground celts and handmade cord-marked pottery.

The archaeological materials unearthed from Nongpok Keithelmanbi were classified into Palaeolithic, Hoabinhian and Corded ware and curved paddle impressed ware cultures (Singh, 1986:1-86). It is interesting to note here that the same type of tools seldom found in other parts of India. Therefore, occurrences of Hoabinhian with microliths may be considered a unique Mesolithic phase developed in Northeast India. However, this statement could only be confirmed by reviewing and comparing the tools with the other state of India and abroad.

As far as Mesolithic artefacts of Northeast India are concerned, neither Indian nor Southeast Asian typological variants are truly represented. However, the morphology of the tools of Northeast India suggests an Indian influence, particularly on the tools of the Palaeolithic phase and a dominance of South and Southeast Asian cultural tradition, is viewed in the Mesolithic and later cultural phases. This is true that culture cannot develop in isolation. But why at one stage of its development, the prevailing dominant cultural tradition fell into decline and thereby making way for another tradition to enter into. This cannot be explained only in terms of cultural diffusion. The ecological, geological and geographical situation must be considered for such interpretation. The geologists are not interested particularly in recent geological history i.e. Quaternary period. However, many geologists (Singh, 1969:1-9; Dutta, 1969: 43-49) pointed out some epeirogenic events occurred in the quaternary period but details are lacking. Sankalia (1974:298) while justifying the peninsular influence on Pleistocene cultures commented: "Geologically the separation of Assam plateau seems to the have been taken place at the end of the Pleistocene or Early in Holocene". The above reasoning justifies that due to the separation of Assam plateau from the mainland of India paved the way for the South and Southeast Asian Cultures. Because of this perhaps, in later prehistoric period Southeast Asian cultural tradition especially the Hoabinhian and Neolithic were dominating in Northeast India. As Northeast India lies nearer to the Hoabinhian complex, it can reasonably be expected that some amount of Hoabinhian cultural influence filtered through Burma via Manipur than to Garo Hills. This has also been justified by the presence of Anyathian cultural evidence recently discovered by Ramesh (1989) at Agartala, Tripura. As far as the chronology of the Hoabinhian culture is concerned many scholars considered the tradition to be of Post-Pleistocene and therefore 'Mesolithic' (Matthews, 1968:94). But Dunn (1970), Golson (1971) and Solheim II (1969) all suggested a Late Pleistocene date for the beginning of the Hoabinhian. But as far as Garo Hills Hoabinhian complex is concerned, no firm chronological ordering in terms of absolute date is available. However, Sankalia (1981: 126) and Rajaguru (1981:5) who worked in Garo Hills proposed a cultural chronology of the prehistoric period of Meghalaya and given c. 10,000-5,000 B.C. date for the Mesolithic culture of Northeast India.

Neolithic Origin in Northeast India

The Neolithic culture of Northeast India is characterised by the predominance of shouldered celts, cord-marked pottery and rice agriculture are more or less similar to the Neolithic cultures of East Asia and Southeast Asia (Dani, 1960). The Neolithic culture of Northeast India has no strict parallels within the Indian Sub-Continents though the shouldered celts have a sporadic distribution in the adjacent areas of Eastern India.

In Northeast India, during the 1960s and 1970s, some important excavations were carried out, one in the North Cachar Hills (1961-1963) and two in the districts of Kamrup (1972-1974) and another in Garo Hills (1967-68). These excavations authenticated the Neolithic assignments of ground stone tools and pottery. In 1963, Goswami and Sharma carried out excavations at Daojali Hading in North Cachar Hills of Assam which have given for the first time stratigraphical occurrence of ground or polished axes and also pottery. Sixty five Stone implements were recovered from the excavations, 60 from the road cutting section and 77 from the surface. The excavated ones comprise of an edged tool, grinding stones, querns, mullers, quartzite pebbles and fossil wood. The raw materials used as shale, sandstone, quartzite and fossil wood. Shale was used for making edged tools and so also fossil wood; sandstone for grinding stones whetstones, querns etc. which are locally available. Out of over 600 potsherds, 595 were of cord-marked variety, 19 of stamped dull red variety, and 11 of brick red variety. The majority of the potsherds are heavily weathered, and those few that were well backed are relatively in good condition. Shapes and forms of vessels are difficult to make out, as the potsherds were found in small fragments (Goswami and Sharma 1963). The Archaeological research team Department of Anthropology, Gauhati University conducted an excavation at the site called Selbalgre-II in Garo Hills (IAR, 1967-1968). The excavation reveals occurrences of ground and polish Neolithic celts and plain hand-made pottery. Rao conducted excavations at the Neolithic site called Sarutaru in Kamrup district, Assam during 1967-73. The cultural contents recovered from the excavations include nine ground stone celts and potsherds. The celts are made of a slate of grey to black colour sandstone of cream to buff colour and are manufactured in two stages: chipping and grinding. The stone tools are classified into two types: (a) Shouldered celts and (b) Round-butted axes. Several potsherds were recovered in association with the stone axes which does not have complete shape. The pottery is hand-made and made of clay mixed with quartz particles. The three ceramic types on the basis of colour are brown, buff and grey. The ceramics are sometimes decorated with cord impressions or basket-impressions in the form of either parallel or crisscross lines with a paddle which is wrapped in cord or matting. The neck or rim portion is plain without any sort of decoration. The ceramic tradition is similar to the ceramics of Daojali Hading of North Cachar Hills, Assam. Marakdola, another excavated site at a distance of one kilometer from the Neolithic site of Sarutaru reveal wheel turned pottery of fine kaolin clay and a shouldered celt. Rao argues for a provisional date about the beginning of Christian era for the Neolithic Sarutaru (Rao, 1973). The other excavated sites like Parsi-Parlo (Ashraf, 1990), and Manipur (Singh, 1993) have yielded numerous potsherds, basically the cord-marked and other hand-made potteries. The Neolithic culture of Northeastern India is distinguished by the predominance of shouldered celts and the characteristic cord-marked pottery. The shouldered tool type has a sporadic distribution in the adjacent states of Eastern India.

Yet, as far as the Neolithic period is concerned, there appears to be no doubt about the relationship between Northeastern India and the countries of Southeast Asia and East Asia. Cord-impressed pottery is the predominant ceramic ware in Northeast India. The occurrences of pottery and stone tools like celts related to agriculture in the same stratigraphic horizons at the sites like Daojali Hading, Sarutaru in Assam, Selbalgre-II in Meghalaya, Parsi-Parlo in Arunachal Pradesh and Phunan in Manipur indicates similarity in the chronology for origin and evolution of pottery and agriculture during the Neolithic period. It is most likely that is the nearest area to China and the Southeast Asian countries, Northeast India was under the strong influence of these cultures during this period. The present-day shifting cultivation in Northeast India, often related to the Neolithic agricultural system, may be an adaptation strategy of the Neolithic people of this area. Roy (1981:193-221) did an elaborate study on the types of artifact from both prehistoric and modern-day slash and burn cultivation. He studied the agricultural implements from the Neolithic sites of the Garo hills, and the tools of ethnographic contexts. According to him, the tools from the Neolithic sites and the ethnographic situation at Garo Hills reveal homogeneity in function. Looking at the tools, it can be presumed that they were used for the primitive type of agriculture resembling the present day shifting cultivation prevalent among many of the populations living in hilly areas. So far we do not have direct palaeo-botanical evidence of cultivated plants in Northeast India to date, but there is ample evidence Neolithic ground and polish tools found an entire region confirms a full-fledged food producing culture. Further, there are various species of wild rice in Northeast India, such as *Oryza rufipogon, Oryza officinalis, Oryza perennis,* and *meyeriana*, which are found in different ecological habitat (Bakalial, 2004). Considering the different varieties of wild and domesticated rice found in this region, Hazarika (2006) argues for an early domestication process of rice in this area. Till date, archaeologists, scholars of the relevant field of expertise have not tried either to understand the potential of modern species of wild and domesticated plants and animals or to trace their origin in Northeast India.

Living Megalithism

Megaliths are a common feature in different parts of the world, including India. Such structures are generally tested in prehistoric times. The meanings are varied, and studies have provided diverse insights into the socio-political, economic and ideological life of prehistoric societies. Majority of these studies are concerned with how they played an important role in the beginnings of early agricultural communities, and creation of complex polities (Renfrew, 1976). In India, however, despite the meanings inherent in them, two independent traditions are seen. One, which is clearly of prehistoric context as found in south India characterised by iron and black-and-red pottery occurring in direct association and hence datable to the Iron Age (1000 BC-1000 AD). The second, found in Eastern and Central India, shows a living tradition with strong cultural connotations. These two groups clearly had no connection at all (Furer-Haimendorf, 1945; Ramachandran, 1971). These megaliths in Eastern and Central India show morphological and functional variations, as well as the diversity of beliefs in contemporary megalithic cultures. Therefore it is difficult to categorise them. In Northeastern India, megaliths are found widely distributed in the Khasi-Jaintia Hills of Meghalaya (Godwin-Austen, 1872; Gurdon, 1914), in Naga-dominated areas of the districts of Chandel, Ukhrul, Tamenglong, Senapati and Churachandpur in Manipur (Singh, 1985; Devi, 2011), in North Cachar Hills and Karbi Anglong districts of Assam (Hutton, 1929; Mills and Hutton, 1929; Bezbaruah, 2004), and in Kohima and Phek districts of Nagaland populated by Angamis and others (Dewar, 1966; Jamir, 1998). In these areas there exists a living tradition among the tribal communities of the erection of megalithic monuments and linked beliefs—this cultural practice associated with the megaliths among living communities is referred to as living megalithism (Marak and Jangkhomang, 2012b). Megaliths in Northeast India have different meanings to different people. For instance, among the Nagas living neighbouring states of Manipur and Nagaland, erection of megaliths takes place after a series of feasts of merit by the merit seeker (Dewar, 1966; Singh, 1985; Jamir, 1998; Devi, 2011). Thus, they act as a symbol of status. Among the Garos of Meghalaya, whenever a new village is set up, the clan members of the founding mother erect a set of menhirs (Marak, 2012), thus acting as foundation stones. Among the Jaintias too there are different meanings inherent in these lithics. However, a few of these structures have now been relegated to the background after the coming of Christianity (Marak and Jangkhomang, 2012b). The study of this culture among the Jaintias gains importance since they are a matrilineal group with megaliths dominating their geo-cultural space. Rao (1991) while discussing the origin and chronology concludes that one has to pay attention to the social and ideological aspects of different megalithic cultures before aiming at establishing affinities and common origin. Several scholars tried to establish the relationship between the megaliths of Northeast India and Southeast India, but there have to be confirmed more precisely with chronometric dates for a better understanding of the chronology shedding more light on the Neolithic-Megalithic relationship.

Prehistoric Cultural Linkage

Geographically and culturally Northeast India interconnects the areas of South Asia, Southeast Asia, and East Asian countries. Therefore, it is worthy to presume cultural linkage within these regions from earliest times. The study was done by Dani (1960) on some Neolithic stray finds suggest that the Neolithic stone tools and pottery have morphological similarities with that of Southeast Asia and China. The occurrence of shoulder ground and polish tools in Northeast India, Bengal, Bihar, and Orissa link these regions with Southeast Asia. Various excavated sites like Daojali Hading, Sarutaru, Selbalgre-II, Parsi-Parlo and Phunan Hills of Manipur have yielded numerous cord-marked wares and other hand-made wares have similarities with the potteries of Southeast and East Asia. These kinds of wares are also found in many eastern and Central Indian Neolithic sites like Koldihawa and Mahagara and even in Nepal (Corvinus, 1996:43-55). At the site of Nongpok Keithalmanbi of Manipur with Neolithic tools and cord-marked pottery, a charcoal sample from the cord-marked ware stratum has been dated to 4,460 ±120 years B.P. The cord-marked pottery and its general decoration pattern can be compared with the Lungshanoid ware decoration of South China (Singh, 1993).

Ramesh (1989) brought to light some artefacts made on silicified fossil wood from west Tripura. The use of silicified fossil wood as a raw material for making tools was earlier recorded by Goswami and Sharma (1963) in Daojali Hading of North Cachar Hills, and recently there are many sites yielding fossil wood artefacts in Lulmai Hills and Chaklapunji area of Bangladesh (2007). The uses of fossil wood for making tools were extensive in the Anythian culture of Burma (Myanmar). This may be considered a sign of cultural links of this region to the Neolithic culture of Myanmar and Bangladesh. The discovery of Hoabinhian artefacts in various sites in Northeast India may again imply connections with Southeast Asian Holocene culture. The Hoabinhian sites are spread over a board region from Southern China, North Vietnam, Malaya, Thailand, Laos, Cambodia, Sumatra, Taiwan and Northeast India (Sharma 1988).

Observation

From the above discussion, it is clear that Northeast India has prehistoric archaeological records belonging to different cultural periods. However due to lack of absolute chronology we still have doubts in placing the development of the various cultural phases in proper stratigraphic sequences. The earliest human occupation and palaeolithic evidence are still doubtful. Though we have the Mesolithic and Neolithic artefacts, the settlement and subsistence pattern is yet to be known properly. Bio-archaeological data is also lacking here. Therefore authentication of domestication of plants and animals is a difficult task. The Megalithic tradition is still persisted among various communities of this region and has remained as an integral part of their socio-cultural and religious life. This region is also lacking Proto-historic cultural phases and hence inferences of the transformation from the prehistoric past to the historical period are also not possible at this stage. To overcome this infamy, more scientific and systematic multidisciplinary approach is required with more chronometric attempts for revealing the prehistoric heritage of Northeast India.

References

Ashraf, AA.1990. *Prehistoric Arunachal: A Study of the Prehistory and Ethno-archaeology of Kamla Valley*, Itanagar; Directorate of Research, Government of Arunachal Pradesh.

Bakalial, D. 2004. *Banaria Dhan* (in Assamese) Guwahati; Prantik.

Bezbaruah, D. 2004. *Megalithic Remains in Karbi Anglong District, Assam: A Study in the Context of Karbi Culture*. Unpublished Ph.D. Thesis, Department of Anthropology, Gauhati University, Guwahati.

Corvinus, G. 1996. 'The prehistory of Nepal after 10 years of research', *Bulletin of Indo-Pacific Prehistory Association*, 14: 43-55.

Dani, AH. 1960. *Prehistory, and Proto-history of Eastern India*, Calcutta: Firma K. L.Mukhopadhyay.

Devi, PB. 2011. *Megalithic Culture of Manipur*. Delhi: Agam Kala Prakashan.

Dewar, S. 1966. 'The ceremony of erecting a Megalith among the Angami Nagas', *Folklore* 77 (4): 264-269.

Driem, GV. 1998. 'Neolithic correlates of ancient Tibeto-Burman migration', In Roger Blench and Matthew Spriggs (Eds.): *Archaeology and Language-II: Archaeological Data and Linguistic Hypotheses*. London and New York: Routledge.

Flemming, A. 1973. 'Tombs for the living', *Man* 8(2):178-193.

Furer-Haimendorf, C.1945. 'The problem of megalithic cultures in Middle India', *Man in India* 25 (2): 73-86.

Ghosh, AK. 1978. 'What happens when the cultural and biological ability of man fails? A case study with the Palaeolithic period in the Garo Hills'. In AC Bhagabati (Ed): *Cultural and Biological Adaptability of Man with special reference of Northeast India,* pp. 6-15. Dibrugarh University.

Glover, Ian C. 1985. 'Some problem relating to the domestication of rice in Asia', In VN Misra, and P. Bellwood (Eds): *Recent Advances in Indo-Pacific Prehistory* pp. 265-74. New Delhi: Oxford and IBH Publishing Co.

Godwin-Austen, HH. 1872. 'On the stone monuments of Khasi Hills tribes', *Journal of the Royal Anthropological Institute* 1: 122-136.

Goswami, MC, and AC Bhagabati. 1959a. 'A preliminary report on the collection of Neolithic tool types from Western Garo Hills', *Man in India*, 39 (4):312-324.

Goswami, MC, and AC Bhagabati. 1959b. 'A typological study of shouldered Celts from Rengchangre (Garo Hills)', *Journal of the Gauhati University*, 10 (2): 105-122.

Goswami, MC, and TC Sharma, 1963. 'A brief report on the investigation into prehistoric archaeology in the N.C. Hills', *Journal of the Gauhati University* 13(2):63-66.

Hutton, JH. 1929. 'Assam megaliths'. Antiquity. 3: 324-338.

IAR: *Indian Archaeology: A Review-1966-67*. New Delhi; Annual Bulletin of Archaeological Survey of India.

IAR: *Indian Archaeology: A Review-1967-68*. New Delhi; Annual Bulletin of Archaeological Survey of India.

Jamir, W. 1998. 'Megaliths in Nagaland', *Purattatva* 28: 104-110.

Mackie, E. 1997. 'Maeshowe, and the winter solstice: Ceremonial aspects of the Orkney grooved ware culture', *Antiquity* 71: 338-359.

Mahanta, HC.1995. *A Study on the Stone Age Cultures of Selbal Valley, West Garo Hills, Meghalaya*. Unpublished Ph.D. Thesis, Gauhati University, Assam.

Marak, Q, and Jangkhomang. 2012b. 'Megaliths, matriliny, and living practices: A study of the Jaintia Megalithic traditions in Meghalaya'. *Indian Anthropologist* 42 (2): 67-82.

Marak, Q, and Jangkhomang. 2012a. 'The sacred stones of Nangbah: A post-processual cultural interpretation of Megaliths'. *Journal of Social Sciences, Humanities and Literature* 1 (2): 62-77.

Marak, Q. 2012. 'Megaliths of North East India'. In TB Subba (Ed.): *North-East India: A Handbook of Anthropology*, pp. 34-53. New Delhi: Orient Blackswan.

Medhi, DK.1980. *Quaternary History of the Garo Hills, Meghalaya*, Unpublished Ph.D.Thesis, Deccan College Post-Graduate, and Research Institute, Pune.

Mills, JP, 1933. 'Assam, as a field of research', *Journal of Assam Research Society* 1 (1): 3-6.

Paddayya, K. 2002-2003. 'The expanding horizons of Indian Archaeology', *Bulletin of Deccan College Post Graduate Research Institute* 62-63: 291-309.

Paddayya, K., and P. Bellwood. 2002. 'South and Southeast Asia', In Berry Cunliffe, Wendy Davies, and Colin Renfrew (Eds): *Archaeology: The Widening Debate*, Oxford University Press.

Ramesh, NR. 1989. *A Study on Geomorphology, Quaternary Geology and Associated Cultural remains of West Tripura District*. Unpublished Ph.D.Thesis, Gauhati University, Assam.

Rao, SN. 1973. 'The Neolithic culture of Sarutaru, Assam', *Bulletin of Department of Anthropology, Dibrugarh University*, 2: 1-9.

Rao, SN. 1991. 'Megalithic Practices among Khasis and Nagas of Northeast India', In JP Singh, and G. Sengupta (Eds): *Archaeology of Northeastern India*, New Delhi: Vikash Publishing House.

Rao, SN, 1979. 'Survival, and continuity of Neolithic traditions of Northeastern India', *Asian Perspective,* 20 (2), 1977.

Roy, SK. 1981. 'Aspects of Neolithic agriculture and shifting cultivation, Garo Hills, Meghalaya', *Asian Perspective,* 14(2): 193-219.

Sankalia, HD. 1974. *Prehistory and Proto-history of India and Pakistan*, Pune: Deccan College Post Graduate Research Institute.

Sharma, HC. and SK. Roy. 1985. 'On the discovery of pebble tools industry in Garo Hills, Meghalaya', In VN Misra and P Bellwood (Eds.): *Recent Advances in Indo-Pacific Prehistory,* New Delhi: Oxford and IBH Publishing Co.

Sharma, HC. 1972. *Prehistoric Archaeology: Stone Age Cultures of Garo Hills, Meghalaya*. Unpublished Ph.D. Thesis, Gauhati University, Assam.

Sharma, TC. 1967. 'A note of the Neolithic pottery of Assam', *Man* 2 (1): 126-128.

Sharma, TC. 1988. 'Discovery of Hoabinhian cultural relics in Northeast India'. In NC Ghosh, and S. Chakraborty (Eds.): *Adaptation and Other Essays, Proceedings of the Archaeological Conference*, Shantiniketan: Research Publication, Biswa Bharati.

Sharma, TC. 1966. *Prehistoric Archaeology of Assam-A Study of the Neolithic Culture.* Unpublished Ph.D.Thesis, University of London.

Sharma, TC. 1991. 'Prehistoric situation in Northeast India', In JP Singh and G. Sengupta (Eds): *Archaeology of Northeastern India*, New Delhi: Vikash Publishing House.

Sharma, TC. 1990. 'The prehistoric background of shifting cultivation', In DN Mazumder (Ed.): *Shifting Cultivation in Northeast India,* Guwahati, Osmos Publication.

Singh, OK. 1993. *Stone Age Culture of Manipur*, Unpublished Ph.D. Thesis, University of Manipur.

Singh, OK. 1985. 'A live Megalithic culture in Manipur'. In VN Misra and P. Bellwood (Eds.): *Recent Advances in Indo-Pacific Prehistory: Proceedings of the International Symposium held at Poona*, December 19-21, 1978, pp. 491-496. New Delhi: Oxford and IBH Publishing Company.

Sonowal, M. 1987. *Studies on the Flake and Blade Industries of Garo Hills, Meghalaya*, Unpublished Ph.D.Thesis. Gauhati University, Assam.

Sundara, A. 1985. 'Cultural ecology of the Neolithic in India', In SB Deo and K.Paddayya (Eds.): *Recent Advances in Indian Archaeology,* Pune: Deccan College Post Graduate and Research Institute.

Worman, EC. 1949. 'The neolithic problems in the prehistory of India' *Journal of the Washington Academy of Sciences*. 39(6): 181-201.

Chapter - 2

The System of Village Council among Tribes of Northeast India: A Preliminary Appraisal

—Dali Dutta and Sarthak Sengupta

The conventional community organisation and the highest administrative body which is control over by the senior are known as Village Council or *Gram Sabha*. This Village Council is normally unregistered and every ethnic group is represented in it. The more isolated the village from government programmes, the more important the Village Council is in organising community development activities. Conventionally, even among democratic tribal communities, women have not taken part in the Village Council, but this is slowly changing.

The village councils constituted at the grassroots level is a body corporate having perpetual succession and a common seal with powers to acquire, hold and dispose of property. The village council consists of members directly elected by the people. The government provides funds to the village council fund from the Tribal Sub Plan and other resources keeping in mind the resources of the government, priorities or development works in other areas.

The village council has the following powers and duties: to prepare village development schemes; to administer proper maintenance of water supply, roads, forest, education and other welfare activities; to help various govt. agencies in carrying out development work in the village; to take development works on its own initiative or on request by the government; to have a loan of money from the government, banks or financial institution for use in the development and welfare work of the village and to reimburse the same with or without interest; and to submit an application for and receive grants-in-aid, donations, subsidies from the government or any agency, etc and to control and disposal of immovable property, etc. The type and pattern of village council system differ from tribe to tribe.

Arunachal Pradesh

Almost all major tribes of Arunachal Pradesh have developed their indigenous type of village councils, which used to perform three-fold functions - judicial, administrative and developmental.

The Adi with its subgroups like Ashing, Bokar, Bori, Karko, Komkar, Milan, Miniyong, Padam, Pailibo, Pangi, Pasi, Ramo, Shimong, Tangam etc., traditionally is under a selected chief who moderates the village council *kebang, libo-keba*, which acts even as a traditional court. The head of the *kebang* is known as *kebang abu, gindo, gam* or *meeloom*. The members are called *kebang ami*. The olden day councils consist of the entire village elder and decisions were taken in a *musup/dere* (village community house) on a majority verdict. The system of *kebang* has got a three-tier structure *viz* the *dolung kebang* or the village *Kebang* and two higher level *kebangs*, the *bango kebang, or dapung* (inter-village council) and the *bogum bokang kebang, bori-bane-kebang* (council of the whole tribe). All the adult males are the members of the *kebang*. The *dolung kebang* is the oldest institution and the other two higher level *kebangs* are the recent origin.

The village council of Aka tribe is called *nyetchi raaj rai* or *melley*. It consists of the *gaonburah* or *nugo*, and his two juniors, the *borah*, the *gibba* and the members of the village community.

Bulyang is the traditional council of the Apatanis. There are three categories of *bulyang: aka bulyang, yapa bulyang*, and *ajang bulyang*. The *aka bulyang* includes the important leaders of the village. These leaders belong to old generation and are consulted on all important matters. The *yapa bulyang* comprises the middle-aged persons who carry out the day-to-day affairs of the village, settle disputes and keep the *aka bulyang* informed all developments. The *ajang bulyang* consists of the young person who acts as messengers and assistants of the *yapa bulyang*. *Bulyang* did play a vital role in maintaining neutrality in war and pacified between two hostile camps by wearing *'aji yatii'* instead of a shield in the battleground.

The traditional village council of the Bangni is known as *glyokum;* members are usually selected by voice vote and consist of village headman with a council of elders.

The village council of Buguns is known as *nimiyang*. The *nimiyang* of a village is constituted by the *gaonbura* and experienced persons (*thapbokhows*) along with the adult individuals of the village. Other two important parts of *nimiyang* are *kachham* and *khoboi.* The *kachham* acts as an assistant to the *thapbokhows* and *gaonburah. Khoboi* is responsible for making sitting arrangement in the venue of the council's meeting. The main function of this council is to restore peace and tranquility in the village.

The traditional village council of the Digaru Mishmi (Taraon) is called *kabai,* which is headed by the *kabai-mai* who maintains peace and harmony with the assistance of few elders - *madyya-mai.*

The most powerful body in the village of Galo is the council of elder's called *keba*. Every Galo village is run by a *keba*. The Galo society is characterised by the three-tier political administration - *dolu keba* (village council); *bane bango keba* (inter-village council) and the bogum *boka keba*, which is the highest *keba*. The *dolu keba* is empowered to decide cases falling within the jurisdiction of their respective villages.

The village council of Idu (Kaman) Mishmis is called as the *abbalah*, which is headed by *abbelaiga* and consists of village elders having wisdom and soundness of judgment. However, the function of the *abbalah* is restricted to judicial matters and it does not cover village administration. *Pharai,* on the other hand, is a council of elders–the members of which represent various clans.

Among the Khamba, a *chappan* (political interpreter), the *shayppon* (head *gam*) and the *thrimpa* (assistant head *gam*) formed the traditional village council called *thrimtamji.*

The Khampti village council is called *mokchup*, *chow-tra* which is governed by the chief (*chowfa*), assisted by *chaofaken, chao moong, chaohootem, chaohoohoo, chaohooson, chao moo* and *tengso*. The judgment is given as per *Thammasat*, in which Khamti customary laws are recorded. The chieftainship is hereditary and the political authority is vested in the village chiefs, besides the chief, the village council consists of people from various sections.

The Khowas' village council is known as *than-ni-minang* which is represented by all the clan elders. Among them, women have also got the right to participate in the council's activities. The village chief is called *bkhao* assisted by two officials called *kachom* and two *khuboi* (village criers).

The Lishu (Yobin) community is governed by *besay* (headman). The Lishu villages are called *chowu,* which usually consists of 5–15 *chohis* (houses) and each is headed by *chown* or *besay* for maintaining peace, law, and order.

The traditional village council of the Memba is headed by *sokpon* or *goba* who is assisted by the *thimpa.* The traditional village council of the Meyors (Zakhring) is headed by the *genpo* who is usually selected by the villagers.

The traditional village council of the Miji is called *malai,* headed by the *nakhau*, other members being *gubo* (assistant) and *phi meriang shamagos* (village elders).

Interestingly, a rich man (*glat kapra*) used to exercise control over the Miju Mishmi (Kaman) villages with assistance from an influential person (*tantong*).

Among the Monpas tribes (But, Chug, Dirang, Kalaktang, Lish, Tawang etc) of Kameng district, all adults of the village elect the village council called *bulu, mangma, tomba, chovenkang* and the council elects the chief known as *akhoo*, *tsorgen (chorgyen)* from among its elected members who exercises power in a democratic manner. The *tsorgen* is the chief of the village and the general assembly is called as *tso tsorgen*. The meeting of the council is held in the house of *tsorgen* or in the *mangkhem* (community hall) or in an open space. The *tsorgen* has his representatives called *tsolba* in each village or hamlet who are also elected. Apart from *tsolba*, he gets a number of messengers or watchman known as *gomis*. The Monpa village council settles the disputes on the basis of the customary law.

The institution of *gingdung* (village chief) of the Nishi and Tagin tries to settle disputes with the help of few village elders (*donkum*) by peaceful negotiation on the basis of customary matters and norms of the society.

The village council of Nocte tribe is variously called as *ngothun, nongwang, ngongthun* or *ngnogthit* which is consisted of the chief and elders. The chief is called as *lowang* who heads the village council. He gives a final decision on an affair after consulting the other members. Apart from the chief, the council consists of the members like *ngongba* (who assist the chief), *ramba* (who functions as a priest), the *tanba* (chief's messenger) and other elderly persons. The Nocte village council maintains law and order, solves disputes within the village and with other villages and also undertakes developmental activities.

Thungdai or mung is the council of the Singpho tribe. The members of the council are known as *singpho silang* or *ningbo ningla*. The council consists of three active members. They are the *gaonburah* as the official representative and other two members selected from among the elder and experienced persons of the village. The entire village attends and takes part in the meeting of the council. More or less the Singpho village council undertakes judicial, cultural and developmental functions for the benefit of the village people.

The village council of Sherdukpen is called as *jungme or bulu,* which consists of the village headman known as *theck akhau or thug-bos,* the ordinary members (*jung me or thumi*), *kacheng* or courier and *chowkidar*. The *jung* decides cases by general agreement but the final decision remains with the *gaonburah* or headman. The Sherdukpen society is divided into two classes – *thongs* (aristocrat) and *chhaos* (commoners). In the village administrative setup, the thongs have a superior position. They have their code of conducts in a written form known as *chatpu-nesey*.

The Tangsas (comprising of a number of sub-tribes like Havi, Jugli, Kimsing, Lungchang, Lungphi, Lungri, Morang, Mosang, Muklom, Rongrang, Sangwal, Sanke, Tikhak, Tonglim, Yongkuk) have got a well-organised village council of elders called differently by different sub-tribes as *khaphua, khanpong, khapo, khangshalang, phove, pheoval, roong-thung, rungwah, lowang ngongwa* etc. The council consists of a leader (called as *phulung wang, kenglang, lungwang, nogwa, ngvajong, mayowaju, phongwa, taadoh, gakhungwelang, walang* or *lowang*) and few members (called as *sangta, khamba, dedwa, lukhap, nokchi, ngunwa, phunwa, powa*) selected by the villagers. The head of the village council is selected from a particular clan, who must be wealthy and intelligent. The other members of the council represent the various clans. The council adjudicates all disputes in the village.

The Wangcho village council (*ngowang*) is well organised for the administration of justice. It is a council of elders called as *wangsu- wangsa, rampo-rampa, ngopa, wangcham*. The council is headed by the village chief called *wangham* who is assisted by *khonsai* (members) with different functions. *Wangcham* acts as a messenger of the chief and the council.

Assam

The traditional village council in each Aiton village is headed by *gaonburah* (*kun haban*), assisted by the *bari chow paw mung*.

The traditional village council of the Boro Kachari is called *hadengra*, headed by *courtgra* who with the help of village elders from different villages (*boro barodal*) settles disputes, and maintains peace and harmony among the people.

The Deori community is governed by a well-constituted village council, locally known as *mel*, constituted with all the elderly members of the village which is headed by *gaonburah*.

Among Dimasa, Burman and Hojai Kachari, the traditional village headman is called *khunang*, elected by the villagers in a formal meeting. He has both executive and judiciary powers. In discharging his duties he is assisted by eight officials – *dilek* (assistant headman), *daulathu, habaisagao, pharai, mantri, hangsebukhu,* and *jalairao*.

The Halam community has two-tier traditional councils; the upper tier (*halam dewan*) is a regional council consisting of several villages and the lower tier (*khoshung* or *khew dewan*) at the village level. The council is composed of *kalim* (headman), *kabur* (assistant headman), *chapia* (messenger), *shengja* (peon) and eight *noktolai* (executive body members).

The village headman among Hajong community is known as *mandal. Jowar* is a Regional Council consisting of few villages. The decision of the *jowar* is final for any kind of disputes.

Every Hmar village is headed by a chief known as *lal,* assisted by few *khawnbawl* and village elders and *tlangsam* (messenger).

The Jaintias inhabiting in Dima Hasao district, socially controlled by village committee headed by *bahekshnong* (headman), who is assisted by few elderly people (*rangshnong*) who are elected by the villagers in general meeting called *durbar shnong*.

The Karbis have three tier traditional self-governing institutions; of which at the apex is the *lingdokpo* or *recho* and his Parliament or council of a minister called *pinpomar*. At the middle level there are twelve *habais* or administrators one each for twelve *longris*' regions, and at the bottom, it is the *mei* or village council. There are three traditional *lingdokpos* with their territorial jurisdiction at Rongkhang, Chinthong, and Amri. Among them the *lingdokpos* of Ronghang as considered to be the supreme. There is a tradition to conduct an annual Royal *darbar* where the *lingdokpos* and also his council are paid tributes, generally in kind, by the *habais* and the other headman of the villages and the *longris*. The council at village level of the Karbis is called *mei* composed of all the elderly male members headed by the *sarthe* or *rongasar* and few *sarso* (assistant *gaonburah*). A *sarthe* never make any decision, as it needs prior consent of the members like *bruteman* (advocate), *mutiyar* (messenger), *pheranke* (cashier), *kurusor* (priest), etc. He can only issue proposals relating to the village affairs in a meeting of the council for its approval. The *mei* plays an important role in regulating the social, economic and religious life of the village.

The Khamiyangs have their own village council called *tra*, which is headed by the *chow ong mung* with assistance from *barik / chowtey mayo* (messenger/watchman). The traditional village council of Khamti is known as *chow-tra*, headed by *chowfa* who is assisted by *chow-sing* and *chowoog-mung*.

A Kuki village council is called *hausa semang pachong,* headed by *kholpa* or *hausa* (chief), two *semang* (priest and counselor) and two *pachong* (blacksmith and carpenter) besides few knowledgeable persons.

Every Matak village in upper Assam is controlled by *gaonburah* who is assisted by *borbura* in discharging his duties. There is also another official called *hazarika* who convene and organizes the meetings.

The traditional chief of a Mishing village was called a *ga:m*. He presided at the sittings of the village *kebang* (the village council), which deliberated upon different matters concerning the well-being of the village community as well as complaints of individual members or groups in the community. The *kebang* was the legal, judicial and executive authority of the community, although the final say on all matters, barring the ones relating to their faith, was that of the *ga:m*. Cases of social and criminal offenses were heard by the *kebang*, and persons found guilty were penalised. The *ga:m* has been replaced with *gaonburah*, a pretty village level agent of the government, since the days of the British.

The village council of the Noctes is known as *nok mork phom*, headed by a *gaonburah* (chief).

The law and order in Rengma Naga village are maintained by *pethinyu* (headman) who happens to be the oldest man of the village, assisted by *athokethunyu* (council members) in *kehonganyu* (council). The traditional village council of Rongmei is known as *paikai*, headed by *paipou.*

The village committee members of the Sonowal Kachari are called *mukhial* or *bara bishava*, headed by *gaonburah*. The other office bearers are *barik* (in charge of prayer hall), *pathak* (reader of religious scriptures), *medhi* (chief of all religious functions), *tamuli* (suppliers of betel-nut at religious functions), *randhoni* (cook), *geetghai* (*husori* singer), *dhanbharali* (treasurer) etc who settled disputes in meeting usually convened in *namghar* (prayer hall).

The secular village organisation of the Tiwa (Lalung) consists of eight village elders (*bura-khel*) which are headed by the *gaonburah* who is assisted by an official called *barika* (messenger). The non-secular organisation of the Tiwa is run by three office bearers namely, *gharbura, zela,* and *hari-kuwari*.

The Turung community of Assam has headman called *merengdingla* who remain in charge of the village administration. The village council constituted of the headman and the elderly villagers.

Zeme village council (*nieu-ndui*) is headed by *mathai diba* (headman), who is assisted by *mathai cheiba* (assistant headman), *tinku pau* (priest), and few youth dormitory (*hangseuki*) representatives (*hangsenge besuteiba peu*), few *paipeu* for looking religious affairs and a few *besuteuba leuma* (village elders) as council members.

Manipur

The chief of the village of Aimol of Manipur is known as *kamsakoi*, his ministers are known as *pasa-kariat,* followed by *maitrempi* who holds the responsibility of settling disputes. The traditional mechanism of social control among Anal was vested in their functionaries called as *khalpu, dopu*, and *thalpu*, who were selected by the village elders.

A Chothe village is organised in a three-tier structure. The three formal groups (*bungkung*) are formed primarily on the basis of age set system. They are *urinta* (highest body), *tangarinta* (looks after customary religious activities, fair, and *luithei* or *nungakluithei*. *Urinta* comprises of seven office bearers - *khullakpa, luplakpa, juh paipa, keirungpa, keirungnapong, hachari*, and *hachari naopong*. *Khullakpa* is the protector of the village. The body of *tangarinta* is subordinate to *urinta* and consists of *pakhangiak, jupai, lomjuihai, lomjuiyaima, lomjuinaha, juhhong, and juh-jong naopong.* Luitheir includes four age-grades like *tangsa, hancha, hithan,* and *leibak;* the first two again has three sub-groups and associated with their youth dormitory.

The village council among Chiru has functionaries such as a chief (*khullakpa*), a religious priest (*sampar*), and a blacksmith (*laishi and thirshreem*).

The Hmars have village council under the village chief (*lal*). Besides elders (*khawnbawl upas*), the chief has some other assistants like the village crier (*tlangsam*)), the village blacksmith (*thirsu*). The court of the chief functioned as the highest legal authority in the village. It tried all cases of petty thefts to rape case and cases involving capital punishment.

The Kacha Naga village council is known as *apai chawang* headed by its chief *chawang* which is hereditary in nature. The village council among the Koirao called the *katammi*, which is headed by a hereditary chief *khullakpa*. Next, to him comes the *liklakpa* who looks after the administration of the village in absence of *khullakpa*. The council is composed of several members selected from different lineage called *sagai* headed by a tan.

The village council of Kabuis is called as *peikai* which consists of *khunbu, khullakpa, luplakpa, mantra, lambu, changbi* etc. It is constituted with the elderly people from every household in the village, clans. The senior priest (*tingkuh*) is the head of the *peikai*. Women do not represent in *pei*. *Pei* is the apex body of the village administration. The function of *peikai* is executive and judiciary rather than legislative. In past, the traditional council of elders was constituted with *banza* and *ganchang* used to deal with religious and secular matters respectively.

Khuo is responsible for the overall administration of a Koireng village. The origin of the village council was shrouded in mystery. It consists of *khullakpa* or *khoreng* (hereditary chief), assisted by *luklakpa* or *tuiran*.

The powers and functions of the village council were well defined. They divided the administrative areas as judicial, religious and developmental functions. These functions are carried out through the various members of the council including the chief.

The Kom tribe has hereditary chiefs called *haisaapa*. Other offices of the traditional council are *sawang* (or *luk lak pa*), *khun pu, punpu (naharakpa)*, *tlangwa* (*pakjanglakpa*), *mantra* and *kathuipa*.

The form of administration in the Kuki society begins from village level to the nation. It comprises *haosa inpi* (lower house) and *upa inpi* (upper house). Among the Kuki society, the chief rules from village council known as *haosa inpi*. The council is composed of the chief and counselors. The chief in council consists of *semang* (village prime minister), *pachong* (defence minister), *lhangsam* (foreign minister with responsibilities of publicity and communication), *thikkheng* (black-smithy), *thiempu* (priest) and *lawmupa* (youths, education, and defence). The size of the Council's member depends on the size or population of the village.

The *semang* is a local term which means the head of ministers at the village level. He is one of the most important members of the village council. He plays the real executive link between the chief and administration. *Pachong* is another official. The village council members, *upas* was appointed by the chief and their duty was to give advice to the chief. Practically the chief would never try any cases without consulting his *upas*. They are selected from the villagers who have tact and wisdom. Besides, they should be well versed in *upas* customary laws and usages of the people. The *upas* is appointed from different sections of the people. The chief counsel was made sure that every section of society is represented. The chief summoned his *upas* to discuss the matter of political importance when receiving proposals from emissaries. He is also accompanied by *upas* on his official visit to another village. The *upas* was given due respect in the village and was exempted from payment of taxes to the chief.

The traditional village council of Lamgang is called *khu purek* which is headed by *kuruwang* and has fifteen other officials. Like *pakhang lakpa* (controller of youth), *chingsandlakpa, ningol-lakpa* (looks after the conduct of women), *anchingba* (commander in war), *yupan* (wine taster), *naharakpa* (controller of children), *selungba, changloi, wangkbarak* and *khulpu* (priest).

Each village of Mao society has its own village court called *makrii kasiina.* Its decision is final and binding. There are no specialised bodies of administration, executive and judicial power all are vested with village authority (*kotsiimei*). The village council is composed of the heads of the clans within the same village. The political system is gerontocratic, led by a chief called *sagung* and the village council is known as *asam katii*. Clan elders are also members of the village council.

The traditional village council of Monsang and Moyon is headed by *eruwngpa* or *iruwang* who is assisted by fourteen elected councilors chosen on a lineage basis. *Senapati* occupies the position next to the *eruwngpa*.

The Maring villages are generally ruled by the chief of administration and rituals *khullakpa* (*khulpu*) with his village council. The village council or by an authority called *yul-ur* or *kho upro* is a body elected or selected comprising of elderly intellect and capable male members of the village. This council is the principal governing body of the village, which maintains the village judiciary court. At present, the Maring society possesses three tiers system- the village court composed within the village, the area court (*chingshanglak*) composed of neighbouring villages and *uparup* assembly, which is composed of whole Maring. The functions of the village council are broadly executive, administrative and judicial.

The Mate village is administered by *housa* (chief) whose position is strictly hereditary. He is assisted by *mantri* and revenue collector, selected from among the village elders. *taangsam* (village crier) duty is to inform the villagers about any messages given by the village authority. The village authority is elected after every three years.

The village council of Tangkhul Naga is known as *hanga*, which is consisted of the *awunga* (headman) being the head of the council and the head of the clans as members (*hangar*). The administrative, executive and judicial functions of the village vest with the Village Council. Though the election is the general principle for the membership of the village council, in most cases they are selected by choice. The total strength of the village council varies according to the total number of houses in a village. The tenure of office of the village authority is three years.

A Tarao village in Manipur is administered by nineteen officials headed by *kurung* (hereditary chief), selected from a specific clan *khulpu*. The officials are *senapati, khullak, lunglak, yupal, khanglak, naharak, loithil, wangkherirak, roumilak, mara-rampu, tongpra, lalchingpa, chingsanglak, mantri, ningolak, sellungba, keiringba,* and *lallupchingba*.

Meghalaya

Each Khasi clan has its own *durbar* or council called *durbar kur*, which is presided by *rangba kur*, the clan headman. The local assembly of the villages of the Khasis had their own *durbar* or council called the *village durbar* or *durbar shnong*. The *village durbar* consists of the male members of the village, the village elders or *basans*. The head of the village council is the village headman, *rangba shnong, sirdar* or *wahadadar*. He presided over the village council. His main function is to see the welfare of the villagers, sanitation, water supply, health, roads and schools which are under the village jurisdiction. The village headman is succeeded by any male members of the village from among the *basans* of the village.

Jaintias have a three-tier system of administration with King (*Syiem*) at the top; the *dolois* (as head of *raid* or *elaka*) at the middle and *wahehchchnong*, the village headman at the bottom who is assisted by the village *durbar* or *durbar chnong*.

Among the Garos, it is the *nokma* who is assisted by two councils, *mela-solbonga,* and *jigma-changga*, the former consisted of the adults from all the *maharis* (small homogenous consanguineous kin group from a common brother) within the *aching* (village or group of villages) for disposing the inter-*mahari* disputes, while the later is the war council.

The village panchayat of Koch tribe is headed by *gaonbura* and composed of the *sirkar* (recorder of the proceedings) and *dakura (*village crier).

Mizoram

The village council of the Chakma area (called as *chawngte*) is composed of members according to the number of houses, three members are to be elected in a village having not more than 50 houses, five members are to be elected in a village having 51 houses or more but less than 150 houses, six members to be elected in a village having 151 houses or more, which includes the president and the secretary. The village council may include a woman member also. The tenure of the elected members is three years. The function of the village council is to settle conflicts and confrontation among villagers, to look after the welfare of the village and villagers.

In past, the Biate are ruled by their customary head *kalim,* assisted by deputy chief *kabur* and each clan has an elder called *thar-thlung-in*, who performs all rituals of the clan. At present, among the Hmar and Biate, the village council is formed through adult franchise. The president is the head of the village council and its office bearers are vice president, secretary, members and the village crier. The president, vice president, and members are elected by the villagers by secret ballot. The village council is the main authority to plan and implement the welfare and developmental activities of the village. Election of the village council is held every three years.

The administrative authority of the Lai community at the grassroots level is the village council. The secretary and the president take the tremendous role. The council can finalise all the civil and criminal cases of the village.

The traditional council of Mara or Lakher tribe has the *abei* - the chief; *macha* – his council of members, *tla awpa* or village crier, *tualituala* (peon), *rotupa* or *karani* (recorder); and *theithaipa* (village priest). Among the Maras there are three classes of courts, these are Village Court, Subordinate District Council Courts, and District Council Courts. All the functions and duties of the courts are discussed in the Lakher Autonomous District.

Among Lusei, Hualngo, traditionally each village had its own chief (*lal*) assisted by a council of elders (*upa*) and *tlangau* (crier) to communicate the decision of chief.

In past, each Pang and Pawi villages were ruled by *lal* with the assistance of *khawnbawl* (two to five advisors), and one each *khawchhir* (recorder), *tlangau* (crier), and *bawlpu* or *thirdeng* (blacksmith).

The administrative control of the Mizo villages is entrusted to elected village councils. They are empowered to look after the village affairs, to punish the guilty persons and to collect land revenue from the villagers.

Nagaland

The population of Nagaland is entirely tribal. There are as many as sixteen major Naga tribes with their own distinctive languages and cultural features. There had been two major forms of village governments in Naga society, one is democratic and the other is autocratic. The village government of Angami is democratic, whereas the Sema and the Konyak have an autocratic type viz. democratic and chieftainships. The governments were run the customary laws and usages. Even today customary laws are considered as the guiding principles of life in society. The village council member is not contested but nominated from each clan for a period of thirty years. The chief of the council is not hereditary but elected by its members. Village Government is known as '*hangvanao*' among Tangkhul, '*putu menden*' among Ao, '*chochomi*' among Sema and '*pangti*' among Lotha. The village council is the apex body in the village of Sangtam Naga, Chakhesang Naga, Yimchungru Naga comprising of the chairman, *gaonburah* and *khel* representatives who are chosen by the villagers. The council is responsible for the administration of village and to maintain law and order besides taking responsibility for the all-around developmental activities.

Chapi is the traditional council of Angami. Among the Ao, *putumenden* or *tatamenden* is the traditional council for social control. The village chief is called *ongre.*

Among the Konyak, they have monarchical system headed by *ahng*, *wang*, meaning status of hereditary King, which was very powerful. The traditional village council among Konyak is called *wang-gho* or *wang-hamyen*.

The informal council of elders among the Kabui Naga is called *pai-kai*, and its head is called *nampau*.

Among the Khiamngan, the *leng* or an old warrior of repute regarded as the head chief of the council of elders.

Among Phom Naga head *barrack* selected or nominated by male members is the senior headman of a village. The traditional village council (*mozaluo*) of the Pochury exists in each village, consists of several clan elders headed by village chief-*kajiry*.

The Rengma have a village chief, but the clan head and elders had a strong influence in the discharge of the chief's duty; and thus not a system of an autocratic chief. The chief is called as *kukughu* or *kekvugu* while the system had no particular name.

The traditional council of the Sangtam Naga called *yukhaba-ka* is constituted by the lineage and clan elders.

The village council (*aphuh hoho*) carries out the administration of justice in the Sumi villages. This is the supreme body of the village. It comprises of the village chief, head *gaonburah* as the chairman, the assistant *gaonburah,* and secretary.

In the Yimchunger community, the traditional village council is *kiu longthsuru*.

The traditional village council of Zeliang Naga called *samka-kebei* which is headed by *tinkupan* or *kadeipeo*. The village council is the powerful body within the village of Zeliang Naga. It comprises the chairman, secretary, *gaonburahs* and *khel* representatives. The village council is responsible for the developmental activities of the village as well as to maintain law and order while administering their village.

Sikkim

The *kyi- dug* constitutes the social organisation of the Bhutia, Drukpa. The main function of the *kyi-dug* is to help its clan members at the time of need. Its office-bearers are elected by the members from amongst themselves.

The Lachenpa and Lachungpa of north Sikkim have the *zumsha* organisation. The village headman (*phipun*) was elected by adult members drawn from each of the family for a term of two years. There are two *gyapons* or *gimbas,* elected by the villagers to help the *pipon*. Women have no right to take part in the election of the *phipun* or *gimba*. Besides the *zumsha*, there was another body of village elders called the *gyemmi*, for aiding and advising the *phipun* in functions involving the community as a whole.

Among the Nepalese of Sikkim, there are various caste organisations generally known as *samaj*, like the *tamang samaj*, the *rai samaj*, the *kami samaj* etc. These councils function as agencies of social control. Among the Limbu, the traditional caste council (*tumyanghang*), which consists of ten elders from different clans (*thibong-yakthung*) is still in vogue.

The Tamang have traditional council (*groi*) consists of elders (*ghanta*) and the Lama of their own community.

Tripura

The traditional political institution of the Chakma was a three-tier system, namely, the Village Council, Anchal Council (covering a wide area of a sub-division) and the Sola-ani Council (the whole territory). The Chakma had a *raja* that was the supreme authority. He used to run the administration with the help of *dewan* (head of the village who is assisted by several officers called *khejas*), *khisa* (aristocrat), *karbari* (assistant to *dewan*), and *ojhai*. The office of the *raja* was hereditary.

The village council of the Halam, and Kaipeng, the community is headed by the *choudhuri* who is assisted by two *khandals* (peons) and a few elders. They also have a council at community level headed by the *rai*. Other posts in the council are those of the *kanchan, galim, aksung, kabur, khoukusung, chapiatom, karma, sengia, tar,* and *planta*.

The Jamatia of Tripura has a well-constituted three tiers system of the council- village (*luku*), regional (*mayal*) and supreme (*hoda*) council. The members are nominated by selections in every five years. The village, regional and supreme headman is called as *choudhury, sardar,* and *akra* respectively.

Social control among Kaloi and Rupini community is maintained through *dian* headed by *choudhuri*. *Rai* is the community level council, where besides *rai* (chief) others are *galim, kamshikak, gabur, jagsum*, and *senga*.

The Kuki, Ralte and Lushai used to have *khawn-bawls* or *lal-upa* (village chief) who would act as a representative of the *lal* (king), and work in tandem with *khaw-pa* (people's representative) and the *khaw-uliens* (village elders), the former two being hereditary.

Social control mechanism among the Magh consists of traditional head called *masugri*, his assistant *choudhuri* and a number of elders

The Mog community has a two-tier system of councils, one is *Pachhu* or *Roa Adalat* and the other one is *Mouja Adalat*. The first one is the village level council. This *Pachhu Adalat* (village council) is constituted with the representation of all the family heads in a village. The second one is a sub-divisional level council. This *Mouja Adalat* can be constituted covering the whole area of a rural development block. The essential qualifications for appointment as judge of both the councils are that he must be a Mog; he must be an honest, intelligent and respectable person; the gender or wealth is not a criterion for the appointment of a judge. There are three judges on each council. One among them is appointed as a chief judge. Appointment of one woman in the panel of judges is obligatory. *Pachhu Adalat* is empowered with the tribal of minor cases like petty quarrel, a dispute over the land boundary. The *Mouja Adalat* is empowered to try all cases and also to give a verdict of punishment of any kind.

Among Noatia, *Choudhuri* is the guardian of traditional values who is assisted by two *khandals* in settling disputes. However, at the community level, to maintain law and order they have a higher appellate association called *hadani-sengawakra*, *hadani-dabeng*, and *khandal*, where one can complain if he/she is not satisfied with *choudhury's* decision.

Every Riang village has one village headman *darbar* called *para choudhuri darbar* and one representative of the village headman known as *choudhury*. They have two tiers of court. These are - *village choudhuri darbar* and *mayal choudhuri darbar*. The *village choudhuri darbar* is constituted by adults (both male and female) living in a village. Each *village darbar* has a *para choudhury* (village headman) and an assistant *para choudhuri* known as *karbary*. Both of these are elected by the adult persons of the concerned village. They may hold their posts until their death or physical inability. *Mayal choudhuri darbar* is constituted by the representative members of the *para choudhury* of the concerned *village darbar*. There are seven *mayal darbars*. The *para choudhury* of the concerned *mayal* selected from the most senior member as the *mayal choudhuri* of their respective *mayal darbar*.

The jurisdiction of the village council of Tripuris is generally restricted within a hamlet locally known as *para*. The village council consists of *choudhury* (village headman), *achai*, *barua*, *khandal* (messenger), *karbari* (secretary) and volunteers. This council is empowered to try petty offenses and to run the village administration.

The tribes of North East India have varied types of village organisation. These are chieftainship, democratic village council, gerontocratic (age set) system, and in few cases very weak forms of such organisation. The village council, whether controlled by the chiefs or by the village elders in a democratic way, are not only judicial organisations but also perform as the main administrative organisations of the village and are supposed to direct all the activities of the village according to their traditional law and custom. In the present day context, however, with the opening up of modern political and administration (Panchayati Raj system), the traditional form of village political system has lost its importance to a great extent, but in some area, it is still continuing.

References

Gopalakrishnan, R. 1995. *Meghalaya Land and People,* New Delhi; Omsons Publications.

Sangkima,1992. *Mizos: Society and Social Change (1890-1947),* Guwahati and Delhi; Spectrum Publications.

Singh, K.S., 1993. *People of India: Sikkim* XXXIX, Anthropological Survey of India, Calcutta; Seagull Books.

Singh, K.S., 1994. *People of India: Meghalaya* XXXII, Anthropological Survey of India, Calcutta; Seagull Books.

Singh, K.S., 1994. *People of India: Nagaland*, Anthropological Survey of India, Calcutta; Seagull Books.

Singh, K.S., 1995. *People of India: Arunachal Pradesh*, Anthropological Survey of India, Calcutta; Seagull Books.

Singh, K.S., 1995. *People of India: Mizoram* XXXIII, Anthropological Survey of India, Calcutta; Seagull Books.

Singh, K.S., 1996. *People of India: Tripura* XVI, Anthropological Survey of India, Calcutta; Seagull Books.

Singh, K.S., 1998. *People of India: Manipur* XXXI, Anthropological Survey of India, Calcutta; Seagull Books.

Singh, K.S., 2003. *People of India: Assam* XV, Part I and II, Anthropological Survey of India, Calcutta; Seagull Books.

Chapter - 3

An Interface of Gender and Ethnicity in Northeast India: An Exploration

—Lucy T. V. Zehol

Introduction

Narratives need to be explored to unravel the truth. The context of this chapter is drawn from two narratives, "the first narrative relates to the rape of a tribal girl in Ukhrul district of Manipur by the Indian Army personnel (read domination) in the 1980's a result of reinforcing stereotype images of tribal women which lead to molestation and rape. The civil societies, particularly women organisations, were up in protest yet the young victim unable to bear the difficult circumstances suicide committed and the army personals ultimately court-martial."

The second narrative relate to the molestation and rape of (tribal) Hmar girls and women in Tipaimukh sub-division of Churachandpur district of Manipur by the Meitei insurgents-UNLF and KCP cadres in 2006 whereby the Rajkhowa Commission was instituted by the Government of Manipur as a result of the tribal civil societies' pressure to 'look' into the matter. For the government (read domination) it was to investigate the authenticity of the 'alleged' molestation and rape of Hmar girls and women, crossed examined the victims in 2008 and the report yet to be made public and justice denied. Civil societies and human right groups have been demanding for the commission report to be made public and the protest continues till date—the 'silence' of the 'Government' (read dominating community) in Manipur a 'deafening sound'. Gender and ethnic stereotyping can both justify domination and subordination and create conditions for their further perpetuation for those situated in the margins and the bottom.

II

Both gender and ethnicity are not clear-cut concepts that make neat compartments where we can insert real human beings. The totality of addressing the understanding of people encapsulates the practical manifestation of concepts like gender and ethnicity. They are powerful constructs that affect the lives of men and women in significant ways. Here the importance of perception comes into play. The sexual image that one has, the resources of society and many other aspects of life may be affected by how one is perceived by society in general. Gender and ethnic stereotyping can both justify domination and subordination and create conditions for their further perpetuation for those situated in the margins and the bottom. To a large extent black feminist and Third World anthropologists have contributed substantially to the study and this chapter is a humble attempt to understand the nuances of how tribal women of Northeast experience an interface of Gender and Ethnicity in their everyday lived experiences."

Contemporary feminists have gone beyond the concept of patriarchy that presupposes the universal subordination of women or at least their subordination where the structures of patriarchy exist; towards an analysis of the internal differentiation of the category of being a woman, as women of particular disadvantages and disabilities. Thus, the concepts of ethnicity and gender need to be clubbed together, rather than be treated as substitutes of one another, in order to make a holistic learning. Relativity is a significant fact to be taken into consideration while understanding the situation of women. Women placed in different situations experience patriarchy in different ways where their class, ethnicity, and social disabilities determine the specific nature of their experience. Thus, gender is not simply a character; it is also a social location that determines the phenomenological experience of what it means to be not just a woman, but a certain kind of woman, in this case, is the narratives of the tribal women of Manipur.

Gender or Ethnicity

Another very important aspect to be considered is which of the two main identities that people possess, the ethnic and the gendered is evoked at any particular point of time and in a particular context. In other words when do people speak in a voice that belongs to their ethnic/racial identity and when do they speak in a voice that specifically refers to their gendered identity. For example, when feminists talk about 'universal sisterhood of women' they are cutting across all ethnic boundaries. Yet at other points of historical time, groups and individual men and women behave like their other social identities, like being black or white, French or Indian. At the same time may be also seen as members of an ethnic group—be it Naga or Hmar or Meitei rather than as men or women.

In foregrounding the ethnic issues, women's specific issues have been sidelined as have sometimes been felt by women participating in larger social movements, like the Dalit movement or the Naga movement. Vasant Moon in *Growing up in India: A Dalit Autobiography* gives an account of how Dalit women, for example, have complained that their rights and specific issues *as women* have been often overlooked in the larger movement against the upper castes and so also the Naga women in the context of the larger Naga political movement against the larger Indian Statecraft. Further, in the context of the Naga women, there is a growing consciousness that urban educated elite women are not sensitive to their (read as common women) in identifying their needs, issues, and areas of conflicts which will remove gender difference rather than heighten them. Many women feel that their struggle is not against *men* but against the *system*.

In many instances, it is found that gender identity overrides that of ethnicity. This is particularly in the case of those women who feel the pinch of being relegated a lower position in social hierarchy for being 'women'. Here, the element of ethnicity takes a back seat or rather is of no consequence. Angela Davis in her book, *Women, Race, and Class* gives an account of white women who entered the Anti-Slavery movement and found that to fight out the menace of slavery; they also had to fight the patriarchy inherent in their own lives. Thus, white women's struggles to free and emancipate their black sisters and brothers were compounded with a struggle *against their own men*. The period around the early nineteenth century, was when white women were faced with the possibility of forging a "powerful alliance between the established struggle for Black liberation and the embryonic battle for women's rights."

It is a fact that in all situations of conflict and oppression of one group by the other, it is the body of women that becomes a site for establishing a power hierarchy. Susan Brown Miller's, now classic work, '*Against Our Will*', documents the violence that has been used against women in various historical times and space. She specifically describes the atrocities committed on the bodies of Vietnamese women, as a deliberate war strategy sanctioned by the US war department. Similarly the rape of black women on the plantations and of Dalit women in the fields of India, women of Northeast rape by the Indian army or the case where the Hmar tribal women of Manipur were raped by the dominant Meitei UNLF and KCP cadres in 2006, are not a matter of sexuality, they are a way in which men of a superior group indicate that they are superior, not to women that are taken for granted but to the *men* of the marginal group. At all historical time periods, each war has been followed by the rape of women of the 'Other' group, as a violation of the bodies of women is an established practice by men to show that they are 'superior'. Even when there is no war, the strategy of rape to subjugate the dominated group is a powerful tool both physical and psychological. Mass media reports are replete with the gory tales of people of one ethnic group raping the women of the other to vent out their anger. In ethnic clashes, women are the targets of avenging each other. The objectification of women sees its worst consequence here.

III

Both gender and ethnicity are powerful constructs that affect the lives of men and women in significant ways. As seen Gender and ethnic stereotyping can both justify domination and subordination and create conditions for their further perpetuation as is the situation for the Hmar and Naga women. Situated in the margins and the bottom the persons who suffer are also privileged with a critical insight into the conditions of their own marginalisation. A deeper understanding of the mystified nature of these constructs will contribute towards efforts to eliminate an unjust system in the Northeast. Over the years, gender and ethnicity have become burning topics of debate and deliberation. Northeast India, a land of multi-ethnicity keeps the discussion on ethnicity alive among the masses as well as among the upper echelons of the society. With each ethnic group being unique and different from the other, the position of women in each is structured as per its traditions, customs, and practices per se. While scholars have attempted to address the realities of gender and ethnicity in northeast India in different writings, what is conspicuous by its absence is a holistic, anthropological research that attempts to understand the juxtaposition of gender and ethnicity.

While different disciplines cater to the study of gender and ethnicity, an anthropological intervention is much needed in order to soundly understand their meaning. The anthropological approach with its emphasis on holistic study attempts to see the interrelatedness or rather the integrative nature of the different facets of human life. Any discussion on gender and ethnicity, taken separately, or together, is only partially addressed if the factor of holism is ignored. Gender and ethnicity, their interface, all this is a part of the larger unit i.e. culture. Within the canopy of culture, there are multiple aspects - family, kinship, polity, economy, religion etc. Any discussion on gender and ethnicity cannot be considered complete unless it explores how the different institutions and structures of the cultural influence gender and ethnicity and how these two influence the others; whether ethnicity is an all-subsuming element which influences the other aspects of culture, and if this is so, then how? How gender construction takes shape as a consequence of the ever-existing customs and traditions, and how the latter, in turn, influence and are influenced by notions of ethnic identity.

The deep-seated, intricately entwined entity i.e. culture is explored by an anthropologist.

Further, as cultures are different from each other, and unique in themselves, the 'look' of gender and ethnicity would be different in each. Anthropologists are careful in not losing out the specifics in the want of generalisations. While generalisations can give an overview, they can be erroneous as well. The anthropological approach calls for an empirical, long-term, intensive study of a community in order to understand the 'seen' as well as 'unseen' facets of that culture; this is exactly the approach which endeavours to suitably address any study on gender and ethnicity.

Concluding Remark

Narratives, as mentioned above, emphasise on the necessity of understanding gender and ethnicity, as they influence each other, rather than as two watertight compartments. There is a need for such anthropological writings that go far beyond and far deeper than the surface understanding of gender and ethnicity.

Acknowledgement

I would like to express my sense of gratitude to the members of the Women Organisations and the NGO's that I was able to interact and share the sense of violation of our dignity and honour because we belong to a particular Gender and Ethnicity.

References

Brown Miller, Susan.1975. *Against our Will: Men, Women, and Rape.* New York: Simon and Schuster.

Davis, Angela. 2011. *Women, Race, and Class.* New Delhi: Navayana.

Moon, Vasant. 2001. *Growing up in India: A Dalit Autobiography*, Translated from Marathi by Gail Omvedt, New Delhi: Vistaar Publication.

Chapter - 4

Salvage Ethnoarchaeological Research in Northeast India: Perspective and Practicality

—*Mayanglambam ManiBabu*

I

The academic stature of present-day archaeology, besides the traditionalist construct of culture-history, owes to the complex processes enriched by a variety of intellectual flows of new and post-processual archaeological epitomes. In contrast to the previous long-run dichotomic and epistemic antinomies, the present status is characterised by the implicit atomisation (Murray, 2017) of past cultural system and cultural processes. Its conceptualisation experienced widely varied research themes, theoretical approaches, and appropriate methodologies. Yet, scholars across the globe generally employ methods conditioned by their regional and local experiences. The essence of prehistoric archaeology as a human science is to unveil the cultural and economic lifeways of those humans lived since its earliest existence on this planet up to the frontiers of documentary history. They are thus more concerned with the tracing and unearthing the remains of the man's past - their proper analysis and giving their meaning. This ever-challenging task is to perform primarily with a simple shovel, pick and spade - unearthing the tangible and solid and fossilised products, the lithic artifacts. This entity, rather, makes Stone-Age Prehistorians, irrespective of conservative and processual, an empiricist (ManiBabu, 2003). In fact 'a stone tool is a sort of map of how human beings thought about their world, harvested resources, and invested time in extracting food and symbolising values and aesthetics' (Lohse, 2008). Stone artifacts were initially studied primarily as indicators of cultural achievements and then of technology and subsistence strategies.

While the issue of interpreting the 'tangible remains' of past human behaviour comes, there has relevance with one of the bipolar propositions in lithic archaeological grammar which states that - archaeological data, being formerly an integral part of socio-cultural entities, 'can not be adequately studied as artificially discrete subsystem separated from the whole circuitry of interaction which was its former context ... (and) should be studied in a socio-cultural and environmental context' (Clarke, 1968:479). The other proposition refers that archaeological data, being now detached from their systemic context, may 'best be studied empirically as a material phenomenon with observable regularities ... in terms of their own attribute systems, away from the distortions of loose presuppositions about their former contexts' (*ibid.*). Both the propositions have merits in their own philosophy. But there may also be an argument that what is detrimental to refer to both the domains in dealing with the finds. The issue deems essential in dealing with both empirically observe characters of the finds in terms of their typo-technology attributes, and also the unseen side of the behaviours and actions (if possible) that were associated with the material objects during their living contexts. This obviously may refer to Schiffer's archaeological (dead) and systemic (living) contexts of the objects. Systemic context labels the condition of an element which is participating in a behavioural system. Archaeological context describes materials which have passed through a cultural system, and which are now the objects of investigation of archaeologists (Schiffer, 1972:157).

It is the first above-mentioned proposition that has relevance in dealing with archaeological data in terms of their previous living systemic socio-cultural domains, and hence it naturally concerns with the ethnographic past. Notwithstanding the temporality in the framework of reference between archaeologists and ethnographers/cultural anthropologists, both share a common goal – to study human culture, the past and the present respectively. This is the traditional academic division. Unlike ethnographers, however, archaeologists work with a very partial kind of evidence: the fragmentary material remains of past human behaviour recorded on excavation or survey. They are to confine to those silent, dumb and mute tangible objects (the material culture) which were made, used and discarded by our past ancestors. Hence, differences lie from other academic fields of humanities. Through this medium with their description and analyses, archaeologists are busied themselves to construct past societies. Besides dealing with their tangible attributes, archaeologists also proceed to interpret the intangible realms that surround these objects–how, why and under what circumstances these objects/materials were made and used. However, it bears little or no signs of gaining the socio-cultural domains of the maker on the basis of the observed characters of an archaeological object. This forms the very challenging task as well as the charm of archaeologists. This natural phenomenon is being faced by all archaeologists through time everywhere. As a way of compensating the 'missing evidence' in the record, comparisons with living or historical known societies have long been part of the archaeological reasoning. Hence, one could describe archaeologists as a special type of cultural anthropologists or ethnographers. However, one of the most difficult tasks for an archaeologist is to know how to interpret the material remains in human terms. Well with the use of many theoretical frameworks archaeologists try to link their excavated evidence to actual human behaviour, and do far more than merely use data different from that used by ethnographers. Direct observations of past human activities are out of question, yet the behavioural realms that surround the archaeological material are to reconstruct somehow in order to have a general picture of the past prehistoric or early historic period, and hence, archaeologists look for incorporating the notions of other allied sciences, especially ethnography, into the archaeological discourse. Studying contemporary people is useful by archaeologists 'since it can produce information not readily attainable through standard interviews' (Kuznar, 1995:1). Thus, to derive the meaning of the archaeological data implicitly or explicitly, the use of ethnographic data reveals as one of the key importance, owing to the fact that collected archaeological finds from the trenches or otherwise are only the material traces of behaviour of the people who made and used them, and not their behaviour itself. Archaeological significances of ethnographic data are hence, to fill these behavioural voids in the record. Gloria London (2000:7) commenting on 'ethnoarchaeological research (as) one of the most powerful tools to aid in recognising the relationship between human behaviour and material culture'...reiterates:

> 'Rather than speculate on the use of fragmentary artifacts or buildings, one sees the complete artifact in use and the person behind who made or uses it. The goal of archaeology is to learn about people, rather than the pots or the building walls, and ethnoarchaeology proves to be an exciting current research strategy toward this purpose' (*ibid.*).

With this basic conceptual background, the present discourse attempts to play up some of the issues and relevancies of ethnoarchaeology (particularly salvage) as a research strategy in getting into the archaeological significances of past lifeways of the indigenous populations of Northeast India-which are, at present in its state of continual change amidst the historical processes of modernisation, globalisation and other developmental works–before it is getting to too late to record the uncontaminated ones.

II

India's northeast-comprising the seven states of Arunachal Pradesh, Assam, Manipur, Meghalaya, Mizoram, Nagaland, and Tripura- is an outgrowth of political and locational appellation, yet its spatial placement amidst the three geographical components of Asia–the South, the East and the Southeast - makes the area a unique meeting place of different ethnic groups. Nestled along the eastern and southeastern extension of the Himalayan mountain range, the region lies amidst the tropical zone inhabited mainly by a large number of indigenous tribal populations of Indo-Mongoloid appellation in different habitats and ecological settings. Endowed with immense natural and human resources different ethnic groups of the region practice different cultures and traditions and within these regulate the lives of the people in their unique ways. It is seen that social, political and cultural systems of tribal people are reflected their myths, stories, folktales, and folk songs. The basic economic scenario of these tribes, till recently was very much dependent on forest for their day-to-day needs, including food, shelter, tools, folk medicine, and in some cases even clothes. As long as the tribes were in control of forest, they had no difficulty in meeting these needs. In turn, they preserved the forest as it was their life support system. Nature, environment, and ecology hence, play the most important roles in their lives. They have developed their religious beliefs and practices around these life-giving forces.

With the advent of the British colonial rule in Northeast India, the beginning of which can be seen with the first Indo-Burmese war and the Treaty of Yandaboo that ended it in 1826 (Allen *et al.,* 1857), the tribal life of the region underwent a process of change. The war itself was thought to be due to the instability that existed in the North East at the beginning of the nineteenth century. The then dominant power in the region, which claimed the Ahom throne, enabled the Burmese to occupy not only Assam but neighbouring Cachar and Manipur as well (Robinson, 1841). Obviously, colonial administration marks the beginning of a new historical period which is the dawn of modernised way of life for the tribals. They began to move away from their traditional way, owing to ignorance, superstitions, and isolation to an alleged brighter and better way of life. In fact, the British restructured the traditional economy into colonial lines, introduced new policies and made efforts to exploit the native natural resources to meet their own imperial interest. Besides, with the progress of industrialisation and modernisation also, the people of the region have undergone substantial change. It is a fact that the religious concepts, terminologies, and practices among the Northeast Indian populations were centred on the traditional animistic faith, but all these groups contribute to somewhat common in them, they are below regular stress from the main prepared religions, like Hinduism and Christianity. Some of this force is intentional as the missionaries work, for instance, among the tribal group is to gain converts. Historical layers of each and every tribe reveal that they converted themselves to Christianity or Hinduism due to outside forces. And these pressures, however, come from the process of integration within a national, political and economic system that brings tribes into increasing contact with other groups and different pseudo-prestigious belief systems. In general, only those tribal pockets that remain geographically isolated from the mainstream are able to retain their traditional cultures and religious faiths for longer periods. Being adapted to the changing atmosphere, almost all Northeast Indian ethnic groups adheres themselves to modernisation and the western norms and practices (modernisation is highly perceived as a Western process) that are gradually being transported across the globe as the acceptable way of behaviour. In view of this, the rich and dynamic indigenous culture has become diluted. However, modernisation is an unavoidable and undeniable factor in any traditional society, to develop is to change, impacts of which cannot only be analysed through either negative or positive. It is a common picture now-a-days among all the Northeast Indian traditional society that people freely engaged themselves with the very domain of modernisation at different levels as a normal course, which has its impact to the traditional worldviews of the people in terms of personality, occupation, lifestyle and traditional and symbolic values, and many more. Yet, a new trend of contra-acculturation modality and desire comes up among the indigenous tribal people, to come back to their pure ideal structures of the past, which they ignored but realised now and feel proud of their beauty and essence, and got repentances of their ignorance before.

It happens to be a great task with some ethnographers trying to record and document the indigenous universe of tribal cultures and traditions. And this has become the only specified core of study with salvage ethnographers towards commemorating, recovering and preserving the remnants of the pure native aboriginal culture the world over before it is entirely effaced and engulfed by modernity and the like. Yet this shall be an obsolete venture to any ethnic group who has had been on its brink of modernised lifeways. Anthropologists and ethnographers are now well aware of the issue that human cultures constantly change as people respond to social, political, economic, and other external and internal influences—that there is no moment when a culture is more authentic or more primitive. They acknowledge that culture is fluid and cannot be treated as isolated in time and space. Just as we should not portray people as primitive vestiges of an earlier stage of human development, we also should not romanticise a culture or idealise another's suffering as more authentic or natural.

Salvage ethnography, as such has been subjected to a conceptual framework which treated aboriginal cultures as entities that stood outside history, uninfluenced by modern western civilisation as they existed in their pure forms. This is met inevitably with their demise once they were drawn into the historical process. Rooted in the ethnographic discourses of the twentieth century the principle of the 'salvage' paradigm' represents a desire to rescue 'authenticity' out of destructive historical change or more implicitly, from those through whose negligence it might be lost. This subject might seem outdated and irrelevant to discussions of contemporary cultural production, where any attempt at 'cultural salvage' can only be greeted with suspicion given the contemporary discourse around Western systems of the objectivation of otherness. The principle of 'salvage' signifies cultural, aesthetic, and institutional practices best discarded as obsolete. Despite Malinowski's tremendous contributions to ethnography and anthropology generally, he was nevertheless a man of his time. A common view in the first half of the twentieth century was that many 'primitive' cultures were quickly disappearing and features of those cultures needed to be preserved (salvaged) before they were lost. Renowned anthropologists such as Malinowski (1932), Radcliffe-Brown (1931), Franz Boas (1928) and many of their students sought to document, photograph, and otherwise preserve cultural traditions in 'dying' cultures among groups such as Native Americans and other traditional societies experiencing rapid change due to modernisation, dislocation, and contact with outside groups. They also collected cultural artifacts, removing property from the communities and placing it in museums and private collections. While referring to Geertz's (1973) pioneered notion of 'thick description' which gives considerable attention to the 'contextual' as well as 'human behavioural' perspectives; and also to Sanday's (1979) proposition of holistic, semiotic and behaviouristic ethnography–it is a great concern for the ethnographers to discuss whether they could set about the original/archaic knowledge of an indigenous people whose culture had been assimilated and acculturated within a larger colonial history.

Ungrudgingly one is to accept with the dictum that modernisation *vis-à-vis* globalisation has made its influence on the Northeast Indian society. Yet there have some domains in terms of technology and material culture, behaviour, ethics, worldviews, etc that have strong natural resentment to a change, owing either to the obtruded part to their inherited ethos or in consonance with the peoples' adaptation strategies to their immediate environment and landscape (both natural and cultural). For instance, change in subsistence economy more particularly with swidden agriculture practiced by a good number of hilly tribes is inconceivable as it centred wholly on the nature of prevailing ecology, landforms, terrains and climatic conditions on one hand, and strong socio-cultural foundations in terms of its organisation of production and in the paraphernalia of technology. The question of modernisation does have no significances in the economic realms of preparing, clearing, tilling the *jhum* sites and also in sowing and harvesting stages. And, in terms of the cultural norms, such as the prevailing system of giving and taking bride price – modernisation or the new religious faith of Christianity has very little influence in its underlying symbolic constructs, norms, and worldviews. Moreover, using the locally available herbs along with rituals is part of the peoples' continuing practices in treating ailments and diseases which were passed on through generations since time immemorial, and it has its great significances with those people settled in the remote hilly flanks with having lesser or no modern medical facilities. Besides these, one could have a number of areas where the human-environment relationship has immense significances, with lesser or no impacts of modernisation. Such are the situations that salvage ethnographers are taking keen interest to document the indigenous ways of life in their uncontaminated forms. The same pulse is also of those archaeologists (the ethnoarchaeologists) who mainly attempted to interpret lifeways of the human past, through the present ethnographic lens, of an indigenous nature. The issue is that field ethnoarchaeological research could no longer collect authentic traditional culture because it no longer existed. Field research in this context could only confuse the cultural record: recent adoptions from modern cultures or cultural distortions caused by oral transmission were taken to be authentic traditions, at times by informants themselves. The archaeological investigation of dispersed indigenous people who remained in the voids of globalisation has thus been out of the question at present.

III

To an archaeologist, studying the past dynamic living contexts of the tangible objects is much more stringent than studying definite characters of the finds in their static archaeological contexts. But in order to reconstruct their past mundane domain, archaeologists have no way out but to deal with these silent objects, the material culture who cannot speak. Obviously, they make no sense by themselves but only acquire significance when interpreted (Gamble, 200: 45). In dealing with these challenges, conventional archaeological practices alone are insufficient, and archaeologists seek for such a way out through ethnography. The main analytical tool used by archaeologists to project modern behaviour into the past is thus the ethnographic analogy. This involves studying modern populations including their material residues and behavioural patterns and comparing this data to archaeologically derived data from sites. It is maintained that since archaeologists have 'no direct access to information about human behaviour' (Trigger, 1989:357), ethnographic information can be employed in interpreting archaeological data with the use of analogy (Spaulding, 1973; Stanislawski, 1978; Stiles, 1977; Gould, 1980; etc.). It was Lewis Binford who rests the importance of the use of ethnographic data in archaeology, its use in the formulation of hypotheses about ancient lifeways in regards to explanations of variability in form, structure and the functioning of cultural systems (Binford, 1968:269). These explanations will, for new archaeologists, hopefully, lead to predictions of behaviour and the generation of universal laws. It is essential to devise ways of inferring the dynamic nonmaterial aspects of 'lived' culture and society from the static surviving physical remains that eventually come to form the 'dead' archaeological record (Binford, 1978). Here lies the meeting point of ethnography and archaeology, giving rise to the development of an academic endeavour within archaeology called 'ethnoarchaeology'. While describing the relationship between archaeology and ethnography, Kluckhohn (1949:46) states that 'archaeology is the ethnography and culture history of past peoples, and its cornerstone is an analogy, (and)...every archaeological reconstruction is analogy based upon a number of...presumptions and assumptions'. Obviously, development of ethnoarchaeology is also guided by a research theme–there is continuity of past identity in the present living context. Kofi Agorsah (1999) thus observed that:

> Ethno-archaeology...consist of a means of explaining the behaviour of past societies on the basis of analytical models derived from observed behavioural or cultural phenomena of living societies, traditional or not. The crucial consideration should be an orientation towards an explicitly well-defined interface between models drawn from modern traditional behaviour and those of the past. (pp. 38-39).

Obviously salvage ethnographic data has relevance in archaeological discourse in fulfilling the very aim of ethno-archaeology, such as, (i) to identify and explain patterns in relationships between human behaviour and its archaeological consequences in the present (O'Connell, 1995), (ii) to provide ethnographic data and explications of those data that are of direct relevance to the interpretation of archaeological materials and to model-building in archaeological practice (Kramer, 1985; Schiffer, 1978; Schwartz, 1978, etc), and (iii) to document patterns in the ongoing society in order to reconstruct past behaviours from their extant material remnants (Rathje, 1978:49).

Miriam Stark (1993) sees ethnoarchaeology, not as a theory but a research strategy for answering archaeological questions in a living society. Though not very much aware of this term which happened to have coined as late as 1900 by J.W. Fewkes, sporadic ethnographic exercises were made from time to time that lien to the very theme of ethnoarchaeology-the use of ethnography to interpret the past. David and Kramer (2001:43) argue that 'ethnoarchaeology (is) developed in order to provide better ethnographic analogies to assist in the interpretation of archaeological data'. And in essence, 'the use of analogy in interpreting archaeological evidence' is ethnoarchaeology (Lynton, 1984: 63). Ethnoarchaeology hence aims at the 'acquisition of ethnographic data to assist archaeological interpretation' (Politis, 2007: 58) and mainly endeavours to establish 'relationships between human behaviour and its archaeological consequences in the present (O'Connell, 1995). Extensive debate on the issue of analogy as the basic tool in ethnoarchaeology persists throughout its journey during the sixties (e.g., Anderson, 1969; Binford, 1968, 1972; Chang, 1967; Clarke, 1968; Freeman, 1968; Munson, 1969) and eighties (Charlton,1981; Gould and Watson, 1982; Crawford, 1982; Lange, 1980; Murray and Walker, 1988; Simms,1992; Stahl, 1993; Wobst, 1978; Wylie, 1982, 1985, 1988, 1989). Though the issue with the use of analogy seemed to decrease with the advent of postmodern theory in archaeology and the subsequent reaction against it by scientifically oriented archaeologists in the 1990s and 2000s (Ravn, 2011), obvious continuity between the prehistoric past and the ethnographic present has always favoured the utilisation of ethnographic data in archaeological interpretation. It is seen that use of analogy or its allied tool was in vogue in all the three paradigmatic domains of archaeological theories-culture history, new archaeology, and post-processual archaeology. A common feature with culture-history archaeology was the use of already existing ethnographic data 'without setting criteria and limitations, and projecting or imposing to a given archaeological case' (Politis, 2015) and made an inference by cross-cultural analogies. With the new theoretical shift from the cultural history to processual or new archaeology during the 1960s with Lewis Binford's 1962 essay ('Archaeology as Anthropology') challenging culture-historians' way of dealing archaeological data (Binford, 1972)-the academic significances of 'ethnoarchaeology' developed and archaeologists started to gather the ethnographic information themselves. And it not only developed as a full academic status but its theoretical and methodological bases also achieved (Ascher, 1968; Binford, 1968; Longacre and Ayres, 1968). Consequently, ethnoarchaeology emerged as a direct result of the development of actualistic studies not favouring the use of ethnographic analogy, but the Middle Range Theory (MRT)-in order to bridge the gap between the dynamics of the living systems and the static nature of the archaeological record (Binford, 1981; Schiffer, 1978). Processualists argue that ethnographical data should only be used for model-building. These 'tested' and approved ethnographically-based models mysteriously transforms to be 'facts', beyond the analogical state. MRT is an ambitious enterprise that can establish links between day-to-day practice and how the archaeological record was formed. Introduction of MRT to archaeology by Binford (1977), borrowing Merton's [1968] sociological theory, was a means of getting contemporary facts from the present to statements about the past.

> 'We must develop ideas and theories (middle-range theory) regarding the formation processes of the archaeological record. Only through an accurate understanding of such processes can we reliably give meaning to the facts that appear, from the past, in the contemporary era' (Binford, 1977:7)

A different strand comes up in the 1980s with the rise of the post-processual or 'contextual' archaeology that never really explored the possibilities of MRT, but carried on seeking to distinguish 'proper' analogies from 'improper' ones. Post-processualists see ethnoarchaeology more as a field of discussion and testing of concepts (Hodder, 1986) rather than a way towards ethnographic analogies or MRT (Binford, 1983), and they put more importance to the issue of context suggesting that questions of relevance, generality, and goodness of fit may strengthen analogies (Hodder, 1982:22). Developed as an academic outcrop through the growing influence of postmodern thought in the social sciences (Bintliff, 1991; Duke, 1995; Watson, 1990), post-processual archaeology developed another ethnoarchaeological perspective to the study of modern material culture. Post-processualists' objective is not to arrive at and explain with, but instead to illustrate the relationship between different data available in one's research and decipher its correlation with human behaviour, present or not (Stark, 1993). The major shift from the processual MRT to post-processual ethnoarchaeology is a step away from simple observations of cause and effect(s) to complex areas of ideology, cosmology or ontology-a shift from how things were done to why they were done. Postprocessual approach to ethnoarchaeological research is more or less 'exploring the symbolic dimensions of material culture' (David and Kramer, 2001:54), and 'material culture studies' (e.g., Conkey, 1989; Hodder, 1986; Miller, 1983, 1985), exploring 'how people construct their material worlds...rather than an adaptive response, culture and material culture are understood in relation to meaning' (Cunningham, 2003:398).

There show another theoretical turn with the cessation of hot deliberations existed between processual and post-processual (for instance, Hegmon, 2003; Johnson, 2006). Commenting this theoretical allegiance as not a defining issue, Hegmon (2003:216) stated that postprocessual emphases of agency, gender, and meaning have been gradually incorporated into the processual mainstream, creating a category best described as 'processual-plus', thereby compromising processual objectives and methods with a greater awareness of postprocessual critiques (Fancher, 2009). Against these backdrops, pursuing salvage ethnoarchaeological research work among the indigenous Northeast Indian populations will have an immense academic yield of prehistoric significance.

IV

With its unique location, Northeast India offers quite a significant arena of archaeological discourse. With India's history of colonial assimilation and acculturation, early archaeological, as well as anthropological researches, were established by non-locales and relate to British scholarship interests. Beginning with the pioneering work of John Lubbock (1867), followed subsequently by many amateurs in the field, the early archaeological research in this region was not, at all, a product of academic tradition. A handful vestigial collection of stone tools by pioneer amateur scholars (Anderson, 1871; Barron, 1872; Godwin-Austen, 1875; Cockburn, 1879; Brown, 1914, 1917, to name a few) could give a firm evidence of prehistoric human settlement in this part of the world. Academic tinge in prehistoric research could be seen with the works of Hutton (1924, 1926, and 1928) and Worman (1949) more particularly with Neolithic archaeology. And it is with the opening of prehistoric archaeology as a specialised course in 1966 for the postgraduate students in Gauhati University, Assam that the academic tempo accelerates with a number of research works by the students and research scholars by conducting field study tour at different corners of the region, more particularly in Meghalaya. Earlier academic ventures by profound local workers (Goswami and Bhagabati, 1959; Goswami and Sharma, 1962, 1963; Sharma, 1966, 1967; Sharma, 1972) in the field of quaternary prehistory, and by subsequent workers in myriad research domains towards attaining an academic archaeological height are noteworthy. In reviewing general research trend in the region, most works are dealing with stone tool prehistory, living megalithism and less with ethnoarchaeological approaches. The present state of studies in the lithic prehistory of Northeast India is at its spatiotemporal dimensions of cultural history. Many times, it is tempted to call for multi-disciplinary research strategies and theories in the approaches concerning with human and social sciences. Taking into account the globally changing prehistoric research paradigms, and also considering the significances that the region has in terms of her geographical proximity and archaeological propinquity with the eastern mainland India and Southeast Asian countries, there need to look for new ventures at all perceptible research areas. However, this does not mean that the work done so far has little significance in structuring her prehistory. In spite of the fact that the traditional and descriptive archaeology is unmistakably the basic foundation of prehistory through the ages, yet new theoretical frameworks could make furtherance in explaining and structuring the prehistoric past with systematic academic tinge. We all should agree that there lacks a large body of information, the lacunae that surround the issues with structuring her prehistory, and for it, all the researchers should share responsibilities. Apparently, one of the reasons behind overlooking the theoretical paradigms in dealing with the issue owed to the workers' flaccid vision with the present scientific and methodological trends, duly conceded with the long-run traditionalist time-space mindset. Besides the activities with shovel and trowel, there need to document other dimensions of past humans, the extraction of which are beyond the limit to that of lithic study.

In essence, ethnoarchaeological works in Northeast India are negligible. Sporadic works on indigenous art and craft (including pottery making culture, indigenous technology, material culture, etc), subsistence economy, megalithic traditions, etc - though claimed to be ethnoarchaeological in nature, do not come at all, within proper methodological and theoretical frameworks. One should be well aware of designing a proper framework for every ethnoarchaeological research, and should not commit mistake with a 'mere accumulation of ethnographic data and the provision of half-baked generalisations with the usual cautionary note 'more needs to be done on this subject', which, in effect obstructing the development of the type of research in ethnoarchaeology that would contribute viable theoretical formulations' (Agorsah, 1990:190). It is also a regular phenomenon with 'many scholars who do ethnographic research and are able to make even the most tenuous link between their material and archaeology have enjoyed the liberty of claiming that they are doing ethnoarchaeology' (*ibid.* 192). In regards to the methodological issues, Gloria London (2000) reckoned -

> Implementing a successful ethnoarchaeology project requires planning and purpose, and addressing issues debated in the archaeological literature must be a key objective of the research. Rather than a fortuitous study of people using a traditional

> technology in the vicinity of an excavation site, a well-planned project involves selection of a suitable community that will provide material to address the issue at hand, be it animal slaughtering with associated patterns of distribution and discard of the bones, house size and contents in relation to family status or population size, etc (p. 6).

As outlined above, contemporary indigenous people still possess some ideal archaeological potentialities. In fact, Northeast India deserves for a wide-ranging ethnoarchaeological radical owing to the fact that indigenous tribal populations in both the plain and hilly flanks still retain some of their traditional adaptive practices interwoven with the traditional mundane domain (amidst modernisation, globalisation, and embracement of alien religious faiths). Mention may be made, for instance, of subsistence economy (swidden and hill-terrace cultivation), landholding pattern, food habit, healing practices, traditional craft (subsistence technologies, carved houses more among the Nagas, hand-made pottery with cord-marked decoration, bark-cloth making, etc), megalithism, disposal of dead, and many more - some of which have Neolithic bearings. Naturally, these strategies, decisions, and actions have essences on archaeological dialogues. In essence salvage, ethnoarchaeological research is the most needed task to be taken up in all possible research areas before its dilution or threatened to be thinned by modern anthropogenic activities. A review article 'On the Scope of the Ethno-archaeological studies in Manipur', ManiBabu (1988-89) has highlighted at least some of the potential research areas in Manipur, such as, in the field of economy, material culture including house type, mortuary practices, megalithism, etc. As the understanding the interaction between humans, things, and their environment, and trying to find areas of interest in interpreting the prehistoric record stand another field of ethnoarchaeology (Gould, 1989), there are potentials of undertaking salvage ethnoarchaeological research on the indigenous ethnic groups of the region. Obviously, ethnography as an excellent mirror to see the key factors involved in past human behaviour basically rests on the notion that as 'societies ... owing to their perceived 'premodern' way of life were deemed appropriate to be compared with archaeological contexts' (Hamilakis, 2011) and 'man in the past was not unlike primitive man studied by the anthropologists' (Orme, 1981:15).

It would be extremely difficult for archaeologists to interpret the archaeological record if they thought that people and cultures of the past bore no resemblance to those of today. It is generally assumed that there has been some continuity through time, thus archaeologists commonly use information from the present to interpret the past. One way they accomplish this is by doing archaeological research on present-day societies-studying the ways in which people live today and the material traces that their activities leave behind. This method of archaeological research is called ethnoarchaeology (Daniel, 2011). However, to highlight research priorities from amongst the myriad potential ethnoarchaeological fields in a region like Northeastern India, where neither is nor was, at any of the arising proper research strategies–is not as cumbersome as searching a small piece of thread over a dark floor. The region stands at its apex of myriad prehistoric research potency. Though many tribal societies of the area are less pristine, yet they offer excellent opportunities for salvage ethnoarchaeologists to work on any of its strains of inquiry. Planned archaeological projects may include various fields (such as settlement and household archaeology, contextual archaeology, the archaeology of body, Marxist archaeology, cognitive archaeology, archaeology of Individual, of wetland, of gender and what not)–in the same manner as one can go for any ethnographic research agenda. As 'our discipline is so broad…(and) none of us can, in his own research, encompass the whole field' (Rouse, 1965),-one can explore potentials of either the Binfordian or Hodderian frameworks (or both) pertaining with the domains of ecological and materialist explanations, or more concerned with a diversity of behavioural insights for a fuller understanding. Besides the fundamental ventures of exploring and excavating more of Stone Age sites, one can go with any of the following fields (but not restricted to), irrespective of research priorities, such as, - (a) human strategy of adaptation and interaction with their habitat in order to recognise behavioural flexibility and diversity (scientific processual framework of man-land relationship), (b) human plurality of knowledge and meaning (humanistic postprocessual framework of human cognition). In regards to the *first* research agenda, one may go with (for example) - food producing and procuring/gathering activities (such as, shifting cultivation, collection of non-domesticated fruits, plants, wood, etc.), settlement strategies (including highland and wetlands), traditional technologies and indigenous craftsmanship (basketry, pottery, fire-making, metal-working technology, etc) to name a few. And for the *second* one, all of the non-material aspects of human culture and behaviour, may come up in terms of cognition, symbolism, contextual framework and meaning of the systems, social organisation, belief systems, and so on. In this regard, the prime area of commonalities between agency theory and evolutionary analysis of human behaviour may also explore especially in relation to the peoples' social and symbolic behaviour. Among myriad fields - traditional subsistence and settlement strategies; and traditional technologies and the organisation of craft production are the main categories for ethnoarchaeological studies in the Asian (Griffin and Solheim, 1990) and South Asian contexts (Sinopoli, 1991). And these are all related to linkages between people and environment. As seen in other parts of the world, the lifeways of the indigenous tribal peoples of Northeast India lean to their immediate environment and their social organisation is woven around the interaction and management with their environment. A few concrete examples that have salvaged ethnoarchaeological potentials may refer to the adaptational pattern of the indigenous people to the surrounding physical environment, thereby creating a 'cultural landscape'. Cultural landscape manifests a social space of human interaction to the physical environment denoting a deep sense of human creativity and variability. And variable physical landscapes always go hand in hand with peoples' dynamic cultural tradition. This is the idea of landscape studies by the post-processual archaeologists. The physical surroundings or the world humans live in may bear different meaning, and different schools of thought are associated with these terms (Shanks and Hodder, 1995). To cite an example of specific research avenue within this paradigm, 'Anthropic Activity Marker' model (Rondelli *et al*., 2014), bears ample scope to extend out in a region like Northeast India where human dependant on natural environment relating to their physical and cultural adaptations is so high. Basically this model has its foundation after a number of initial studies concerning to the definite areas people recurrently use of their landscape or living space for specific activities (Kent, 1987; Kroll and Price, 1991), the physical manifestation of which this might be archaeologically identified (Hodder and Orton, 1976; Halstead *et al.,* 1978; Hassan, 1978). Concerning more with the identification of these anthropogenic areas through the analysis of dispersions of macroscopic materials (especially lithic and faunal remains), such analyses were soon fully integrated into archaeological methodology (Lancelotti *et. al.,* 2017:339). Indeed, a number of studies (Barba and Bello, 1978; Barba, 2007; Manzanilla and Barba, 1990; Ortiz and Barba, 1993; Middleton and Price, 1996) could realised that the enduring use of space produces distinctive patterns of evidence in the deposit, in particular, the enrichment and/or depletion of chemical and/or physical elements, which directly represent the result of the activity that produced them. If the enduring use of space produces distinctive patterns of evidence, ethnoarchaeology and experimental archaeology drive the inferential reasoning that creates the model(s) connecting the concentration of particular proxies with a specific activity (Barba and Ortiz, 1992; Middleton and Price, 1996; Pecci, 2003; Pecci *et al.,* 2013). A relevant example that be cited, mainly seen mainly in the hilly flanks of Manipur, Meghalaya, Mizoram and Nagaland is that phenomenon of exploiting the naturally-occurring rock boulders toward manifesting practical and prestige technologies. This obviously reflects the worldview of the respective tribal group, and the art that surrounds the system is transmitting through generations since earliest times till today. Mention may be made of two significant features seen among some indigenous tribal populations in Manipur, such as, the traditional way of using large hewn or natural stone blocks and boulders– (i) as material manifestation of symbol of a man's status in the society by way of erecting these as megalithic monuments (as prestige technology) and (ii) as perimeter of one's habitation boundary area/forest land, or as practical technology to make a sloppy habitation site into a plain level so as to make them easier to make shelters, etc. The peoples' way of management of stone boulders reflects the kin centric relationship that an indigenous culture maintains with their natural resources, thereby creating a cultural landscape. The materiality of such large stones in its living archaeological contexts manifest the peoples' worldview of society, status, landscape, territoriality and what not; and could make ethnographic postulates operable to the archaeologists towards highlighting prehistoric cultural landscapes (ManiBabu, 2014). Appropriate salvage ethnoarchaeological tool in such attempts is subject to the context of the research area and the gravity of data in hand.

Another important issue within the perspective of the cultural landscape is the domain of space syntax of megaliths, some preliminary works of which have also been attempted (ManiBabu, 2014; Philip and ManiBabu, 2015) on some megalithic sites located in the Naga inhabited villages in Manipur. Through the space syntax research on the distributional pattern of megaliths, a spatial ontology can be inferred on the relations between spatial configuration and the social functioning of space of monuments. It is observed that 'a spatial cognition to the erection and placement of monuments based on a correlative arrangement between environment and human movement exist where the spatial distributions of monuments are related with the spaces where there is a maximum accessibility of human movement' (ManiBabu, *op. cit.*). Obviously, if a landscape comprising of these characters along with other tangible traces of human activity - such as post-holes, associated habitation debris, landform modifications attributable to man, etc. - are found distributed over a deserted area, this has great salvage ethnoarchaeological potentialities toward shedding light on 'settlement archaeology' of the area on the basis of the present ethnographic postulates on how the present tribal people interact with their surrounding environment. With this, other human aspects related to subsistence, polity, society and many others can also be addressed accordingly subject to the nature of data in hand.

Beyond such salvage ethnoarchaeological domains, another interesting and intriguing area is in terms of various crafts and technologies for myriad subsistence pursuits. Peoples' strategies to procure and produce food entails various processes suitable to the environment where they settled-the landform, climatic stipulation, potentials of natural resources and many more. Hunting and fishing activities by the tribal people in Manipur, for instance, entail to the development of myriad strategies in accordance with their immediate environment. Making of different kinds of fishing implements and appliances, such as, baskets, nets, snares, spears, traps, etc are all the resultant technologies which gave way with different locational character, nature, and content of water-bodies. The same is in the hunting practices also. Some unique hunting strategies seen in bygone days among the Tangkhul Nagas of the north-easterly Ukhrul District in the State of Manipur is very much a part of the hunters' skill in their food procuring strategies. Besides using the long hairs of a horse's tail for trapping wild birds, such as pheasants, wild-fowls, doves and other birds of medium size (Shimray, 1976: 19) they used to develop a trapping techniques (called 'Vakhong') to catch a particular small bird (locally termed as 'Shiri' of about eight inches long) using a large number of big *uningthou* trees (*Phoebe hainesiana* Brandis; Family: *Lauraceae*) grown in the nearby forests.

'There, high on the trees, small basins were made by axing out into the main or big branches, and put water in them. The birds while feeding on the fruits of the trees, immediately saw the water, and felt convenient to get a drink from the artificial tanks where traps had been laid. Baskets–full of birds were caught in that way. This trap was meant only for a particular species of birds–eight inches long. In spite of its small size, it makes a delicious dish' (*ibid.*).

Another most challenging practice connected with food producing economy among the hill tribes of Northeastern India, Southeast Asia and Highlanders of Pacific and beyond, which has salvage ethnoarchaeological significances, is the 'slash-and-burn' system of cultivation. Besides its genesis to the Neolithic period, this agricultural practice possesses a number of archaeological implications in terms of its adaptational character in a hilly environment, its application of simple technology, and other traceable corresponding activities in archaeological contexts. Since salvage ethnoarchaeology may proceed at various levels of complexity depending on the ultimate use to which the data are to be put (Binford, 1967, 1968; Gould, 1968; White, 1967 etc), the present issue is to identify and accumulate specific material and/or behavioural traces of subsistence activities that will remain as part of the archaeological features. The general operational character of shifting agriculture permits archaeologists to identify vast traces of cultivators' activities, which are deemed available in the activities area, such as - (a) traces of charcoal pieces and ashes dispersed over and beneath a sloppy hilly soil, (b) perimetric features that mark the boundaries of cultivated plots small rock boulders in rows or otherwise, spatial distribution of accumulated medium-to large-sized rock boulders over an area put together while preparing *jhum* fields so that these may not affect the soil or otherwise, managing to get wider space for sowing seeds, (c) material traces of temporary huts constructed in the *jhum* fields-its foundational floors, along with those activities concerning cooking and eating, such as structure of a hearth constructed mainly with a composite of three medium-sized stones placed each in a triangular equidistance pattern so that a cooking vessel can fit to place over it, (d) raised ramparts that facilitates farmers to make strict vigil over the crops grown from a raised height, and many more items - such as betel, cigarettes and playing cards, pieces of old/torn cloth, combs, sandals, batteries, etc. Regarding the first character, obviously 'ephemeral surface fires may prove difficult to detect after the wind blows the remains around...On the other hand, when the earth is scooped out very deeply and fires burn for a long time, it is easier to detect and recognise as human controlled actions, possibly many years or millennia afterwards' (Mallol *et al.*, 2007). Some ethnoarchaeological approach to soil micromorphology with the goal of obtaining reference material on anthropogenic fires (Goldberg and Whitebread, 1993; Wattez, 1992) are significant to mention with this issue.

All these attempts are but- (i) to document visible archaeological signatures that could give an ethnographic postulate of activities related to man's interaction with their physical surroundings, and (ii) to situate the dynamic archaeological past through the static ethnographic present against the backdrop of the present salvage ethnoarchaeological pursuit. It is, however, a problem with archaeologists' to translate inanimate objects and features into a model of behaviour. Although the problems are substantial they are not insuperable. The idea of studying how past peoples disposed themselves upon the land in order to understand the nature of their social, political, and economic structure-what Parsons (1972:128) aptly terms the 'sociology of architectural remains'- goes back at least to the explorers and amateur archaeologists of the nineteenth century.

V

To a wider extent, it is not inconceivable that the life-ways and traditional knowledge systems of some tribal populations in Northeast India are still retaining its archaic character in terms of their mundane domain amidst the exogenic pressure of modernisation and globalisation. Likewise, a handful of their endemic worldviews are seen alive still, obviously keeping on transmitting through generations since bygone days. Hence it is not a farfetched excuses that native peoples' adaptational pattern, some elements of their cultural behaviour and worldviews may be looked at as natural analogues of the past-inherited through the medium of 'memes', the continually inherited 'cultural genes' or an entity of 'cultural replicator that is capable of being transmitted from one brain to another' (Dawkins, 1976:210). Examples of 'memes' include ideas, habits, skills, inventions, ways of making pots, building arches and ways of doing things that we copy from person to person by imitation (Dawkins, 1976; Dennet, 1995). 'Artefacts can be viewed as the products of culturally transmitted information (cultural instructions or 'memes'), in conjunction with the physical capacities or motor habits of the makers as well as stochastic factors, working upon materials found in the environment' (Tschauner, 1996). Construing past human behaviour through the contemporary living peoples has bearings on a construct that-humans' favourable strategies (including other socio-cultural paraphernalia) are developed in order to adapt to the continuing ecosystem since the earliest past, and these are unmistakably transmitted through the 'memes' in a continuing process. Indigenous communities have kept their cultures alive by passing on their worldview, their knowledge, and know-how, their arts, rituals, and performances through generations. Obviously peoples' present life-ways being transmitted at least in memetic principle may have a little stock of the earlier accomplishment and skill, and obviously, these reflect the natural analogs for the past and also direct means of understanding extended survivals of the earlier human system, providing us with information about the totality of the past. It is asserted that the purpose of using ethnography in interpreting archaeological features, however, is not to extrapolate contemporary situations and human behaviour back into the past, but to provide a framework through which we can formulate a new working hypothesis for a better understanding of the archaeological record. As 'the most confident interpretation of a prehistoric artifact comes from the discovery of a similar or identical implement used by a living people (Anderson, 1969), ethnographic analogy utilises the ethnographic record as a source, or analog, for making inferences about the unknown subject of past human behaviour. The 'ethnographic present' thus creates a sense of place as 'allochronous' (Fabian, 1983) in archaeology, and especially the ones who have used ethnoarchaeological studies unreflectively and uncritically, have often treated local people (and their agricultural practices) as examples of pre-modern situations, as living in another time. Hence, ethnography as an excellent mirror to see the key factors involved in past human behaviour rests on the notion that as 'societies...owing to their perceived 'premodern' way of life were deemed appropriate to be compared with archaeological contexts' (Hamilakis, 2011) and 'man in the past was not unlike primitive man studied by the anthropologists' (Orme, 1981:15).

Yet another issue comes up on whether salvage ethnoarchaeologists need to go to the field to do their own ethnography, and if so why can't they rely on the data collected by the ethnographers? Ethnography being 'a portrait of a people' and 'a written description of a particular culture, the customs, beliefs, and behaviour (is) based on information collected through fieldwork' (Harris and Johnson, 2000), and ethnographic research focuses on cultural interpretation, for the purposes of description or extension of social theory – the data of which are typically gathered through participant observations and interviews. It is a fact that while using ethnographic data in describing and interpreting archaeological finds, archaeologists are more concerned with the resultant concrete features caused by the human action that goes to the realm of archaeological context than the features and activities of contemporary people. In normal courses, ethnographies usually ignore the physical manifestation of resultant activities related to the dynamic aspects of human lifeways. Core areas of archaeological significances, such as, disposal and discarded patterns and minute details of human activities (that give rise to tangible traces), details of spatial relations of physical vestiges of socio-economic activity, variation in artefact forms, human interaction with material culture and its cultural domains, minute activities of disposal pattern and many more, are not usually recorded in normal ethnographies. Hence, archaeologists who use ethnographic analogy clearly express their defeat with the ethnographic data.

> ...ethnography is inadequate for archaeological purposes because the literature describes either ideal types without a description of the range of variation or detailed material items without behavioural correlates or because it describes no material items i.e. no results of behaviour (Ascher, 1962:360).

Owing to these situations, archaeologists have often turned to conducting their own studies of living peoples, directed at use, discard and manufacture of material items (Gould, 1971: 144). Moreover, in attempting to capture as much indigenous behaviour as possible, salvage ethnographers usually oft to document those behaviours that still differentiate the group under study from surrounding groups or western populations (Wobst, 1978:304). Hence some areas concerning broader cultural aspects like, regional and inter-regional processes are found undocumented. Since the basic information relevant in reconstructing the past, such as, seeking the material consequences for human behaviours, their proper documentation in order to evaluate the meaning and models that surrounds the tangible and intangible cultural systems and many more of archaeological significances are not at all furnished as well as ignored in normal ethnographies-it is well better to go for their own functional ethnography.

The foregoing discourse could highlight the significance of pursuing salvage ethnoarchaeological studies on the indigenous peoples of Northeast India as a domain of restructuring and heightening the existing image of the archaeological entity, the information of which may not likely be available in the near future. Systematic investigations, with properly constructed research design, will, however, be needed to pull together suitable data, after duly selecting an appropriate community or an area of research prior to their change, alteration or destruction with anthropogenic activities. There is enormous depth in archaeological discourse to make inroads in areas to immediate human concern, and ethnoarchaeology happens to be the right path facilitating archaeologist to get the intangible domains of the tangible archaeological finds and features. It is hoped that bold ventures along the 'hyper pluralistic' ethnoarchaeological tract by serious archaeologists, having expertise in the science of man, can give a laudable contribution towards structuring an overall prehistoric archaeological profile of Northeast India in the days to come.

References

Agorsah, EK. 1990. 'Ethno-archaeology: The search for a self-corrective approach to the study of past human behaviour'. *The African Archaeological Review*, 8: 189-208.

Agorsah, EK.1999. 'Ethno-archaeological consideration of social relationship and settlement patterning among Africans in the Caribbean diaspora'. In JB Haviser (Ed): *African Sites: Archaeology in the Caribbean.* pp. 38-64. Princeton: Marcus Weiner Publishers.

Allen, BC.; EA. Gait; CG. Allen; and HF. Howard. 1857. *Gazetteer of Bengal and Northeast India.* (Reprinted 1979). Delhi: Mittal Publications.

Anderson, J. 1871. 'The stone implements of Yunan with a notice of a Bronze Axe-like weapon from the Sanda Valley. Report on the expedition to western Yunan via Bhamo', Calcutta, Appendix C: 410-415.

Anderson, KM. 1969. 'Ethnographic analogy and archeological interpretation'. *Science* 163: 133-138.

Ascher, R. 1961. 'Analogy in archaeological interpretation'. *Southwestern Journal of Anthropology,* 17 (3): 317-325.

Ascher, R. 1968. 'Time's arrow and the archaeology of a contemporary community', In KC Chang (Ed): *Settlement Archaeology*, pp. 43-52. Palo Alto: National Press.

Barba, L. 2007. 'Chemical residues in lime: Plastered archaeological floors'. *Geoarchaeology,* 22 (4): 439-452.

Barba, L., and A. Ortiz. 1992. 'Análisis químico de pisos de ocupación: un caso etnográfico en Tlaxcala, México'. *Latin American Antiquity*, 3: 63-82.

Barba, L., and G. Bello. 1978. 'Análisis de fosfatos en el piso de una casa habitada actualmente'. *Notas Antropológicas,* 24: 188-193.

Barron, LTD. 1872. 'Note on the stone implements from the Naga Hills'. *Jr. Royal Anthrop. Inst.*, 1: 61-62.

Binford, LR. 1967. Smudge Pits and hide smoking: The use of analogy in archaeological reasoning. *American Antiquity,* 32*:* 1-12.

Binford, LR. 1968. 'Methodological considerations of the archaeological use of ethnographic data'. In RB Lee, and I. DeVore (Eds.): *Man the Hunter*, pp. 268-273. Chicago: Aldine.

Binford, LR. 1972. Archaeological reasoning and Smudge Pits – revisited'. In LR Binford (Ed.): *An Archeological Perspective*. pp. 52-58. New York: Seminar Press.

Binford, LR. 1977. *For Theory Building in Archaeology*. New York: Academic.

Binford, LR. 1978. *Nunamiut Ethnoarchaeology.* New York: Academic Press.

Binford, LR. 1981. 'Behavioral archaeology and the Pompeii premise'. *Journal of Anthropological Research,* 37:195-208.

Bintliff, J. 1991. 'Postmodernism, rhetoric, and scholasticism at TAG: The current state of British Archaeology'. *Antiquity,* 65:274-278.

Boas, F. 1928. *Anthropology and Modern Life.* New York: W.W. Norton and Co., Inc.

Brown, JC. 1914. 'Grooved stone hammers from Assam, etc'. *Jr. Asiatic Society of Bengal.* X (4): 133-143.

Brown, JC. 1917. *Catalogue Raisonne of the Prehistoric Antiquities in the Indian Museum, Calcutta.* Simla: Government Press.

Chang, KC. 1967. 'Major aspects of the interrelationship of Archaeology and Ethnology'. *Current Anthropology,* 8: 227-243.

Charlton, TH. 1981. 'Archaeology, ethnohistory, and ethnology: Interpretive interfaces'. *Advances in Archaeological Method and Theory* 4: 129-176.

Clarke, DL. 1968. *Analytical Archaeology.* London: Methuen and Co. Ltd.

Cockburn, J. 1879. 'Notes on stone implements from Khasi Hills, etc'. *Jr. Asiatic Society of Bengal.* XLVIII (II): 107-109.

Conkey, MW. 1989. 'The place of material culture in contemporary anthropology'. In AL Hedlund (Ed): *Perspectives on Anthropological Collections from the American Southwest: Proceedings of a Symposium*. pp. 13-31. Anthropological Research Papers, No. 40. Tucson: Arizona State University Press.

Crawford, H. 1982. 'Analogies, anomalies and research strategy'. *Pal'eòrient* 8: 5-9.

Cunningham, JJ. 2003. 'Transcending the 'obnoxious spectator': A case for processual pluralism in Ethno-archaeology'. *Journal of Anthropological Archaeology,* 22: 389-410.

Daniel, H. 2011. 'Contribution of ethnographic/ethnoarchaeological investigations to Northeast African Archaeology'. *ITYOPòIS*, 1: 187-191.

David, N. and C. Kramer 2001. *Ethnoarchaeology in Action*. Cambridge: Cambridge University Press.

Dawkins, R. 1976. *The Selfish Gene.* Oxford: Oxford University Press.

Dennett, DC. 1995. *Darwin's Dangerous Ideas: Evolution and Meanings of Life.* New York: Simon and Schuster.

Duke, P. 1995. 'Working through theoretical tension in contemporary archaeology: A practical attempt from Southwestern Colorado'. *Journal of Archaeological Method and Theory*, 2: 201-229.

Fabian, J. 1983. *Time and the Other: How Anthropology Makes its Object.* New York: Columbia University Press.

Fancher, JM. 2009. 'An ethnoarchaeological analysis of small prey bone assemblages produced by forest foragers of the Central African Republic'. Unpublished Ph. D. Thesis. Washington State University.

Fewkes, JW. 1900. 'Tuseyan migration traditions'. *Bur. Am. Ethnol.* 19 Annual Report.

Freeman, LG., Jr. 1968. 'A theoretical framework for interpreting archaeological materials'. In RB Lee, and I. DeVore (Eds.): *Man the Hunter*, pp. 262-267. Chicago: Aldine.

Gamble, C. 2001. *Archaeology: The Basics.* New York: Routledge.

Geertz, C. 1973. *The Interpretation of Cultures: Selected Essays*. New York: Basic Books, Inc., Publishers.

Godwin-Austen, HH. 1875. 'A celt found in the Khasi Hills at Shillong'. *Proc. Asiatic Soc. Bengal.* p. 158.

Goldberg, P. and I. Whitebread. 1993. 'Micromorphological studies of a Bedouin tent floor'. In P Goldberg, DT. Nash, and M. Petraglia, (Eds.): *Formation Processes in Context.* Monographs in World Archaeology, Vol. 17. pp. 165-188. New York: Prehistory Press.

Goswami, MC., and AC. Bhagabati 1959. 'A typological study of shoulder celts from Rengchangiri (Garo Hills)'. *Jr. Univ., Gau.* X (2): 105-122.

Goswami, MC., and TC.Sharma 1962. 'A brief report on the investigation into the prehistoric archaeology of North Cachar Hills'. *Jr. Univ., Gau.* XIII (2): 63-66.

Goswami, MC., and TC. Sharma 1963. 'Further report on the investigations into the prehistoric archaeology of North Cachar Hills'. *Jr. Univ., Gau.* XIV (2): 45-47.

Gould, RA.1968. Living Archeology: The Nataraja of Western Australia. *Southwestern Journal of Anthropology,* 24: 101-122.

Gould, RA. 1980. *Living Archaeology,* Cambridge: Cambridge University Press.

Gould, RA. 1989. 'Ethno-archaeology and the past: Our search for the real thing'. *Fennoscandia Archaeologica,* VI: 3-22.

Gould, RA., and PJ Watson. 1982. 'A dialogue on the meaning and use of analogy in ethnoarchaeological reasoning'. *Journal of Anthropological Archaeology,* 1: 355-381.

Gould, RA. 1971. 'The archaeologist as ethnographer: A case from the western desert of Australia.' *World Archaeology,* 3: 143-177.

Griffin, PB., and WG. Solheim II. 1990. 'Ethno-archaeological research in Asia'. *Asian Perspectives,* 28: 145-162.

Halstead, P., I. Hodder, and G. Jones. 1978. Behavioural archaeology and refuse patterns: A case study'. *Norwegian Archaeological Review*, 11 (2): 118-131.

Hamilakis, Y. 2011. 'Archaeological ethnography: A multitemporal meeting ground for archaeology and anthropology'. *Annu. Rev. Anthropol.,* 40: 399-414.

Harris, M. and O Johnson. 2000. *Cultural Anthropology*, (5th ed.), Needham Heights, MA: Allyn and Bacon.

Hassan, FA. 1978. 'Sediments in archaeology: Methods and implications for palaeoenvironmental and cultural analyses'. *Journal of Field Archaeology*, 5 (2): 197-213.

Hegmon, M. 2003. 'Setting theoretical egos aside: Issues and theory in North American Archaeology'. *American Antiquity,* 68(2): 213-243.

Hodder, I. 1982. *The Present Past-an introduction to Anthropology for Archaeologists.* London: B.T. Batsford, Ltd.

Hodder, I. 1986. 'From ethnoarchaeology to material culture studies'. *Dialoghi Di Archeologia,* 3:93-97.

Hodder, I., and C. Orton. 1976. *Spatial Analysis in Archaeology*. Cambridge: Cambridge University Press.

Hutton, JH. 1924. 'Two Celts from Naga Hills'. *Man* XXIV (15): 20-22.

Hutton, JH. 1926. 'A Naga Hill Celt'. *Jr. Asiatic Soc. Beng.,* XXII: 133.

Hutton, JH. 1928. 'Prehistory of Assam'. *Man in India,* VIII (4): 228-232.

Johnson, MH. 2006. 'On the nature of theoretical archaeology and archaeological theory'. *Archaeological Dialogues,* 13(2): 117-132.

Kent, S., (ed.) 1987. *Method and Theory for Activity Area Research: An Ethnoarchaeological Approach.* New York: Columbia University Press.

Kluckhohn, C. 1949. *Mirror for man.* USA: McGraw-Hill.

Knapp, AB. 1996. 'Archaeology without gravity: Postmodernism and the past'. *Journal of Archaeological Method and Theory,* 3:127-158.

Kramer, C. 1979. *Ethnoarchaeology: Implications of Ethnography for Archaeology*. New York: Columbia University Press.

Kramer, C. 1985. 'Ceramic ethnoarchaeology'. *Annual Review of Anthropology* 14:77-102.

Kroll, EM, and TD. Price. 1991. *The Interpretation of Archaeological Spatial Patterning*. New York: Springer.

Kuznar, L. 1997. *Reclaiming a Scientific Anthropology*. London.

Kuznar, LA.1995. 'Awatimarka: The ethnoarchaeology of an Andean Herding community'. Harcour Brac, FortWorh, TX.

Lancelotti, C.; A. Pecci and D. Zurro. 2017. 'Anthropic activity markers: Archaeology and ethnoarchaeology'. *Environmental Archaeology*, 22(4): 339-342.

Lange, FW. 1980. 'Prehistory and hunter/gatherers: The role of Analogs'. *Midcontinental Journal of Archaeology* 5: 133–147.

Lohse, ES. 2008. 'Measuring prehistoric strategies: Flakes, symmetries, and balance in Stone Tools'. *http://www.isu.edu/%7Elohserne/lohseCHAG9.htm.* Retrieved on September 24, 2008.

London, G. 2000. 'Ethno-archaeology and interpretations of the past'. *Near Eastern Archaeology,* 63 (1): 2-8.

Longacre, WA and JE Ayres 1968. 'Archaeological lessons from an Apache Wickiup'. In SR Binford. and LR. Binford (Eds): *New Perspectives in Archaeology*. pp. 151-159. Chicago: Aldine Publishing Company.

Lubbock, J. 1867. 'The stone age, stone tools in Upper Assam'. *Athenaeum* (June 22): 822.

Malinowski, A. 1932. *Argonauts of the Western Pacific: An Account of Native Enterprise and Adventure in the Archipelagoes of Melanesian New Guinea.* London: Routledge and Kegan Paul.

Mallol, C, FW Marlowe, BM Wood, and CC Porter. 2007. 'Earth, wind, and fire: Ethno-archaeological signals of Hadza fires'. *Journal of Archaeological Science*, 34:2035-2052.

ManiBabu, M. 1988-89. 'On the scope of the ethnoarchaeological studies in Manipur'. *Regional Integration,* XII and XIII (1): 37-42.

ManiBabu, M. 2003. 'Morphological characterisation of prehistoric stone artifacts'. *The Oriental Anthropologist,* 3(1):9-17.

ManiBabu, M. 2014. 'Making sense of stones: Wealth, status and indigenous management strategy' In K Jose and GK. Bera (Eds.): *Indigenous Resource Management in North East India.* pp. 192-217. New Delhi: Osmons Publications.

Manzanilla, L, and L. Barba. 1990. 'The study of activities in classic households. Two case studies from Coba and Teotihuacan'. *Ancient Mesoamerica,* 2: 299-307.

Merton, RK. 1968. *Social Theory and Social Structure*. New York: Free Press.

Middleton, W and D. Price. 1996. 'Identification of activity areas by multi-element characterisation of sediments from modern and archaeological house floors using inductively coupled plasma-atomic emission spectroscopy'. *Journal of Archaeological Science* 23: 673-687.

Miller, D.1983. 'Things ain't what they used to be'. *Royal Anthropological Institute Newsletter,* 59:5-7.

Munson, PJ. 1969. 'Comments on Binford's Smudge Pits and Hide smoking: The use of analogy in archaeological reasoning'. *American Antiquity,* 34: 83-85.

Murray, T. 2017. 'The origins of cultural history in prehistoric archaeology: Rethinking plausibility and disciplinary tradition'. *World Archaeology,* 49(2): 187-197.

Murray, T., and MJ. Walker 1988. 'Like WHAT? A practical question of analogical inference and archaeological meaningfulness'. *Journal of Anthropological Archaeology,* 7: 248-287.

O'Connell, JF. 1995. 'Ethno-archaeology Needs a general theory of behavior'. *Journal of Archaeological Research*, 3 (3): 205-255.

Orme, B. 1981. *Anthropology for Archaeologists: An introduction*. London: Duckworth.

Ortiz, A., and L. Barba. 1993. 'La química en el estudio de áreas de actividad'. In *Anatomía de un Conjunto Residencial Teotihuacano en Oztoyahualco*, pp. 617-660. Mexico City: UNAM.

Pecci, A. 2003. 'Los alimentos y sus residuos químicos. Arqueología experimental para entender actividades prehispánicas'. *Quaderni di Thule III*: 75-83.

Pecci, A., MÁ Cau Ontiveros, C. Valdambrini, and F. Inserra. 2013. 'Understanding residues of oil production: Environmental archaeology' 341 Downloaded by [47.29.211.40] at 05:40 16 November 2017 'Chemical analyses of floors in traditional mills'. *Journal of Archaeological Science* 40 (2): 883-893.

Philips, M. and M. ManiBabu, 2015. 'Megalithic monuments in Manipur: A discourse on space syntax analyses'. Paper presented at the 45th *Annual Conference of the Indian Anthropological Society,* (23-25 May 2015). University of Calcutta, Kolkata.

Politis, GG. 2007. *Nukak - Ethnoarchaeology of an Amazonian People*. Walnut Creek, CA: University College London Institute of Archaeology Publications.

Politis, GG. 2015. 'Reflections on contemporary ethnoarchaeology'. *Pyrenae,* 46 (1): 41-83.

Radcliffe-Brown. AR. 1931. *The Social Organisation of Australian Tribes.* Melbourne.

Rathje, WL.1978. 'Archaeological ethnography: Because sometimes it is better to give than to receive'. To RA. Gould (Ed): *Explorations in Ethnoarchaeology*. pp. 49-76. Albuquerque: University of New Mexico Press.

Ravn, M. 2011. 'Ethnographic analogy from the Pacific: Just as analogical as any other analogy', *World Archaeology,* 43(4): 716-725.

Robinson, W. 1841 (1975). *A Descriptive Account of Assam*, New Delhi: Sanskaran Prakasan.

Rondelli, B., C. Lancelotti, M. Madella, A. Pecci, A. Balbo, J. Ruiz Perez, F. Inserra, C. Gadekar, MÀ Cau Ontiveros, and P. Ajithprasad. 2014. 'Anthropic activity markers and spatial variability: An ethnoarchaeological experiment in a domestic unit of Northern Gujarat (India)'. *Journal of Archaeological Science*, 41: 482-492.

Rouse, I. 1965. 'The place of 'peoples' in prehistoric research'. *The Journal of the Royal Anthropological Institute of Great Britain and Ireland*, 95(1):1-15.

Sanday, PR. 1979. 'The ethnographic paradigms(s)'. *Administrative Science Quarterly* 24 (4): 527-538.

Schiffer, MB. 1972. 'Archaeological context and systemic context'. *American Antiquity,* 37(2): 156-165.

Schiffer, MB. 1978. 'Methodological issues in ethnoarchaeology'. In RA Gould (Ed): *Explorations in Ethnoarchaeology*, University of New Mexico Press, Albuquerque, 229-247.

Schwartz, DW. 1978. 'Forward'. In RA Gould (Ed): *Explorations in Ethnoarchaeology.* pp. 229-247. Albuquerque: University of New Mexico Press.

Shanks, M. and I. Hodder, 1995. 'Processual, postprocessual and interpretive archaeology'. In I Hodder; M. Shanks; A. Alexandri; V. Buchli; J. Carman; J. Last; and G. Lucas (Eds): *Interpreting Archaeology*, pp. 3-29. London and New York: Routledge.

Sharma, HC. 1972. *Stone Age Cultures of the Garo Hills*. Unpublished Ph. D. Thesis. Gauhati University, Assam.

Sharma, TC. 1966. *Prehistoric Archaeology of Assam – A Study of Neolithic Cultures*. Unpublished Ph.D. Thesis, University of London.

Sharma, TC. 1967. 'A note on the Neolithic pottery of Assam'. *Man* II (1): 126-128.

Shimray, YK. 1976. 'Tangkhul language and culture'. In BB Singh (Ed): *An Introduction to Tribal Language and Culture of Manipur (7 Tribes).* pp. 1-30. Imphal: Manipur State Kala Akademi.

Simms, SR. 1992. 'Ethno-archaeology: Obnoxious spectator, trivial pursuit, or the keys to a time machine?' In L Wandsnider (Ed.): *Quandaries and Quests: Visions of Archaeology's Future*. pp. 186-198. Southern Illinois University, Center for Archaeological Investigations, Occasional Paper No. 20.

Sinopoli, CM. 1991. 'Seeking the past through the present: Recent ethnoarchaeological research in South Asia'. *Asian Perspectives* 30(2): 177-192.

Spaulding, AC. 1973. 'Archaeology in the active voice: The new anthropology'. In CL Redman, (Ed.): *Research and Theory in Current Archaeology.* pp. 337-354. New York: John Wiley.

Stahl, AB. 1993. 'Concepts of time and approaches to archaeological reasoning in historical perspective'. *American Antiquity,* 58: 235-260.

Stanislawski, MB. 1978. 'If pots were Mortal' In RA Gould (Ed): *Explorations in Ethno-archaeology,* pp. 201-228. Albuquerque: University of New Mexico Press.

Stark, M.1993. 'Re-fitting the 'cracked and broken façade': The case for empiricism in postprocessual ethnoarchaeology'. In N Yoffee and A. Sherratt, (Eds): *Archaeological Theory: Who Sets the Agenda?* pp. 93-104. Cambridge: Cambridge University Press.

Stiles, D. 1977. 'Ethno-archaeology: A discussion of methods and application'. *Man* (NS), 12(1): 87-103.

Trigger, BG. 1989. *A History of Archaeological Thought.* Cambridge: Cambridge University Press.

Tschauner, H. 1996. 'Middle range theory, behavioural archaeology, and post-empiricist philosophy of science in archaeology'. *Journal of Archaeological Method and Theory*. 3: 1-30.

Watson, R. 1990. 'Ozymandias, king of kings: Postprocessual radical archaeology as critique'. *American Antiquity,* 92:673-89.

Wattez, J., 1992. *Dynamique de Formation des Structures de Combustion de la Fin du Pale'olithique au Ne'olithique Moyen.* Paris: Universite' de Paris I.

White, JP 1967. 'Ethno-archaeology in New Guinea: Two examples. *Mankind*, 6: 409-414.

Wobst, HM.1978. 'The archaeo-ethnology of hunter-gatherers or the tyranny of the ethnographic record in archaeology'. *American Antiquity,* 43: 303-309.

The Woman, EC. 1949. 'The Neolithic problem in the prehistory of India'. *Jr. Washington of Science.* 39(6): 181-201.

Wylie, A. 1982. 'An analogy with any other name is just as analogical: A commentary on the Gould-Watson dialogue'. *Journal of Anthropological Archaeology*. 1(4): 382-401.

Wylie, A. 1985. 'The reaction against analogy'. *Advances in Archaeological Method and Theory,* 8: 63-111.

Wylie, A. 1988. 'Simple analogy and the role of relevance assumptions: Implications of archaeological practice'. *International Studies in the Philosophy of Science,* 2: 134-150.

Wylie, A. 1989. 'Archaeological cables and tacking: The implications of practice for Bernstein's Options beyond Objectivism and Relativism'. *Philosophy of Social Science,* 19: 1-18.

Chapter - 5

Bio-cultural Perspective of Reproductive Health among the Women of Northeast India

—Juri Borah and Sarthak Sengupta

The word 'health' embodies a broader concept which encompasses the reproductive health too. Reproductive health can be considered as the vital, indispensable and also the most crucial facet of general health. Health is defined by World Health Organisation as "a state of complete physical, mental and social well-being and not merely the absence of disease or infirmity" (WHO, 1948). The definition of reproductive health by the United Nation (1994) is expressed with a slight modification of the definition of WHO on health. Accordingly, reproductive health is defined by the International Conference on Population and Development (ICPD) as "a state of complete physical, mental and social well-being and not merely the absence of disease or infirmity, in all matters relating to the reproductive system and to its functions and processes". Ersheng and Shah (1997) mentioned that although scores of researchers' use the term reproductive health, yet the word is observed to be ill-defined in many such works. In this regards, he tried a step forward with WHO's definition of reproductive health and gave emphasis on some further aspects that include the ability of the people to bear healthy children, safe regulation of fertility according to their own choice and also maintaining their sexual relationships by averting the fear of contracting diseases. This definition of reproductive health is encouraged for balancing the views in regards to the diseases to be precluded in both the sexes, male and female. However, an improvement in the concept of ICPD is also documented in the WHO's literature on reproductive health (1998) that tries to overcome the limitations of the earlier definition that was put forward by United Nation (1994). The new definition of WHO (1998) on reproductive health is "it refers to a spectrum of conditions, events, and processes throughout life, ranging from healthy sexual development, physical comfort and closeness and the joys of childbearing to avert disease and death. Profoundly life-affirming and life-threatening conditions make up reproductive health. Perhaps more than with any other health condition, the social, psychological and physiological factors are inter-related in reproductive health, which WHO views as crucial to overall health".

The right to health is one of the basic human rights. Women have been historically discriminated against, they are a vulnerable section whose health concerns need to be prioritised, understood and researched. With the fast changes brought about by globalisation and the consequential new economic order, there is an augment in the need for academic studies to be focused on the area of women's health. The gendered aspects of women's health, women's access to healthcare facilities, the impact of new reproductive technology on women's reproductive health, the rise in sexually transmitted diseases among women, health problems of working women, the vulnerability of women belonging to marginalised sections with respect to health problems of tribal, health concerns of women with disabilities are some of the issues which requires proper understanding. There is a rising need to include gender dimensions in the healthcare policies and programmes by the government and to review the existing programmes and policies as per the international standards.

After the attainment of menstruation period, the reproductive role of a woman approaches the postmenopausal period with the experience of some vital processes like conception, childbirth, breastfeeding and also the child-rearing process. Therefore, each and every stride in women's life has to get notable attention among the people since failure to deal with anyone step may set the scene for the later hazardous condition to their reproductive health in particular and overall health in general. However, any reproductive health-related problem arises during the reproductive years may be a reflection in the later stages of life.

Menstruation, an unavoidable and universal reproductive phenomenon starts off the reproductive phase of a woman's life and become momentous to them. As such, any menstrual dysfunction in adolescent stage may affect the normal life of an adolescent, youth as well as adult women (Mohite *et al.,* 2013). Non-maintenance of hygienic practice during menstruation period is susceptible to various kinds of gynaecological morbidity (Kumar and Srivastava, 2011; Krishnakumai and Arun, 2012; Garg *et al*., 2012; Juyal *et al*., 2012). Menstruation disorders are considered to be the most commonly occurring gynaecological problems among the married women (Balachander *et al*., 1993). Although the consequences of very poor health care services among the women residing in the rural areas are documented by many earlier studies, in urban areas also women's reproductive health condition is far from satisfactory (Agarwal *et al.*, 2007).

Reproductive Tract Infections (RTI) is one of the treacherous rudiments for fetching poor reproductive health conditions. Although both male and female are the victims of different reproductive tract infections, the proportions of sufferers with RTI's are reported to be more among the women counterparts. The prevalence of Reproductive Tract Infections and a myriad of gynaecological problems bring a miserable condition among the women. Women are basically reluctant to seek treatment and suffer silently with RTI's for prolonged time periods. Many of them draw a parallel gaze about their sufferings with the inevitable part of womanhood. However, they also have hesitation and inhibition for sharing their sufferings with the doctors and remain unresponsive up to that stage when the problem alarms the serious symptoms. Beginning of the RTI in case of the female is observed in the lower genital tract which has the chance of producing some symptoms like abnormal vaginal discharge or leucorrhea, pain at the genital organ, and itching and burning sensation during urination (Ravi and Kulasekaran, 2013). Out of various symptoms associated with Reproductive Tract Infections, abnormal vaginal discharge is considered as the most common variety (Kumari *et al.*, 2000; Kulkarni and Durge, 2005; Kaur and Kapoor, 2014). Various factors like cultural restrictions, dependency, poor awareness, improper infrastructure, lack of focused counseling services and also gender inequalities are observed as responsible sources behind their enduring nature towards this suffering (Wasserheit *et al.*, 1989; Younis *et al.*, 1993; Gittlesohn *et al.*, 1994; Oomman, 1996; Bhatia *et al.*, 1997 and Joshi *et al.*, 2008).

Menopause is one of the unavoidable and universal milestones in a woman's life. It is considered as the transition period from reproductive to the non-reproductive stage. Hence, it introduces women to a new phase of life. The stages of Reproductive Ageing Workshop classification divided menopause stages into three categories; postmenopausal, that is no menstrual bleeding in the previous twelve months; perimenopausal as those who did not have menstruation in the previous two months or those who experienced increasing irregularity of menses and premenopausal as minor changes in cycle length (Soules *et al.*, 2001). Menopausal age is a subject of variation, individual-wise, and community-wise and also according to the geographical distribution. A variety of bio-social variables are assumed to be allied with early and late menopause. It encompasses the factors like menarcheal age, age at first childbirth, parity, education, socio-economic status, dietary habits, body size and shape, blood pressure, etc.

Many internal, as well as external factors, may challenge an individual's ability to maintain reproductive health. Apart from having the predetermined genetic susceptibility to a particular disorder or disease, socio-cultural factors are also equally responsible for the maintenance of impartial reproductive health. As such, depend on diverse bio-social factors reproductive health status of the women shows inconsistency among the masses geographically as well as community-wise. In this regard, the role of anthropologists is acknowledging because anthropologists traditionally deal with the variation among different ethnic groups.

The importance of the issue of the reproductive health of women came into a focal point among the scholars after the International Conference on Population and Development (ICPD) in Cairo, Egypt (1994) and also following the International Conference on Women held in Beijing (1995). Since then, studies on the reproductive health of the women inhabiting in the different parts of the world have been continuing with diverse perspectives. In the Indian scenario also studies on different aspects of the reproductive health of women are also increasingly gaining attention among the scholars.

Studies on the reproductive health of women in North East India are very scrappy and relatively less as not much of attention is paid to the problem of maternal and child health (Krishnakumari and Arun, 2012). Maximum numbers of the works so far reported are also not from the viewpoint of an anthropologist. Among few limited notable works, mention may be made of Meitei *et al.,* (2005), who had worked on the awareness and prevalence of Reproductive Tract Infections in few districts of North East Indian states. Both the males and females in the majority of the districts in the northeastern part of India have relatively poor knowledge about Reproductive Tract Infections. The level of awareness of RTI among males and females have observed only in 11 and 9 districts respectively out of 34 districts from north-eastern states in India. Their study reveals the spacious gap in between the level of knowledge and prevalence of RTI's among the female population in comparison to the males.

Chanu (2007) observed a higher proportion of different obstetric problems in her study among the Lois women in both the rural and urban areas of Imphal West District, Manipur. The proportions of problems are although observed to be higher in the rural areas, the urban set up is also not the exception in this regard. Increasing proportions of obstetric problems as per the increased maternal age were reported by her study which seems to decrease with increased household income and paternal education. She also mentioned the significant role of maternal education on obstetric mortality. Her study acknowledged the Loi women of Manipur for their awareness and participation up to a great extent during their pregnancy period. However, the higher proportions of the women availed antenatal care is in urban setup than in rural areas.

Chakraborty and Hazarika (2011) studied the status of misconception and knowledge about the HIV/AIDS epidemic and some of its proximate socio-demographic determinants among the married women of reproductive age group (15-49 years) in Assam, India. Their study covers 27 districts of Assam based on the data taken from the District Level Household and Facility Survey, Phase III (DLHS-III) conducted by International Institute for Population Studies (IIPS), Mumbai, India during 2007-2008 at the national level. Statistically significant improvement in the proportion of individuals with good conception regarding knowledge about HIV/AIDS both in rural as well as urban areas of Assam were reported in the study. But the women from the rural area, belonging to scheduled tribe category and also the Muslims can be considered as the vulnerable section of the overall population of the region.

Reproductive health of Andro women of Manipur (Krishnakumari and Arun, 2012) shows the relatively higher incidence of Reproductive Tract Infections (RTI) among them. Interestingly, the women don't take bath during their menstruation period for the fear of polluting the surroundings. As such, the comparatively higher occurrence of Reproductive Tract Infections was documented among those Andro women who don't wash their private parts during periods. Their study pointed out the uses of unclean and old linen cloths among the population and reiterate ignorance, poverty, low educational level as the root causes. The Andro women refer their health problems relating to reproductive organs and functions as women's illness instead of reproductive illnesses.

Gogoi and Prusty (2013) tried to examine the prevalence of reproductive health complications and treatment seeking behaviour among tribal women in North East India based on District Level Household and Facility Survey-3 (DLHS-3) data. Their study reveals that tribal women were reporting less awareness about RTI/STD's but non-tribal women reporting comparatively more complications than tribal women. Only a few women use to go to a public source for treatment seeking, while a high proportion of women do not receive any treatment for their problems. Among the tribal population studied, the relatively higher incidence of abnormal vaginal discharge is recorded from Meghalaya, followed by Assam in the north-eastern states of India.

Hazarika and Chutia (2013) worked among the Deori and Mishing women of Assam to understand their rate of abortion, stillbirth and reproductive risk. Their study confirmed the worsening of reproductive health conditions and loss of reproductivity of tribal women. Among four districts covered (Dhemaji, Dibrugarh, Lakhimpur, and Sibsagar of Assam), relatively higher abortion rate (both voluntary and involuntary) among the Deori and Mishing have been recorded in the Dhemaji district while Lakhimpur district witnesses the lowest. They reported that the ratio of stillbirths to total births in the case of Deori decreases from 2010 to 2012. The researcher mentioned that the reason for such decreasing trend in stillbirth is due to the increasing health awareness amongst the childbearing Deori women. Though, both the communities have been suffering from various reproductive health-related problems like involuntary abortion, severe anemic condition, blood diseases, high and low blood pressure, jaundice, high fever, problem associated with uterus, postpartum complication, vaginal bleeding, sterility, cesarean, and stillbirth; the number of Deori women suffering from such reproductive health problems has been found to be relatively higher than that of the married Mishing women.

Sarmah (2014) studied various reproductive health-related issues such as the prevalence of both infectious and non-infectious diseases, awareness regarding health and diseases, the use of health services, the quality of healthcare services, marital and sexual behaviour among the Bodo-Kachari women in North Guwahati area, Assam. Among the Bodo-Kachari women, various reproductive diseases like dysmenorrhea, irregular menstruation, menorrhagia, and hypomenorrhea were found as widespread. The frequency of dysmenorrhea is more prevalent among both the unmarried and married Bodo-Kachari women. Among the married women, the frequency of irregular menstruation is common. She mentioned higher incidence of the symptoms of convulsion, followed by vaginal bleeding and prolonged labour pain at the time of delivery as the common reproductive complications among the Bodo Kachari women in Assam. Her study also documented the comparatively higher incidence of home delivery for which she considered poverty, lack of education, lack of transportation and interruption of husband or family members in institutional delivery as the basic causes. Interestingly, awareness levels with regards to HIV/AIDS were found to be increased along with education and impact of health awareness campaigning, media influences through radio and television among the studied population.

Baidya *et al.* (2014) studied the prevalence of various reproductive health problems and also the knowledge with regards to reproductive health and healthcare-seeking behaviour among rural adolescent girls of Mohanpur block of West Tripura district. The respondents belonged to the age group of 10-19 years. Enormous reproductive health-related complications like dysmenorrhea, menstrual irregularity, menorrhagia and pre-menstrual syndrome have been reported among the rural adolescent girls from West Tripura district. Among all the aforementioned menstrual related problems, the prevalence of dysmenorrhea was found to be excessively high. Among them, the absence of adequate knowledge and correct understanding with regards to puberty changes, STDs and HIV/AIDS are recorded. Moreover, the adolescent girls always silently suffer the pain and the associated discomfort during menstruation.

Shahani (2014) studied the existing practices on sexual and reproductive behaviour in relation to the knowledge and attitudes, operating socio-economic and cultural factors as well as the perception and awareness level pertaining to the healthcare services among adolescent girls' of Meitei-Pangals from East Imphal, Manipur. The majority of the Meitei-Pangal girl respondents have not heard about the RTI/STD but they have heard about HIV/AIDS through the sources like radio, TV, and NGOs etc. Even though they are aware of HIV/AIDS, they are not at all conscious about the use of condoms and others preventive measures of HIV/AIDS. During pregnancy time, the majority of the women do not visit health centres for basic antenatal check-ups. They are not aware of the balanced diet also. The frequency of the contraceptive users is very limited among them and as a result, they face an unplanned pregnancy. High rates of teenage pregnancy are quite common and most of the married women experience motherhood within the first year of their married life. High-risk of STIs/RTIs and poor nutritional status have also become common reproductive and sexual health problems among the married Meitei and Pangal women. The majority of the Meitei and Pangal girls perceive menstruation as disgusting and as a curse. The discussions on reproductive and sexual health-related issues are considered as taboo in Meitei-Pangal society, young people are hindered from actively seeking counsel for their needs. The girls, in general, hesitate to share their reproductive health problem with their mothers also. Seeking abortions are common among both married as well as unmarried adolescent girls to avoid social condemnation. Low rates of educational attainment, limited sex education and inhibited attitudes towards sex are considered as responsible towards ignorance about sex and reproduction among them.

Deka *et al.* (2015) carried out a community-based cross-sectional study among the adolescent girls of 10-19 years residing in the urban slums of Guwahati city to assess their menstrual health, hygiene practices, and their health-seeking behaviour. A large section of the adolescent girls was suffering from dysmenorrhea and only a few of the sufferers preferred seeking treatment. The symptom of Reproductive Tract Infection is found as noticeably higher among the girls belonging to the age group of 15-19 years than the girls belonging to 10-14 years of age group. Only an insignificant proportion of the girls were found to use disposable sanitary napkins during menstruation while most of them prefer to use the old pieces of cloth. They reuse the same piece of cloth by washing. Few reasons for not adopting modern medical treatment are: did not feel necessary, high cost of treatment, long waiting time, not knowing the source of treatment, treatment facility far off and embarrassment to go for treatment.

Chanu and Arunkumar (2015) studied the traditional knowledge regarding reproductive healthcare among the Thadou tribe of Manipur. Their study revealed vast uses of medicinal plants among the Thadous. Now-a-day, due to the process of urbanisation and cultural contact as well as the widespread use of western medicines in the state, the situation of medicinal pluralism can be seen, causing a threat to the continuation of indigenous knowledge tradition among the Thadou younger generation. The traditionally practiced indigenous reproductive healthcare system as a means of survival in Thadou community, however, exists even today and in spite of easily accessible modern medical facility, Thadou women still practice some indigenous medicines during menstruation and pregnancy period. During menstruation period a girl is not allowed to mingle with the boys or men as it will affect the womb. Likewise, a pregnant woman is not allowed to attain funeral ceremony since they believe that it causes miscarriage. They do floor moping even in the third trimester of pregnancy for easy delivery, but in the early stage of pregnancy, they are debarred from carrying heavy loads. During the time of delivery, the women keep their legs in straight position while sitting with a belief that it will heal the wounded portion very fast and keep the right body-image even in the later stage. Hot boiled chicken soup is also given to the woman up to seven days from the date of delivery after taking bath with hot water for quick recovery of the body. Moreover, chicken, as well as boil food without any chilies, is also served to the mother during the delivery time.

A study on age at menopause, prevalence of menopausal symptoms and also the awareness and attitude towards menopause and treatment seeking behaviour among women attending Guwahati Medical College and Hospital, Assam was conducted by Alakananda along with her associates (2015). Their findings reveal the widespread occurrence of postmenopausal symptoms like muscle and joint pain, fatigue, hot flush, insomnia and night sweat. Though the frequencies of the sufferers are quite high, yet there was a lack of awareness among the masses towards their own problems. In the early postmenopausal period, the symptoms linked to vasomotor, psychosomatic and urogenital are more frequently observed, whereas psychological symptoms (except depression) and some rare menopausal symptoms like weight gain and dryness of skin became dominant among women in the late postmenopausal period. Although the ethnic variation in the studied samples may be one reason behind this finding, yet another reason is accounted as the habit of adaptation of the women towards their sufferings after passing substantial times. In a comparison of menopausal symptoms with mean duration since menopause, the frequency of the symptoms was found to decrease in accordance with higher duration. They observed the profound role of education, occupation, monthly income and lifestyle on the postmenopausal health of the women. The occurrence of menopausal symptoms is quite high among the women having no education, unemployed and also among those belongs to lower income group categories. Poor living conditions are supposed to be the root cause for their ill postmenopausal health which affects on their nutritional and mental status.

Sarma (2015) conducted her study among the working and non-working women of 38 to 60 years of age living in Guwahati, Assam to know about their postmenopausal health-related problems as well as the influence of the various socio-cultural factors on the same. A good proportion of the women from both the groups reported the sufferings of several postmenopausal symptoms. Among the non-working women, the frequencies of both psychological and vasomotor symptoms are more prevalent in comparison to the working women. The occurrences of urinary and musculoskeletal problems are quite common in both the samples under consideration. Hence, joint pain and backaches and also changing weight are observed as the common symptoms among them.

Patar *et al.* (2015) tried to evaluate the gynaecological problems among unmarried adolescent girls belonging to age group 10-19 years attending the outpatient department of Gauhati Medical College, Guwahati. Most common gynaecological problems that have been causing sufferings to the respondent adolescent girls were menstrual disorders which are followed by vaginal discharge and ovarian tumor. Among the menstrual disorders, most common were menorrhagia, followed by oligomenorrhea, dysmenorrhea, metrorrhagia, amenorrhoea, and polymenorrhea. Most of the adolescent girls have shyness and hesitation to disclose their sufferings and are unaware of their bodily changes too.

Borah and Sengupta (2015) tried to evaluate few components of reproductive health aspects of women like the availability of appropriate healthcare services and family planning, healthcare delivery and health-seeking behaviour, gynaecological and obstetric related health problems, beliefs and practices associated with ante and postnatal care among the Dibongiya Deori women of Lakhimpur district of Assam. Their study reveals relatively low awareness among the Dibongiya Deori women towards their reproductive health condition. The frequency of spontaneous abortion and also the incidence of death at infant stage was found to be high in the studied population. Quite a good number of the Dibongiya mother has been experiencing gynaecological problems like white discharge, menstrual problems like hypermenorrhea, hypomenorrhea irregular bleeding, dysmenorrhea and obstetric problems like pregnancy complications. Since they consider menstruation as unholy and as such its associated disorders are not yet recognised as derailing issues. The frequency of family planning adopters among them is significantly low. The women are not aware with regards to the prevalence of AIDS and other sexually transmitted diseases. Most of the women only heard about the word AIDS and have the misconception that transmission of AIDS is possible due to the indulgence of multiple sex partners. Now-a-day, however, people are showing interest towards the modern medical facility and as such avails prenatal care during pregnancy. A lot of ethnomedicines are also used by the Dibongiya Deori women to get relief from reproductive health-related problems.

Sonowal and Sonowal (2017) conducted investigation among the Sonowal Kacharis of Dibrugarh district of Assam to have an idea about their indigenous preventive strategies against pregnancy, childbirth and also postpartum complications. They reported the use of diverse phytotherapy among the Sonowal Kachari women for treating their problems such as bleeding after childbirth, postpartum abdominal pain, postpartum hemorrhage and inadequate lactation.

It is apparent from the above discussion that each and every ethnic group has some unique distinctiveness in respect of biological and cultural perspectives. Ironically, in North East India, women from the deprived and marginalised sections experience differential access to modern healthcare facilities. There is also a need to explore and understand the health concerns of women belonging to marginalised sections since they are doubly vulnerable to discrimination.

The present appraisal records inadequate knowledge on reproductive health issues among most of the ethnic groups in North East India. Studies pertaining to reproductive health status from diverse perspective divulge the lack of awareness among the adolescent girls and the women towards their health condition and have poor reproductive health as an outcome. Although a little preventive strategy is in the process, however, the people have to proceed further. Establishment of the medical institution with the improved medical facility at an affordable price will be helpful for the people to move forward in this regards.

Studies on post-menopausal women referred in the present chapter also record the frequent incidence of several vasomotor, psychological, psychosomatic, physiological, urogenital and sexual discomforts. Therefore, proper nutrition and dietary practices, support, counseling, and health education are important to prevent further medical and mental health issues associated with the menopausal transition. Early recognition of the symptoms will enable the people to reduce the feeling of discomfort so that a good health condition she can lead. Since drastic hormonal changes during the menopausal transition are basically liable for their health problems, apposite care and cooperation from both husband and other family's member are of immense value to tackle this period easily.

More scientific works to assess the severity of the symptoms are of utmost importance in filling knowledge gaps and for the improvement of the health of the population which would markedly bring an effective environment in the society as a whole.

References

Agarwal, P.; MM. Singh and S. Garg, 2007, 'Maternal health-care utilisation among women in an urban slum in Delhi', *Indian Journal of community medicine,* 32: 203-205.

Alakananda; N. Das and BP. Das, 2015, 'Age of menopause and menopausal symptoms among women attending Gauhati Medical College and Hospital, Guwahati, Assam: A cross-sectional study', *Scholars Journal of Applied Medical Sciences*, 3(7c): 2621-2629.

Baidya, S.; M. Debnath and R. Das, 2014, 'A study of reproductive health problems among rural adolescent girls of Mohanpur block of West Tripura district', *Al Ameen Journal of Medical Science*, 7(1): 78-82.

Balachander, G.; SS. Raghaver and P. Rajaram, 1993, 'Gynecological problems in adolescent', *The Journal of Obstetrics and Gynecology of India*, 43:599-604.

Bhatia, JC.; J. Cleland; L. Bhagavan and NS. Rao, 1997, 'Levels and determinants of gynecological morbidity in a district of South India', *Studies in Family Planning,* 28: 95-103.

Borah, J. and S. Sengupta, 2015, 'Reproductive health of the Dibongiya Deori women of Lakhimpur District, Assam', *Anthropos India*, 1(2): 197-204.

Chakraborty, S., and PJ. Hazarika, 2011, 'Misconception and knowledge regarding HIV/AIDS among married women in the reproductive age group in Assam, India', *World Applied Sciences Journal*, 15(7): 966-972.

Chanu, TJ., 2007, *A Study of Reproductive and Child Health among the Lois of Imphal Valley*, An unpublished Ph.D. thesis submitted to the Department of Anthropology, North Eastern Hill University, Shillong.

Chanu, TJ., and MC. Arunkumar, 2015, 'Traditional reproductive health care practices and knowledge: A case of the Thadou of Manipur', *IOSR Journal of Humanities and Social Science*, 20(7): 86-88.

Deka, C.; AC. Baishya and J. Ojah, 2015, 'A study of reproductive health and health-seeking behaviour of adolescent girls residing in urban slums of Guwahati city', *The New Indian Journal of OBGYN*, 2(1): 51-55.

Ersheng, G. and I. Shah, 1997, 'Reproductive health research: progress and policy implications', In *Progress of Social Science Research on Reproductive Health*, pp. 1-8, Shanghai; China Population Publishing House.

Garg, R.; S. Goyal and S. Gupta, 2012, 'India moves towards menstrual hygiene: Subsidized sanitary napkins for rural adolescent girls-issues and challenges', *Maternal and Child Health Journal*, 16(4): 767-774.

Gittlesohn, J.; KK. Holmes and P. Pilot, 1994, *Listening to Women Talk about Their Health: Issues and Evidence from India*, New Delhi; Har-Anand Publications.

Gogoi, M., and RK. Prusty, 2013, 'Reproductive health complications among tribal women in India: A special focus on northeast India', *Etawah Journal of Social Sciences*, 8-14.

Hazarika, P. and N. Chutia, 2013, 'Abortion incidents, stillbirth and reproductive health risk of Deori and Mishing women in northeast India', *International Journal of Scientific and Technology Research*, 2(8): 259-266.

Joshi, A.; M. Dhapola and PJ. Pelto, 2008, 'Gynaecological problems: Perceptions and treatment-seeking behaviours of rural Gujarati Women', In MA. Koenig; S. Jejeebhoy, JC. Cleland and B. Ganatra (Eds.), *Reproductive Health in India New Evidence*, pp. 133-158, Jaipur; Rawat Publications.

Juyal, R.; S. Kandpal; J. Semwal and K. Negi, 2012, 'Practices of menstrual hygiene among adolescent girls in a district of Uttarakhand', *Indian Journal of Community Health*, 24(2): 124-128.

Kaur, J., and AK. Kapoor, 2014, 'Perceptions and knowledge about leukorrhea in a slum dwelling South Asian Community', *Journal of Family and Reproductive Health*, 8(1): 45-52.

Krishnakumari, P., and MC. Arun, 2012, 'Reproductive health of women in Andro', *Journal of the Anthropological Society of Manipur India*, 1: 121-130.

Kulkarni, RN., and PM. Durge, 2005, 'A study of leucorrhoea in reproductive age group women of Nagpur city', *Indian Journal of Public Health*, 49(4): 238-249.

Kumar, A. and K. Srivastava, 2011, 'Cultural and social practices regarding menstruation among adolescent girls', *Social Work in Public Health,* 26(6): 594-604.

Kumari, S.; I. Walia and A. Singh, 2000, 'Self-reported uterine prolapse in a resettlement colony of North India', *Journal of Midwifery Women's Health,* 45(4): 343-350.

Meitei, MH.; K. Latashori and Ksh. Gopal, 2005, 'Awareness and prevalence of reproductive tract infections in north-east districts of India', *Health, and Population-Perspective and Issues*, 28(3): 132-145.

Mohite, RV.; VR. Mohite; SM. Kumbhar and P. Ganganahalli, 2013, 'Common menstrual problems among slum adolescent girls of Western Maharashtra, India', *Journal of Krishna Institute of Medical Sciences University,* 2(1): 89-97.

Oomman, NM., 1996, *Poverty and Pathology: Comparing Rural Rajasthani Women's Ethno-Medical Models with Biomedical Model of Reproductive Behaviour*, An unpublished Ph.D. thesis submitted to John Hopkins University, USA.

Patar, J.; BP. Das, MK. Bora, 2015, 'Evaluation of gynaecological problems among adolescent girls attending gynaecology outpatient department in Gauhati Medical College and Hospital', *Scholars Journal of Applied Medical Sciences*, 3(7D): 2729-2732.

Ravi, RP., and RA. Kulasekaran, 2013, 'Trends in reproductive tract infections and barriers to seeking treatment among young women: A community-based cross-sectional study in South India', *American Journal of Epidemiology and Infectious Disease,* 1(4): 53-58.

Sarma, J., 2015, *A Study of Completed Fertility and Postmenopausal Health of Working and Non-Working Assamese Women of Guwahati, Assam,* An unpublished Ph.D. thesis submitted to the Department of Anthropology, Gauhati University, Assam.

Sarmah, L., 2014, *Reproductive Health Seeking Behavior among the Bodo-Kachari Women in North Guwahati Area, Assam*, An unpublished Ph.D. thesis submitted to the Department of Anthropology, Gauhati University, Assam.

Shahani, R., 2014, 'Adolescence and reproductive behaviour: A study of Meitei-Pangals of Manipur', *International Journal of Scientific and Research Publications*, 4(9): 1-5.

Sonowal, S. and R. Sonowal, 2017, 'Traditional knowledge of medicinal plants using during pregnancy, childbirth and postpartum healing: A study among the Sonowal Kacharis of Dibrugarh district, Assam', In A. Zaman and M. Sharma (Eds.), *Anthropological Aurora of North East India*, pp. 161-169, New Delhi; Adhyayan Publishers and Distributors.

Soules, MR.; S. Sherman; E. Parrott; R. Rebar; N. Santoro; W. Utian and N. Woods, 2001, 'Stages of reproductive aging workshop (STRAW)', *Journal of Women's Health and Gender-Based Medicine,* 10: 843-848.

United Nation, 1994, *Report of the International Conference on Population and Development,* Cairo.

Wasserheit, J.; JR. Harris; J. Chakraborty; BA. Kay and KJ. Mason, 1989, 'Reproductive tract infections in a family planning population in rural Bangladesh', *Studies in Family Planning,* 20: 69-80.

World Health Organisation, 1948, *Constitution of the World Health Organisation*, Geneva, 1(1).

World Health Organisation, 1996, *Research on the Menopause in the 1990s* [WHO Technical Report Series No. 866], Geneva: WHO.

World Health Organisation, 1998, *Sexual and Reproductive Health Research Priorities for WHO*: 1998-2003.

Younis, N.; HN. Khattab; H. Zurayk and A. Farag, 1993, 'A community study of gynecological and related morbidities in rural Egypt', *Studies in Family Planning,* 24(3): 175-186.

Chapter - 6

Living on the Edge: The Missing Status of Mishing in Arunachal Pradesh

—Ratna Tayeng

Introduction

The chapter attempts to offer a logistic account of the controversial issues related to the citizenship problem of Mishing tribe and their relationships with the neighbouring tribes. This problem is by and large a product of the post-colonial boundary making the initiative. The fact is after independence, Indian government paid little attention to indigenous cultural groups and ethnic boundaries in drawing out the administrative region which profoundly impacted the socio-political landscape and created cultural fragmentation and disunion within and between the two bordering states.

At the same time, various socio-political movements emerge partly from believing that their ethnonationalism identity gives a sense of social security, distinct identity and opportunity which keep them vigilant to stress on protection against the taking of scarce resources by others. As a result, members of Mishing population inhabited in the border regions found themselves trapped in a dilemma of marginalisation and deprivation. They were isolated in the context of state policies, which is a state of their own.

According to Lego (2012: 3), "the root of the present problem of statelessness of the Mishing in Arunachal Pradesh lies in the creation of Assam-Arunachal Pradesh Border in 1951. The minority Mishing people living in Arunachal Pradesh fall prey to the plan of Gopinath Bordoloi, who convinced the gathering at Sadiya to join Assam instead of remaining in the state of Arunachal Pradesh (then NEFA). In the Sadiya plebiscite 1951 chaired by Gopinath Bordoloi, the then Chief Minister of Assam, the major fraction of the Mishing community preferred to join Assam side.

Podmeswar Doley's eagerness to remain with his (their) own racial brothers were defeated by other Mishings. Gopinath Bordoloi seeing a ripe opportunity arbitrarily annexed the major part of the Mishing inhabited territories for Assam. That put the minds of Arunachal Pradesh Mishings in oscillation, and in the minds of their Adi cousins sprouted out a feeling of disgrace against them. Subsequently, in the land where their forefathers were born, people began to consider them as outsiders or refugees".

In a state like Arunachal Pradesh, government designated "Scheduled Tribe" status is very important. In fact, the lion's share of public employment, business and trade licenses, and even the right to seek elected office are reserved for members of the Scheduled Tribes. Nearly 80 per cent of the government job is reserved for them only. In the Legislative Assembly except one, 60 seats are reserved for Scheduled Tribes. According to Baruah (2003:45), "This protective discrimination regime is the result of incremental policy-making going back to colonial times when policy instruments were devised to protect vulnerable aboriginal peoples living in isolated enclaves-once described as 'backward tracts'."

Now the situation is that though Arunachal Pradesh Mishings have the right to vote in state elections, they are indirectly or directly prevented from translating their potential voting power into effective policy-making. Because they are hardly represented in state politics, which makes them unable effectively to represent their voices and grievances. Even if some try to contest the election, I was told that they made to step down by their neighbouring people very often. As a minority, they cannot even speak about it. More importantly, their main problem such as lack of basic amenities like road connectivity, school, and healthcare facility in their areas remain unattended. In fact, during rainy seasons most of the Mishing areas remain cut off from the rest of the state. The Government of Arunachal Pradesh has totally failed to do anything for them due to lack of representation in Assembly to raise their problems.

Mishings and their neighbours

As a non-native in a homeland that does not want them, many find a welcome hand holding out only suffering and pain. Although the Mishing of Arunachal Pradesh considers themselves as natives of the soil, so far the dominant natives of state don't consider them as native. One apprehension among dominant native is that once Mishing is given Scheduled Tribe status, it will open a Pandora's Box to demand Scheduled Tribe status in the state among Deoris, Nepalese, Karbi, and Chakma-Hajongs etc. To most of the dominant natives, they are outsiders and migrant labourers.

This discrimination and deprivation resulted in a variety of forms of adaptation, which gave rise to many negative psychological consequences that are reflected in terms of quality of life and well-being. This state of affairs reflects not a sudden engagement between Mishing and non-Mishing but a longstanding relationship built up over many years. The processes by which Mishing groups are categorised and labeled affect how they are treated in society and how they are seen and represented. The term Mishing itself is contentious to many neighbouring tribes. It is often loaded with highly pejorative meanings in many contexts. For example, in Adi, the word 'Mishing' often carry overtones of a derogatory nature, the word becoming interchangeable with overtly racist terms such as 'Mishing–Mipak' or 'Abil' (slave).

In an interview with a Galo gentleman[1] noted "If Mishings are given Scheduled Tribe status today, Deori and Nepali will ask for it tomorrow. When Arunachal Pradesh was demarcated, they were given the choice to pick and choose between Assam and NEFA. The majority chooses Assam as a result land were also re-demarcated for them into Assam. So, in the course of time, if any Mishing left behind in Arunachal Pradesh, it is their problem, why we suffer.

Recently, Adi Bane Kebang (apex organisation of Adi) has appealed the state Govt. for granting them as Adi. Giving Scheduled Tribe status to them is a state issue and it will affect us all. ABK has no right to decide our future, let other tribes of the state decide whom to include in our Arunachal Pradesh. We are Mongolian race, but we cannot simply go to Mongolia and claim our rights there. Maybe they want a larger population in the name of Adi, want to create another constituency and want to demand another district. If at all they are to be given Scheduled Tribe status, they should be given as Mishing tribe. Why they tagged us as Adi. If they are interested in number why doesn't Adi become Mishing since Mishings are more in number? It's saddening to see how many outsiders want to take a dip in our little plate. When almost all the tribes of the state are striving to protect their ethnic purity and cultural uniqueness, it is sad to learn that the ABK is contaminating its own tribe by trying to include the Mishings into its fold, whose members also taking pride in being called an Assamese, rather than being called a tribal of Arunachal Pradesh. Such a move should be thwarted and nipped in the bud.

The overall image of Mishings among the tribes of Arunachal Pradesh is similar. I have conducted a number of interviews with the person belonging to Galo, Apatani, and Nyishi tribe. I found that people hailing from these tribes were outrightly opposed to the notion of giving Scheduled Tribe status to Mishing. For them, Mishing had been just another Assam tribe that needs to be treated as an outsider. A person belonging to Nyishi tribe once noted "I agree that Mishing is Tani, but they are Tani people from Assam and we are Tani from Arunachal Pradesh. They have become so diluted due to mixing with Assamese. Even, genetically, they might have diluted from the original stock, they allowed themselves to interbreed with non-Tani races. So, most of them have lost their racial purity. We cannot call all of them as a son of Abotani. They lost their original identity and hence shouldn't be considered as Tanis anymore. Possession of Scheduled Tribe status doesn't qualify them as Tanis".

The reason for non-accepting them as native are of course many, but it also partly arises from the fear that Mishings once accepted might develop an intention to reclaim the territories their forefathers left behind. Again, the word Mishing immediately associates Mishing from Assam, in the mind of the dominant native of the state and somehow creates a perception, however false, that they are a population who has the option to return to their land of origin. This myth of a 'double homeland' makes them soft targets of ethnic group assertions fighting over available scarce resources often leading to loss of home, hearth, and livelihood.

The image of Mishings among the Adi of Arunachal Pradesh is also by and large similar. They are often stereotyped, sometimes called as "Mipak" (slave) and often accused of petty cheating. Every Adi man knows tales of trickery and cheating while traveling through Sadiya road done by some Mishing. As a result, some Adis avoid any relations with Mishing altogether. Among Adis, there is also a perception that if an Adi man does not get a wife, he will look for Mishing woman. Mishing women as considered as easy-going for marriage because most of them are poor. Some other Adis have a sympathetic perception about them and maintain social relations but such sympathy is inconsistent and only lasts as long as the Mishing remain within their designated stereotype.

In recent years a dialogue is going on for an inclusion of the Mishing of Arunachal Pradesh in the list of Scheduled Tribes of Arunachal Pradesh at par Adi tribe. The ABK leaders consider Mishing as part of their stock. Hence, numbers of cultural exchange programmes have taken place in the border region between Adi and Mishing. In April 2013, a huge crowd gathered at Sirki Nane Lotta at Jonai town where the two-day cultural meet was organised by the Adi-Mishing Lemo Kebang (AMLK) to fostering unity and brotherhood between Adi and Mishing.

The very nature of the Adi-Mishing issue is very delicate. Many would think that it's a ploy by the Adis to increase their political stronghold, especially the Nyishis since today they are at the topmost hierarchy of the Tani pyramid. Galos and Apatanis would also follow suit because if we look into the history of these two tribes, they have always been a staunch defender of their distinctiveness in their respective tribes.

This is not to say that all Adis are in support of inclusion of Mishing within Adi fold. In an interview with one of the student leaders of AdiSU (All Adi Student's Union), Mr. Onong Gao (name changed at his request) remarked that "Some clans of the Mishing are indeed Adi but they forsook their true identity, that is being an Adi, ages ago. Now they already have their own unshakeable religious faith of their own and have a vast difference in ritual and traditional practices from Adi. That is why they never eat or taste the beef. As a result, there are two numbers of community hall (Dere/ Mosup) at Oyan, one for Adis and one for Mishings. The majority of them are not Adi and many Mishing identify them as Adi. I don't understand why some of our people reluctant to agree that Adis is Adis and Mishings are Mishings. Moreover, the majority of the Mishings looks like Assamese now. Very few have tribal looks. If Adi includes Mishing then that day is not far when other tribes will be surprised to the non-tribal looks of Adi. Till now Adi and Apatani are regarded as the most charming and beautiful tribes of Arunachal Pradesh. We Adis had already made the greatest blunder by losing the state Capital and now heading for another historical blunder by trying to consolidate Mishing with us. ABK leaders must realise that there must be something really needed to be done for the socio-economic welfare of Adi society rather than this useless issue at this point in time".

What is more interesting is that once the Mishing left the hill areas they were only known for unpleasant activities. Even in the known history, they were often accused of treachery and theft. Lego (2005) also noted in many instances where many Adis were poisoned when they visited the Mishing areas. He further noted how young people were often advised not to go to the Mishing area and not to speak the truth in the olden days. Even today, Mishing are often alleged of indulging in various kinds of black magic.

It is a fact that many Adi thinks Mishings to be dishonest, complicated, and opportunistic. The Mishings themselves are to some extent, responsible for the sad part of the story. When I was about to conduct fieldwork, my parent was so worried that I am going to stay with Mishing, they gave me lots of advice. When I went back home and told them about their hospitality, they still were not ready to accept.

"The relationship between Adi and Mishing has always been unequal. Although, the Mishings hail from the same stock as the Adis ethnically and culturally the political relationship between them was far from equal. The Adis claimed supremacy over the Mishings and regarded them as their slaves and thus they had only a subordinate political status and were subjects of tribute to the Adis. Once the exactions became more taxing, the only recourse left for the Mishings was to move to a safer place, which was the plains area of Upper Assam. The oppressive relationship between the Adis and the Mishings was thus, the main cause of the emigration of the Mishings to the plains of Assam in search of peace, protection, and land" (Pegu, 2005: 55-56).

"After the end of Ahom rule, the situation changed gradually under the British rule in Assam. After the British occupation of Assam, many Mishings found it to their advantage to move away from the vicinity of the Adi lands. Encouraged by the attitude of new authorities and feeling a sense of security and protection, they began to defy the Adis, some even moved down to remote places beyond the easy access of the Adis" (Lego, 2005, III). This annoyed the Adis and they continued to attack and plunder the Mishing villages, even their villages were well within the British territory. In such a situation, the British government was compelled to send several expeditions against the Adis. "In 1889-90 Adis from Yomsing and Ledum village raided a Miri (Mishing) village in the British territory. Subsequently, a blockade of the whole Adis was ordered and carried out" (Chakrabarty, 1971:54).

Thus, the common identity of Mishings is based on a history of perceived victimisation at the hands of their neighbours. It is, therefore, understandable that identification with the Mishing heritage would be associated with greater criticism of Arunachal society. The people of Arunachal have been reluctant to acknowledge the existence of Mishing people, and it has discouraged the formation of a Mishing identity among the Arunachal Mishing population.

Real and unreal Mishing

In a country like India, constitutional category, legal and formal category matter a lot. It tells where one belongs, part of the member, who is legal and who is illegal, who is native and who are non-native. To prove that they are real native since 1997 family dossier was carried out in all the Mishing inhabited villages. As per the government order, the year 1947 was fixed as the cutoff year. So, only Mishings whose ancestors have resided within present-day Arunachal boundaries before 1947 were considered as bona fide Mishing. They now called themselves as pure Mishing, sometimes called as Dakdung. According to Pao (2009), they are called Dakdung because of the stand-up in their land and could resist all the attacks from various Tani groups of Arunachal Pradesh. The Mishing afraid of other

Tani group and migrated to the Ahom Kingdom is known as Daktok (tainted Mishing who run away from their land). While these formal categories have nothing to do with the person's identity, they have subsequently affected the realm of their social life.

Regarding the political status of Mishing in Arunachal Pradesh, Mr. Ponil Bori responded: "There is a general perception that Mishing is coming from Assam and settling here in Arunachal Pradesh. Mishings have always been an integral part of Arunachal Pradesh. We are as much a part of Arunachal Pradesh as the other tribes residing here. We all have migrated from some other place. If we start saying who is who then we all are refugees here. Some Mishings went down in Assam to settle and the majority of them stayed back in their motherland, their home.

The issue of Scheduled Tribe problem did not arise until the 1970s. Till the 1970s, they were enlisted as Abor Galong, Abor Padam, Abor Minyong, Abor Pasi, Abor Miri etc. The authority maintained no prescribed format of certificate; it entirely depends on the officer concerned. Especially in East Siang, the official issued such certificates as per their convenience. But after the 1980s as competition has grown tougher, problems emerge for the necessity Scheduled Tribe certificate in the government-sponsored entrance like MBBS, APJEE, and other job examination Scheduled Tribe became popular and necessitate and policy of excluding non-Scheduled Tribe which are not included in the list of APST became attention.

A few years back there was a commission, Ringu Commission, where Gegong Apang (the then Chief Minister of Arunachal Pradesh), along with other members of many Banggos opinions was taken at Namsing, Oyan, Mer, Gadum. The commission, later on, proposes the name of three tribes and sent for recognition to Govt. of India, which was headed by Omen Moyong Deori. There was an attempt to include the name of Deories, and Khamiyang tribe along with Mishing, into APST which led to violent opposition from All Arunachal Pradesh Student's Union. In the year 2006, however, state Government formed a committee under the Chairmanship of Lombo Tayeng (the then Minister of Public Health Engineering and Water Supply, Govt. of Arunachal Pradesh) to look after the feasibility to grant Scheduled Tribe status to the Mishings residing in the state. But the findings and recommendations of the committee were never made public. Since 2007 they are considered as Adi tribe. We have no other choice.

Mishing who settled in Arunachal has every right to claim their citizenship in Arunachal Pradesh. The granting of recognition to the Mishing and their descendants who have settled in Arunachal Pradesh since time immemorial is based on the fact that they fulfill the existing criteria laid down by the law of the land. The law of the land and the available documents prove that some Mishing fulfills the criteria laid down by the govt. in Arunachal Pradesh and the Mishing people have no business to prove that. To that end, we have submitted to the Govt. the Settlement Order issued to the Mishing people by the Deputy Commissioner of the East Siang, the appointment orders of Mishing *Gaon Buras* prior to the statehood of Arunachal Pradesh. What more is there to prove?".

The experiences, which trigger these emotions of deprivation among Mishings of Arunachal Pradesh, are not much different from those experienced by their relatives in Assam. Mr. Daniel Kumbang (name changed at his request) from Bahir Jonai, Assam noted "Our Mishing tribe is a pendulum for Arunachal Pradesh and Assam. Assam says we are migrants from Arunachal Pradesh. Arunachal Pradesh says we are migrants from Assam. We are well aware that indigenous Mishings of Arunachal Pradesh are seeking Scheduled Tribe status, which is denied until this day. We know several Arunachal Pradesh tribes mistreat our brethren and giving a hard time there. We want to help but we are helpless. The problem arises from the false assumption that Assam Mishings will come to Arunachal Pradesh once Arunachal Pradesh Mishings are given Scheduled Tribe status. If there were no Arunachal Pradesh and the state boundary, there would not have been such a problem. Taking our peacefulness for granted, we are divided into Arunachal Pradesh Mishing and Assam Mishing.

Unfortunately, our people in Arunachal Pradesh are taking the identity of the 'Adi'. I feel that there is no point trying to create a new Mishing identity. Arunachal Pradesh Mishing should stop identifying as an Adi. Our people have a huge respect for Adi but most of Adi doesn't have any respect for our tribe in their heart. I have been too many Adi places and had some friend as well. What I found is that most of Adi never considers us as brothers.

Most unfortunate thing is that educated Mishings of Assam have forgotten their mother tongue and educated Mishing of Arunachal Pradesh have forgotten their community's name. So the former is asking their sons and daughters to speak Assamese and the latter is asking to become Adi. By looking at the present situation, I can guess that Mishing people living in Assam will call themselves as Assamese and that of Arunachal Pradesh will call themselves as Adi. "I have seen Mishing people are used as a vote bank by the Arunachal Pradesh politicians. They treat Mishing as how politicians treat illegal immigrant in Assam."

Oken Pao (name changed at his request) from Oyan village, Arunachal Pradesh noted: "Being seen as an outsider is one of the biggest problems

Mishing of Arunachal Pradesh facing. Mental suffering is worse than the physical illness, and it is the worse illness in the world. We are as indigenous as any other indigenous tribes of this state. But unfortunately the State Government yet to recognise us as Scheduled Tribe of Arunachal Pradesh (APST). Due to nonrecognition, we are lagging behind in every sector of education, economy and social activity. Most of the people of Arunachal Pradesh treat us as outsiders illegally settled in Arunachal Pradesh.

Due to this, we do not have the liberty/courage to buy or own a land outside our own traditional lands for which we are always seen with suspicion. We are also not given trading license, gun license etc as we are considered as non-APST and while on allotment of some contract works in various departments or by political allotment, our people hardly get a chance to participate. We are even denied the rights to have a land allotment in urban places in Arunachal Pradesh. Every community needs a place of worship, after all, India is a secular state, and unfortunately, we are not given space or a place to build a Namghar in Pasighat. We even consulted the Deputy Commissioner of East Siang also, but no concrete step has been taken so far".

There is no doubt that Arunachal Pradesh Mishings have suffered discrimination in the hand of Arunachal society. Inequities such as those described above continue to existing in great part because of a lack of Arunachal Pradesh Mishings representation in decision-making bodies. With the rise of Mishing-educated generation, some Arunachal Pradesh Mishings began the process of mobilisation for equal rights without much success. For example, in the last few years, a student organisation known as All Mishing Student Union of Arunachal Pradesh (AMSU) is being active in the region. It is the sister organisation of the Takam Mishing Porin Kebang (All Mising Student Union) which have its headquarters in Assam. Recently, on 24 December 2013, they organised a movement where a large number of Mishing assembles at Ruksin, near the Assam-Arunachal Pradesh border demanding the state government to recognise Mishing as one of the bona fide tribe of the state. They also raise voice against the taking of Adi ST and advocated for retaining their ethnic identity at all cost.

The organiser of the Mishing Bachao Andolan, Mr. Suresh Pao (name changed at his request) noted "For last 30 years we are neglected and discriminated by Government of India and Government of Arunachal Pradesh. The reason for discrimination is that we Mishing are mostly dark and look like non-tribal. So on racial looks, we have kept aside, politicised, and discriminated. There are many tribes in Arunachal Pradesh, who migrated recently from other states and country, such as Singpho, Khampti,

Yobin etc, who have more tribal looks, all were provided APST but we Mishing who is originally from Arunachal Pradesh are still living as stateless.

We are made to become Adi to get Scheduled Tribe certificate and PRC. If my ancestor were Mishing then how can I proclaim to be Adi? The human being, by nature all free, equal, and independent, no one can put out of this estate and subject to the political power of another without his own consent. For those who have taken the Adi identity, let them be Adi. Those who have not taken the Adi identity let them be Mishing. I was scolded by Mishing officers and seniors for demanding Scheduled Tribe certificate for Mishing living in Arunachal Pradesh. I try to explain them, but our elders are stubborn. I accept that our Mishing and Adi have a common ancestor. But not only Adi, our Mishing also shares a common ancestor with Galo, Tagin, Hill Miri etc. The unity among Adi-Mishings people is very appreciable efforts. But I reject the terms and conditions that Mishing living in Arunachal Pradesh will be treated as a sub-tribe of Adi or Arunachal Pradesh Mishing can only get a Scheduled Tribe certificate from Arunachal Pradesh as Adi tribe is an insult to our Mishing Tribe, which is the second largest tribe of North East India. Our Mishing tribe is not a sub-tribe. Mishing and Adi are both Tani people but Mishing cannot be Adi and Adi cannot be Mishing.

I always stood firm from my childhood with my head held high and sang our song "India is my country, all people are my brothers and sisters" but some of my brothers say I am not from Arunachal Pradesh, I am a refugee. For Arunachal Pradesh Mishing, the most important question is our survival. We are loyal citizens of Arunachal Pradesh, but at the same time, we requested that it recognises us as APST and enables us to be a rightful citizen. The authorities do not want to grant APST status to us. We are still not represented in the Arunachal Pradesh assembly. We don't have right to have our own MPs and MLAs. I born here, my father and grandfather were the original inhabitants of this land. Then why people and govt. do not understand this".

All of the important concerns related to life in Arunachal Pradesh discussed above, can be related to a broad theme of instability in Arunachal Pradesh borderland. Whether talking about residency, employment, education or their social life, Arunachal Pradesh Mishing identified the uncertainty of their lives, and in particular, worries for the future, as the primary cause of their suffering. Instability was present in a large number of domains of everyday life in Arunachal Pradesh and was connected to suffering and poor psychosocial well-being. Unfortunately, the issue of political marginalisation along the Assam-Arunachal Pradesh borderlands has failed to raise any serious response. Moreover, intervention for reducing political marginalisation requires political will, constitutional safeguards, and effective enforcement mechanisms. So far, both the state governments and central government hardly has developed or has any good policy for the upliftment of these fractured communities. Rabinowitz (2001:75) once noted "Being a trapped minority is undoubtedly a predicament, an undesirable situation imposed on the minority against its will. Being smaller and poorer, the opportunities for trapped minorities to change their situation are few. This does not mean, however, that the predicament is finite".

With the recent submission of a memorandum by Adi Bane Kebang (ABK) in 2007 to Chief Minister of Arunachal Pradesh demanding Scheduled Tribe status for Mishing people under the Adi, the issue has escalated into a major controversial issue among the socio-political circles of the border state. The move that has been strongly seconded by Adi Students' Union (AdiSU) is resented by the apex student body of the state All Arunachal Pradesh Students' Union (AAPSU) and Student Union Movement of Arunachal[2] (SUMA). The AAPSU said that there was "no question of granting the status to Mishing people since they were already recognised in the state of neighbouring Assam". On the similar line, a noted academician of Arunachal Pradesh, Nani Bath (2010) argues that "APST status cannot just be granted to the Mishing of Siang as Mr. Gegong Apang wanted. It is difficult to ascertain the reasons as to why the PRCs were granted by the Government of Arunachal Pradesh to those categories of people who are not considered as the natives of any district of Arunachal Pradesh". Though, the Mishings insist on being treated at par with the local indigenous peoples. This is, however, not acceptable to the indigenous peoples. Whatsoever, the truth, the reality is that Arunachal Pradesh borderlands and the people who reside there continue to bleed because of neglect and a complete vacuum of governance. They are still struggling to get recognition as a Scheduled Tribe of Arunachal Pradesh despite the fact that they were aboriginal inhabitants of this land.

Conclusion

This accidental boundary making took place in 1951. Mishing people were asked to choose where they want to stay. The majority of them chose to stay in Assam since plebiscite was taken at Sadiya in the heart of Assam. The majority of them voted in the hope that with the new political set up and new rules, their social economic condition might change. Those few choosing to stay in Arunachal Pradesh were wanted to keep a foothold in their ancient homeland. Unfortunately, many those who stay in Arunachal Pradesh have lost their time and space. Subsequently, in the land their forefathers were born, people began to consider them as outsiders or refugees.

The overwhelming belief that majority of the Mishings lived in Assam had a profound impact on the Mishing experience in the Arunachal Pradesh. For Mishing, now, they had three options available to them. They could join the Mishing of Assam or they could continue to pursue their distinct political identity or they could choose to self-identify as Adi. It is unlikely that they will be able to go for the first option since the State Govt. are radical and inclined towards accommodation of them within their respective territory. If they identify themselves with Mishing referred to in Mishing historical documents, then they have to recover their history. If they claim to be descendants of the Adis, then they have to re-write their history again.

Notes

1. Interview was conducted on 23/12/2013 at Likabali.
2. Student Union Movement of Arunachal (SUMA) is a recently formed student organisation of Arunachal Pradesh. Formed on 23 January 23 2013 and headed by Biri Tabing as the President and Unti Umbrey as General Secretary.

References

Baruah, Sanjib, 2003. 'Citizens and denizens: Ethnicity, homelands, and the crisis of displacement in Northeast India', *Journal of Refugee Studies* 16 (1): 44-66.

Chakravarti, BC., 1971. *The Evolution of India's Northern Borders*, London; Asia Publishing House.

Lego, Lomti, 2012. *The Missing Identity of Arunachal Mishing*, Ajit Pertin, Naharlagun, Arunachal Pradesh.

Pao, Kaling, 2009. *Agrarian Economy on Siang Valley: A Case Study on Oyan Village of East Siang District*, Arunachal Pradesh, an unpublished M.A. Dissertation submitted to Arunachal Institute of Tribal Studies, Rajiv Gandhi University, Arunachal Pradesh.

Pegu, Lakhi Nath, 2005. *Mishing Socio-Religious Life; Continuity and Change*, An unpublished Ph.D. thesis, submitted to Department of History, Arunachal University, Arunachal Pradesh.

Rabinowitz, Dan 2001. 'The Palestinian citizens of Israel, the concept of trapped minority and the discourse of trans-nationalism in Anthropology', *Ethnic and Racial Studies* 24(1): 64-85.

Other sources:

A memorandum submitted by Adi Bane Kebang to the Hon'ble Chief Minister, Arunachal Pradesh, 2007.

AAPSU accuse govt of being soft on refugee and non-indigenous population, *The Arunachal Times*, 28/09/2010, p. 1.

Bath, Nani, Native Vs Non-Native: Need for a Comprehensive Policy, *The Arunachal Times*, 28/09/2010, p. 1.

Chapter - 7

Population Composition of the High and Low Altitude Monpa of Arunachal Pradesh

—D. K. Adak, T. Baruah, P. Bharati, P. Kashyap, J. Phukan and P. Chetry

Introduction

Men have been familiar since long with the fact that the conditions of life are usually harder and breathing is more difficult in high altitude areas than in low altitude ones, and that striking functional and morphological differences exist between high and low altitude populations. An appreciable proportion of the world population live permanently at elevations of 3000 m or higher and are exposed to a harsh environment, known as "high altitude", which in reality comprises a constellation of stresses, namely, hypobaric hypoxia, cold, rugged terrain, high dosage of ultraviolet radiation, iodine deficiency, limited natural resources etc., (Gupta *et al.*, 1989).

The composition of the population is the internal structure of a human population with respect to one or more demographic attributes or traits at a particular point in time. The word 'composition' in population literature is often used as a synonym of 'distribution' or 'structure'. To the demographers, the study of population composition constitutes a basic and the most relevant field of study (Misra, 1982). The study of population composition acts as an indicator of its current population dynamics (Chachra and Bhasin, 1998).

Population composition has been studied widely in India in different areas (Basu, 1969; Ghosh, 1976; Talukdar, 1979; Rao, 1989; Narhari, 1991; Reddy, 1991; Adak and Gharami, 2001; and many others). However, not many reports are available on this line on high altitude population (Gupta *et. al.,* 1989). Moreover, there is no such report in North-East India. Hence, an endeavour has been made in the present chapter to deal with certain aspects of population composition of the Dirang and Tawang Monpa, a low and high altitude population of Arunachal Pradesh.

Material and Methods

A door-to-door survey was conducted using structured schedule during May-June, 2014 for Tawang Monpa and during May-June, 2015 for Dirang Monpa. The data were collected from 309 and 500 households of the Dirang and Tawang Monpa respectively.

Dirang Monpas are Buddhist by religion, who is one of the sub-groups of Monpa tribe. They inhabit the hilly terrain (1600 m) of West Kameng district of Arunachal Pradesh. The district experiences moderate to heavy rainfall and in the winter, it experiences severe cold. Dirang Monpa residing in Dirang town and its surrounding areas were selected for the study.

Tawang Monpas are also Buddhist. Like Dirang Monpa they are one of the sub-groups of the Monpa tribe, who are high altitude (3048 m) people. They inhabit the hilly terrain of Tawang district of Arunachal Pradesh. These district experiences moderate to heavy rainfall and in the winter it experiences frost and snowfall. For the present study, Tawang Monpas residing in Tawang town and its surrounding areas were selected.

Results

Age and sex distribution

Table 7.1a: Distribution of population by age and sex: Tawang Monpa

Age groups (in years)	*Male*		*Female*		*Total*		*Sex Ratio*
	No.	*Per cent*	*No.*	*Per cent*	*No.*	*Per cent*	
0-4	62	5.76	62	6.17	124	5.96	1000
5-9	75	6.96	70	6.97	145	6.96	933.33
10-14	73	6.78	70	6.97	143	6.87	958.9
15-19	102	9.47	100	9.95	202	9.7	980.39
20-24	117	10.86	154	15.32	271	13.02	1316.24
25-29	141	13.09	136	13.53	277	13.3	964.54
30-34	86	7.98	72	7.16	158	7.59	837.21
35-39	90	8.36	94	9.35	184	8.84	1044.44
40-44	62	5.76	62	6.17	124	5.96	1000
45-49	74	6.87	89	8.85	163	7.83	1202.7
50-54	63	5.85	37	3.68	100	4.8	587.3
55-59	37	3.44	26	2.59	63	3.02	702.7
60-64	30	2.79	7	0.7	37	1.78	233.33
65-69	17	1.58	11	1.09	28	1.34	647.06
70-74	11	1.02	6	0.6	17	0.82	545.45
75-79	25	2.32	5	0.5	30	1.44	200
80-84	8	0.74	3	0.3	11	0.53	375
85-89	3	0.28	-	-	3	0.14	-
90 & above	1	0.09	1	0.1	2	0.1	492.31
Total	**1077**	**100**	**1005**	**100**	**2082**	**100**	**933.15**

Age and sex distribution are the building blocks that construct the composition of a population. The age structure and sex distribution of Tawang Monpa people as on May 2014 are presented in Table 7.1a. Of the total population, an excess of males relative to females is observed. The number of total males is 1077 and the number of females is 1005. As the age increases, the number of individuals gradually increases among the males from 0-4 years to 25-29 years age group. The number of individuals gradually decreases from 30-34 years age group in the same sex. Whereas, among the females, the number of individuals gradually increases from 0-4 years to 20-24 years age group. The number of individuals gradually decreases from 25-29 years age group in this sex. It is interesting to note that while 30 individuals are recorded among the males in 60-64 years only seven individuals are recorded among the females in this age group.

Table 7.1b: Distribution of population by age and sex: Dirang Monpa

Age groups (in years)	*Male*		*Female*		*Total*		*Sex Ratio*
	No.	*Per cent*	*No.*	*Per cent*	*No.*	*Per cent*	
0-4	46	7.00	46	7.03	92	7.02	1000.00
5-9	64	9.74	58	8.87	122	9.31	906.25
10-14	68	10.35	48	7.34	116	8.85	705.88
15-19	57	8.68	77	11.77	134	10.22	1350.88
20-24	58	8.83	90	13.76	148	11.29	1551.72
25-29	86	13.09	72	11.01	158	12.05	837.21
30-34	47	7.15	71	10.86	118	9.00	1510.64
35-39	58	8.83	44	6.73	102	7.78	758.62
40-44	41	6.24	46	7.03	87	6.64	1121.95
45-49	39	5.94	30	4.59	69	5.26	769.23
50-54	25	3.81	35	5.35	60	4.58	1400.00
55-59	23	3.50	11	1.68	34	2.59	478.26
60-64	20	3.04	15	2.29	35	2.67	750.00
65-69	10	1.52	4	0.61	14	1.07	400.00
70-74	8	1.22	2	0.31	10	0.76	250.00
75-79	5	0.76	2	0.31	7	0.53	400.00
80 & above	2	0.30	3	0.46	5	0.38	1500.00
Total	**657**	**100.00**	**4**	**100.00**	**1311**	**100.00**	**995.43**

Age structure and sex distribution of Dirang Monpa people as on May 2015 are presented in Table 7.1b. Of the total population, males and females are recorded almost in equal number. The number of total males is 657 and the number of females is 654. As the age increases, the number of individuals gradually increases among the males from 0-4 years to 10-14 years age group. A sudden increase is perceptible in the 25-29 years age group. The number of individuals gradually decreases from 30-34 years age group in this sex. Whereas, among the females, the number of individuals gradually increases from 0-4 years to 25-29 years age group. The only exception is noticed in 10-14 years age group in which an opposite trend is perceptible. The number of individuals gradually decreases than in this sex.

Sex ratio

Misra (1982) says, "the study of sex-ratio in a population is important primarily because of two reasons: firstly, analysis of the sex-ratio can help in drawing several inferences regarding the dynamics of demographic phenomena; and secondly, it has bearing upon the marriage rate, death rate, birth rate and even on the rate of migration directly". The relative strength of the males and females in number in a population is commonly measured by sex-ratio. This is a basic measure in demography, genetics, and epidemiology. In the present study, the sex-ratio has been considered as the number of males per 1000 females [(females/males) ×1000]. In case of sex-ratio values, an increasing trend is perceptible in the Tawang Monpa from 5-9 years to 20-24 years age group. However, from 50-54 years to 80-84 years age group a dismal picture is noticed. This might be due to small sample size in many age groups (Table 7.1a). In case of sex-ratio values, no definite trend (increasing or decreasing) is perceptible among the Dirang Monpa. This might be due to small sample size in many age groups (Table 7.1b). However, overall sex-ratio is found to be 995.43, which is indicative of the almost equal number of total individuals in both the sexes in this population.

Population pyramid

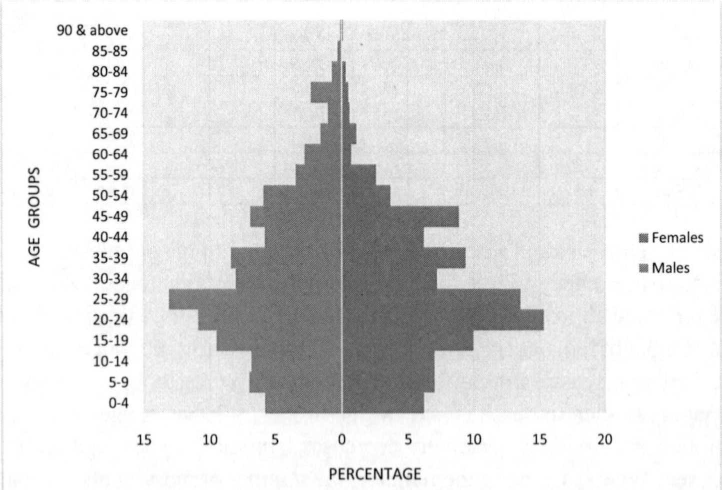

Fig.7.1a: Population pyramid: Tawang Monpac.

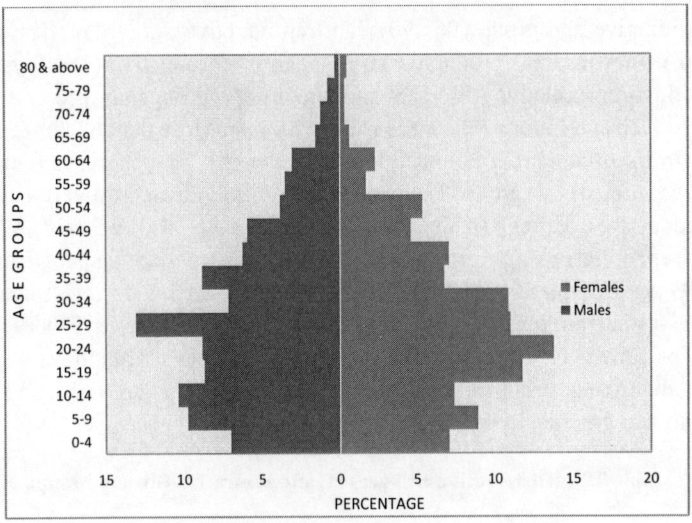

Fig. 7.1b: Population pyramid: Dirang Monpa.

The age structure of Tawang Monpa neither suggests a trend of progressive type population growth nor a trend of stationary type population growth. This may readily be appreciated visually from the illustration portraying the age pyramid (Figure 7.1a) of the population group. However, a constriction at the base of the population pyramid, suggests a recent fertility decline or increased infant mortality. The age structure of Dirang Monpa people also, suggests neither a trend of progressive type population growth nor a trend of stationary population growth. This may readily be appreciated visually from the illustration portraying the age pyramid (Figure 7.1b) of the population group.

Sex-ratio in pre-reproductive, reproductive and post-reproductive age groups

In Table 7.2a and Figure 7.2, the sex-ratio values in pre-reproductive (0-14 years), reproductive (15-49 years) and post-reproductive (50 years and above) age groups are presented for Tawang Monpa. More than 66 per cent of the individuals fall in reproductive (male: 62.40 per cent; female: 70.35 per cent) age group. The percentage of individuals is lowest in post-reproductive age group (male: 18.11 per cent; female: 9.55 per cent). While pre-reproductive age group falls in between in this respect (male: 19.49 per cent; female: 20.10 per cent). A trend of gradual decline is noticed in sex-ratio from reproductive (1052.08) to post-reproductive (492.31) age groups. However, sex ratio value is found to be considerably lower in pre-reproductive age group (961.90) than reproductive age group. The sex-ratio values in pre-reproductive (0-14 years), reproductive (15-49 years) and post-reproductive (50 years and above) age groups are presented in Table 7.2b and Figure 7.2 for the Dirang Monpa. More than 62 per cent of the individuals fall in reproductive (male: 58.75 per cent; female: 65.75 per cent) age group. The percentage of individuals is lowest in post-reproductive age group (male: 14.16 per cent; female: 11.01 per cent). While pre-reproductive age group falls in between in this respect (male: 27.09 per cent; female: 23.24 per cent). A trend of gradual decline is noticed in sex-ratio from reproductive (1113.99) to post-reproductive (774.19) age groups. However, sex ratio value is found to be considerably lower in pre-reproductive age group (853.93) than reproductive age group. These findings are shown graphically in Figure 7.2.

Table 7.2a: Distribution by age, sex, and sex-ratio: Tawang Monpa

Age-group(in years)	*Male*	*Female*	*Total*	*Sex-ratio*
Pre-reproductive (0-14 years)	210(19.49)	202(20.10)	412(19.79)	961.90
Reproductive (15-49 years)	672(62.40)	707(70.35)	1379(66.23)	1052.08
Post- reproductive (50 & above years)	195(18.11)	96(9.55)	291(13.98)	492.31
Total	**1077(100.00)**	**1005 (100.00)**	**2082 (100.00)**	**933.15**

Figures in parenthesis indicate percentage values.

Table 7.2b: Distribution by age, sex, and sex-ratio: Dirang Monpa

Age-group (in years)	*Male*	*Female*	*Total*	*Sex-ratio*
Pre-reproductive (0-14 years)	178(27.09)	152(23.24)	330.(25.17)	853.93
Reproductive (15-49 years)	386(58.75)	430(65.75)	816(62.24)	1113.99
Post- reproductive (50 & above years)	93(14.16)	72(11.01)	165(12.59)	774.19
Total	**657(100.00)**	**654(100.00)**	**1311 (100.00)**	**995.43**

Figures in parenthesis indicate percentage values.

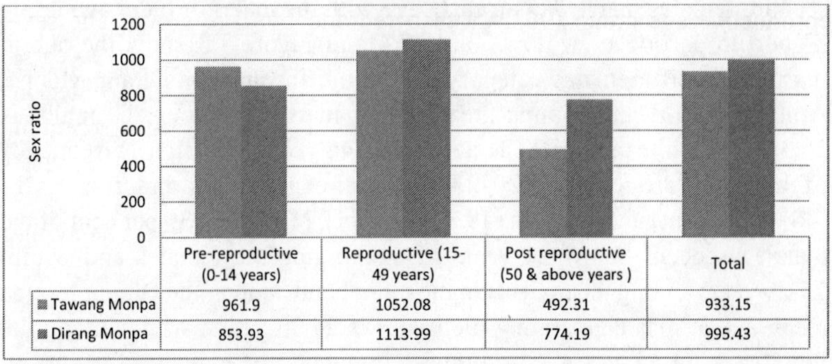

Fig. 7.2: Sex-ratio in pre-reproductive, reproductive and post-reproductive age groups.

Population characteristics

Some population characteristics of the Tawang and Dirang Monpa are presented in Table 7.3. Among the Tawang Monpa, it reveals a relatively high index of aging (31.07). This might be due to a lower rate of mortality among the aged in this population. Child-women ratio among them is 17.54, suggesting a declining trend of fertility. The young dependency ratio is found to be 26.72, while old dependency ratio is 8.30. On the other hand, the Dirang Monpa also reveals a relatively high index of aging (23.33). This might be due to a higher rate of mortality among the aged in this population. Child-women ratio among them is 23.00, suggesting an increasing trend of fertility. The young dependency ratio is found to be 36.26, while old dependency ratio is 7.80.

Table 7.3: Some population indices among Tawang and Dirang Monpa

Indices	*Tawang Monpa*	*Dirang Monpa*
Index of aging	31.07	23.33
Young dependency ratio	26.72	36.26
Old dependency ratio	8.30	7.80
Total dependency ratio	35.02	44.06
Child women ratio	17.54	23.00

Age at marriage

Misra (1982) says the age at marriage in India showing an upward trend continues. Still the age at marriage is quite low in India in comparison with other developing and especially with the developed countries. The social and health status of a woman is adversely affected by her low age at marriage. There are few factors involved in this matter. First, cohabitation and childbirth at immature age cause unfavourable physical effects and second, females married at an early age with the males of older age imply higher proportion of widow. Table 7.4 and Figure 7.3 show the age at marriage in different age category among the Tawang and Dirang Monpa. Among the Tawang Monpa mean age at marriage among the males is 25.3 years; while among the females is 21.44 years. The highest frequency of marriages occurs in 20-24 years age group among the males (40.04 per cent) and females (48.32 per cent). More than 30 per cent of the marriages occur below 20 years of age among the females and within 25-29 years among the males. On the other hand, among the Dirang Monpa mean age at marriage among the males is 24.73 years; while among the females is 21.68 years. The highest frequency of marriages occurs in 25-29 years age group among the males (48.25 per cent) and in 20-24 years among females (45.16 per cent). More than 30 per cent of the marriages occur below 20 years of age among the females and within 25-29 years among the males in case of Tawang Monpa. Side by side, among the Dirang Monpa more than 30 per cent of the marriages occur below 20 years of age among the females and within 20-24 years among the males.

Table 7.4: Age at marriage

Age at marriage	*Tawang Monpa*				*Dirang Monpa*			
	Males		*Females*		*Males*		*Females*	
	No.	*Per cent*	*No.*	*Per cent*	*No.*	*Per cent*	*No.*	*Per cent*
Below 20	43	8.56	163	32.15	22	6.98	95	30.65
20-24	201	40.04	245	48.32	120	38.10	140	45.16
25-29	154	30.68	82	16.17	152	48.25	70	22.58
30 & above	104	20.72	17	3.35	21	6.67	5	1.61
Total	**502**	**100.00**	**507**	**99.99**	**315**	**100.00**	**310**	**100.00**

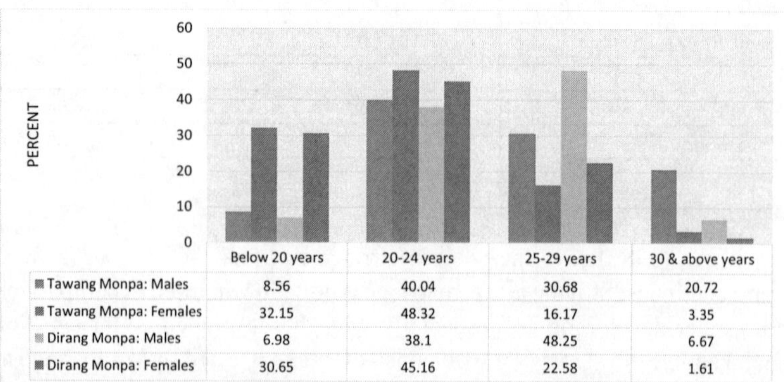

Fig. 7.3: Age at marriage.

Marriage distance

It is seen from Table 7.5 and Figure 7.4 that among the Tawang Monpa more than 23 per cent of the marriages occur in the same area/village in this population. Highest per cent (45.56 per cent) of marriages occur within 1-5 km. However, a good per cent (16.17 per cent) of the marriages took place within 6-10 km. Next are the marriages within 11-15 km. In which 6.51 per cent of the marriages took place. In other distance categories, very low frequency of marriages occurred. Mean marital distance among the Tawang Monpa is 8.22 km. While among the Dirang Monapa more than 28 per cent of the marriages occur in the same area/village among this population. Highest per cent (32.70 per cent) of marriages occur within 1-5 km. However, a good percent (26.99 per cent) of the marriages took place within 6-10 km. In other distance categories, very low frequency of marriages occurred. Mean marital distance among the Dirang Monpa is 5.33 km.

Table 7.5: Marriage distance: Tawang and Dirang Monpa

Distance (in Km)	*Tawang Monpa*		*Dirang Monpa*	
	No.	*Per cent*	*No.*	*Per cent*
0	119	23.47	89	28.25
1-5	231	45.56	103	32.70
6-10	82	16.17	85	26.99
11-15	33	6.51	15	4.76
16-20	9	1.78	10	3.18
21-25	4	0.79	3	0.95
26-30	7	1.38	2	0.63
31-35	3	0.59	0	-
36-40	6	1.18	3	0.95
40+	13	2.57	5	1.59
Total	**507**	**100.00**	**315**	**100.00**

Reproductive performance

In order to find out the completed family size, the Tawang and Dirang Monpa women, who are aged 45 years and above, married once and lived continuously in wedlock till attainment of 45 years of age has been taken into consideration. Completed family size is shown in Table 7.6 for the studied population groups. Completed family size among the Tawang Monpa is 4.16±0.08. It is further seen from Table 7.6 that the mean number of surviving children to those women is 3.84±0.08. Side by side, completed family size among the Dirang Monpa is 4.60±0.06 and the mean number of surviving children to those women is 4.32±0.07.

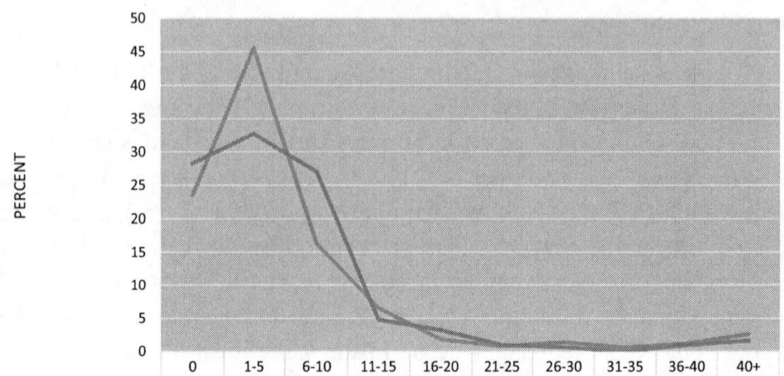

	0	1-5	6-10	11-15	16-20	21-25	26-30	31-35	36-40	40+
Tawang Monpa	23.47	45.56	16.17	6.51	1.78	0.79	1.38	0.59	1.18	2.57
Dirang Monpa	28.25	32.7	26.99	4.76	3.18	0.95	0.63	0	0.95	1.59

Fig. 7.4: Marriage distance (in km).

Table 7.6: Completed family size

Population	*No. of mothers*	*No. of live births*	*No. of surviving children*	*Mean no. of live births per mother (±S.E.)*	*Mean no. of surviving children per mother (±S.E.)*
Tawang Monpa	134	558	514	4.16±0.08	3.84±0.08
Dirang Monpa	78	359	337	4.60±0.06	4.32±0.07

Table 7.7a: Number of live births and surviving children to all married women by age groups: Tawang Monpa

Age groups (in years) of mothers	*No. of married women*	*No. of live births*	*No. of surviving children*	*Mean no. of live births ± S.E.*	*Mean no. of Surviving children ± S.E.*
15-19	6	4	4	0.67±0.21	0.67±0.21
20-24	51	64	62	1.25±0.15	1.22±0.14
25-29	81	175	168	2.36±0.16	2.27±0.15
30-34	54	147	135	2.72±0.08	2.50±0.08
35-39	77	282	260	3.66±0.11	3.38±0.10
40-44	56	212	197	3.78±0.10	3.52±0.10
45-49	78	334	310	4.28±0.11	3.97±0.10
50+	56	224	204	4.00±0.12	3.64±0.12
Total	**459**	**1442**	**1340**	**3.14±0.06**	**2.91±0.06**

Table 7.7b: Number of live births and surviving children to all married women by age groups: Dirang Monpa

Age groups (in years) of mothers	*No. of married women*	*No. of live births*	*No. of surviving children*	*Mean no. of live births ± S.E.*	*Mean no. of Surviving children ± S.E.*
15-19	4	3	3	0.75±0.25	0.75±0.25
20-24	20	35	32	1.75±0.10	1.60±0.11
25-29	35	76	70	2.17±0.08	2.00±0.04
30-34	60	179	174	2.98±0.09	2.90±0.07
35-39	50	188	179	3.76±0.13	3.58±0.12
40-44	47	190	179	4.04±0.13	3.81±0.13
45-49	32	142	134	4.43±0.09	4.19±0.11
50+	46	217	203	4.72±0.08	4.41±0.10
Total	**294**	**1030**	**974**	**3.50±0.07**	**3.31±0.06**

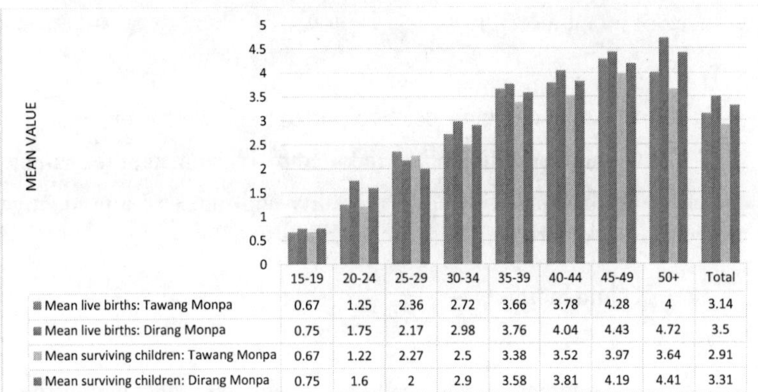

Fig. 7.5: Mean live births and surviving children according to age groups of mothers.

Mean number of live-births and surviving children of all married women by age groups has been furnished in Table 7.7a and 7.7b and Figure 7.5 for Tawang and Dirang Monpa respectively. It is found that the mean number of live births per Tawang Monpa mother is 3.14±0.06. It is also noticed that mean number of live births increases with advancement of age. Mean the number of live births increased from 0.67±0.21 for the mothers in the age group of 15-19 years to 4.00±0.12 for the mothers aged 50 years and above. Mean number of surviving children increases from 0.67±0.21 in the age group of 15-19 years to 3.64±0.12 for the women aged 50 years and above. Like mean number of live births, in case of a mean number of surviving children also the mean number increases with advancement of age.

Mortalities

Mortality plays an important role in determining the age-sex structure of a population. Reduction in mortality in infancy and early childhood results in the prolongation of lifespan, which in turn results in a 'young' age distribution. Different mortalities occurred among the Tawang and /Dirang Monpa are dealt in this section. The measure of infant mortality used in this study was calculated following the method suggested by Khan (1987). To calculate the index of the infant mortality all births, which took place during 12 months prior to the interview, were excluded from the analysis, as they did not have one full year of experience. The index thus obtained is similar to infant mortality rate (IMR) estimated from a cohort but is different from a period (one year) rate. It averages the period IMRs over the entire reproductive period of women included in the sample. Garma (1983) in Mexico has adopted a similar approach with quite useful results.

$$\text{Index of infant mortality} = \frac{\sum Idi}{\sum Bi} \times 1000$$

Where

Idi = Total number of infant deaths reported by ith woman of the sample

Bi = Total number of live births reported by ith woman of the sample

Following this, index of child mortality and index of reproductive wastage were also derived. These are as follows:

$$\text{Index of child mortality} = \frac{\sum Cdi}{\sum Bi} \times 1000$$

Where

Cdi = Total number of child deaths (1-4 years) reported by ith woman of the sample

Bi = Total number of live births reported by ith woman of the sample

$$\text{Index of reproductive wastage} = \frac{\sum Rwi}{\sum Ci} \times 1000$$

Where

Rwi = Total number of reproductive wastage (abortion and stillbirths) reported by ith woman of the sample

Ci = Total number of conception reported by ith woman of the sample

Table 7.8. Record of conception, pregnancy wastage and fertility

Population	*No. of mothers*	*No. of conception*	*No. of reproductive wastage*	*Mean reproductive wastage*	*No. of live births*	*Average live births*
Tawang Monpa	59	469	2	.02	442*	.14
Dirang Monpa	94	043	5	.01	030**	.50

*Inclusive of 5 twin births; **Inclusive of 2 twin births

Average live births among the Tawang and Dirang Monpa are 3.14 and 3.50 per mother respectively (Table 7.8). It can be mentioned that to calculate this value mothers of all ages are considered. However, mean of reproductive wastage is found to be 0.02 among the Tawang Monpa and 0.01 among the Dirang Monpa.

Table 7.9: Infant and child mortality

Population	*No. of live births*	*No. of infants died (0-1 year)*	*No. of child died (1-4 years)*	*Index of infant mortality*	*Index of child mortality*
Tawang Monpa	442	8	4	0.22	0.51
Dirang Monpa	030	5	8	3.98	7.18

Infant and child mortality (Table 7.9) among the Tawang Monpa are 40.22 and 30.51 respectively. Infant and child mortality on the other hand are 33.98 and 27.18 among the Dirang Monpa. Thus, both infant and child mortality are comparatively higher among the Tawang Monpa than their counterpart.

Discussion

The Tawang and Dirang Monpa are the sub-groups of the Monpa tribe. The Tawang Monpa inhabit at high altitude, the hilly terrain of the Tawang district of Arunachal Pradesh. The age structure of both the studied populations suggests neither a trend of progressive type population growth nor a trend of stationary population growth. However, a constriction at the base of the population pyramid of the Tawang Monpa suggests a recent fertility decline or increased infant mortality.

Physiological studies on humans to high altitude suggested a reduction of sperm count and an elevated number of abnormal spermatozoa in males and delayed menarche as well as disturbances of the menstrual cycle in females and reduced birth weight. Early human studies on native high-altitude populations, especially in the Andes, tend to correspond to the above-mentioned observations by showing reduced fertility, higher neonatal and infant mortality, slower physical growth rate and higher hematological values compared to low altitude populations (Gupta *et al.,* 1989).

The mean live births were lower among the Tawang Monpa (3.14) than their counterpart, the Dirang Monpa (3.50). It is interesting to note that mean live births among the Tawang Monpa was lower than the high altitude Sherpa (3.91) residing in Nepal (Table 7.10 and Figure 7.6). The Tawang Monpa show lower fertility than the Sherpas of low altitude too. However, the low altitude Sherpa of Mungpoo shows more or less similar mean live births with present population.

Table 7.10: Fertility measures: comparative data

Population	*Area*	*Altitude (m)*	*Mean no.of live births per women*	*Mean no. of surviving children per women*	*Source*
Sherpa	Upper Khumbu Nepal	3500-4050	3.91±2.09	2.49±1.82	Gupta et. al., 1989
Sherpa	Kalimpong, India	11000-1500	44.74±3.15	33.88±2.59	-do-
Sherpa	Rango, Kalimpong, India	-do-	55.16±3.33	33.90±2.41	-do-
Sherpa	Echhay, Kalimpong, India	-do-	3.67±2.76	3.14±2.34	-do-
Sherpa	Munsong, Kalimpong, India	-do-	4.53±3.15	3.60±2.60	-do-
Sherpa	Lava, Kalimpong, India	-do-	5.16±3.19	4.22±2.60	-do-
Sherpa	Labdah, Darjeeling, India	-do-	4.43±2.98	3.74±2.44	-do-
Sherpa	Mungpoo, Darjeeling, India	-do-	3.17±2.10	2.69±1.88	-do-
Lepcha	Kalimpong, India	-do-	4.12±2.70	3.63±2.51	-do
Tawang Monpa	Tawang, Arunachal Pradesh	3048	3.14±0.06	2.91±0.06	Present study
Dirang Monpa	Dirang, Arunachal Pradesh	1600	3.50±0.07	3.31±0.06	Present study

But the Sherpa of Rangoo and Lava, both in Kalimpong show higher mean live births than that of the Tawang Monpa. Though the mean live births of the Tawang Monpa is lower than high altitude Sherpa, mean surviving children is higher (2.91) than that of the said population (2.49). Like high altitude Sherpa, the low altitude Sherpa of Mungpoo also shows lower mean surviving children (2.69) than that of the Tawang Monpa. The Sherpa of Lava (4.22) show the highest mean of surviving children among all the population groups. Physiological studies on humans to high altitude suggested a reduction of sperm count and an elevated number of abnormal spermatozoa in males. Low live births among the high altitude Monpa is indicative of altitudinal stresses on biological traits in highlander Tawang Monpa.

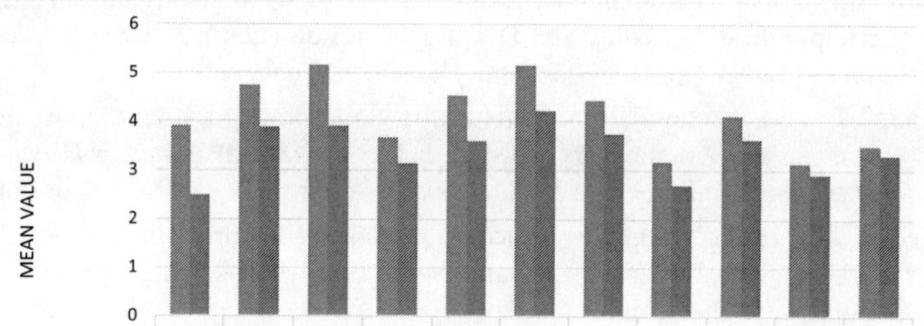

	Sherpa, Upper Khumbu, Nepal	Sherpa, Kalimpong, India	Sherpa, Rango, Kalimpong, India	Sherpa, Echhay, Kalimpong, India	Sherpa, Munsong, Kalimpong, India	Sherpa, Lava, Kalimpong, India	Sherpa, Labdah, Kalimpong, India	Sherpa, Mungpoo, Darjeeling, India	Lepcha, Kalimpong, India	Tawang Monpa, Tawang, Arunachal Pradesh, India	Dirang Monpa, Dirang, Arunachal Pradesh, India
Mean live births	3.91	4.74	5.16	3.67	4.53	5.16	4.43	3.17	4.12	3.14	3.5
Mean surviving children	2.49	3.88	3.9	3.14	3.6	4.22	3.74	2.69	3.63	2.91	3.31

Fig. 7.6: Fertility measures: comparative data.

Acknowledgements

This study was undertaken as a part of ICMR funded project (IRIS ID: 2010-07150). The wiling co-operation of the subject is highly appreciated.

References

Adak, DK. and AK. Gharami, 2001. 'A study on the population composition of the Ladiya of Sagar District, Madhya Pradesh' *South Asian Anthropologist*, 1, 2:83-89.

Basu, A. 1969. 'The Pahira: A population genetical study'. *Am. J. Phys. Anthrop.*, 31: 399-416.

Chachra, SP. and MK. Bhasin, 1998. 'An anthropo-demographic study among the caste and tribal groups of central Himalayas: I. Population Structure'. *J. Hum. Ecol.*, (5):405-416.

Garma, I.O.G.Y. 1983. 'Some factors associated with infant mortality in Mexico'. *Infant and Child Mortality in the Third World.* Inter Centre Cooperative Research Programme. Project No. 1: Final Report. CICRED, WHO/OMS, Paris.

Ghosh, AK. 1976. 'The Kota of the Nilgiri Hills: A demographic study'. *J. Biosoc. Sci.*, 8: 17-26.

Gupta, R., A. Basu, IG. Pawson, P. Bharati, B. Mukhopadhyay, S. Mukhopadhyay, SK. Roy, PP. Majumder, SK. Bhattacharya, KK. Bhattacharya, and SK. Das, 1989. 'Altitude and human biology: A comparative study of Himalayan, Andean and Ethiopian data'. In A. Basu and R. Gupta (Eds.): *Human Biology of Asian Highland Populations in the Global Context*, Calcutta; Indian Anthropological Societies Occasional Papers.

Khan, ME. 1987. 'Infant mortality in Uttar Pradesh'. *Social Change*, 17, 3: 52-64.

Misra, BD. 1982. *An Introduction to Study of Population*. New Delhi; South Asian Publishers Pvt. Ltd.

Narhari, S. 1991. 'Population structure and genetic demography in four Yerukala groups'. In K.N. Reddy and D.V. Raghava Rao (Eds.): *Population Structure among Tribes*. pp. 187-206. Tamil University; Thanjavur.

Rao, VR. 1989. 'Population structure of Naik Gond of Chandrapur district, Maharashtra: A preliminary analysis'. In K.S. Singh (Ed): *Genetical Demography of Indian Population*, pp. 19-30. Kolkata; Anthropological Survey of India.

Reddy, KN. 1991. 'Population structure of Irulas of Nilgiris'. In K.N. Reddy and D.V. Raghava Rao (Eds.): *Population Structure among Tribes*. pp. 1-28. Tamil University; Thanjavur.

Talukdar, S. 1979. 'Genetical demography of two Dule Bagdi demes'. *Man in India*, 59:43-69.

Chapter - 8

Morpho-genetic and Behavioural Traits among the Sherdukpens of Arunachal Pradesh

—Haobijam Vokendro S.

Introduction

Arunachal Pradesh is the largest state in the North East India occupying 13th position in terms of area of the 28 states of India. The state is home to 26 tribes. The major tribes of the state are Adi, Apatani, Galo, Monpa, Nyishi, Nocte, Tagin, Wancho etc. Because of its multi-cultural and multi-lingual ethnic compositions, Arunachal Pradesh is considered as a paradise for anthropological studies. British missionaries and administrators, native scholars, scholars from outside the state and abroad have been studying these various groups of ethnic people. Not only anthropologists, sociologists, historians, political scientists, economists, and educationalists study these people from different perspectives based on varying interests and by adopting various approaches. However, studies on biological and genetic aspects of the tribes are very limited.

The Sherdukpens is a Mongoloid and Buddhist tribe distributed in four neighbouring villages in West Kameng District, Arunachal Pradesh. An attempt is being made in this chapter to describe the distribution of ABO and Rh blood groups, cerumen types, and few morphological and behavioural traits among the Sherdukpen tribe of Arunachal Pradesh by selecting a sample village.

Material and Methods

ABO and Rh (D) blood samples were collected from 116 individuals of the Sherdukpen tribes of both sexes from the Thongre village. The samples were analysed for ABO and Rh (D) blood groups following Race and Sanger

(1962). Allele frequencies were calculated according to Mourant *et al.* (1976). An attempt is also being made to observe the cerumen types- dry and wet. Various morphological and behavioural traits, viz., arm folding, hand clasping, hyper-extensivity of thumb, finger length pattern, dimple cheek, leg folding, toe formula, earlobe, cleft chin, tongue folding and tongue rolling and hypertrichosis were also collected from randomly selected 40 males and 40 females of the village in order to examine the distribution of such traits among the population.

Results and Discussion

The result of ABO blood groups is shown in Table 8.1. It is observed from the table that the tribe shows a distribution trend of A > B > O > AB. The homogeneity test (X^2= .9002, d.f. 3) shows that the population is in genetic equilibrium in respect of the ABO blood group frequency distribution. The occurrence of high frequency of A blood group is also found among the Apatani and earlier work on Sherdukpen (Goswami and Das, 1990), among the Meiteis of Manipur (Singh *et al,* 1986) and the Brahmins of Manipur (Yaiphaba *et al*, 2010).

Table 8.1: ABO blood groups and allele frequencies among Sherdukpens

Phenotypes	*Observed number*	*Per cent*	*Expected number*	*Allele frequencies*
O	20	17.24	19.99	O = 0.4152
A	48	41.38	44.51	A = 0.3306
B	32	27.59	32.01	B = 0.2542
AB	16	13.79	19.49	-
Total	**116**	**100.00**	**116**	

X^2= 0.9002, d.f. 3

Table 8.2: Rh (D) phenotypes and allele frequency among the Sherdukpens

Phenotypes	*Number observed*	*Per cent*	*Allele frequencies*
Rh (D) +ve	114	98.27	D = 0.8687
Rh (D) -ve	2	1.73	d = 0.1313
Total	**116**	**100.00**	**1.0000**

It is observed that Rh (D) +ve phenotypes are 98.27 per cent among the Sherdukpens (Table 8.2). The frequency of allele D and d are found to be 0.8687 and 0.1313 respectively. Very limited works on Rh (D) blood group analysis was done among the tribes of Arunachal Pradesh. Some of the works on Rh (D) blood group analysis were carried out among the Adi of Pasighat (Kar, 1975; Nath *et al.,* 2000); Taraon Mishmis of Lohit (Duarah,1979); Digaru Mishmis (Kotal *et al.*, 2003).

Table 8.3: ABO blood groups and alleles among some tribes of Arunachal Pradesh

Population	*No.*	*Phenotype*				*Allele*			*X^2 with Sherdukpen (d.f. =3)*	*Reference*
		A	B	AB	O	A	B	O		
Sherdukpen	116	41.38	27.59	13.79	17.24	0.3306	0.2542	0.4152	-	Present study
Nocte	332	31.62	16.57	4.22	47.59	0.199	0.110	0.691	*39.492	Goswami and Das, 1990
Wancho	330	35.15	16.67	6.36	41.82	0.234	0.123	0.643	*36.063	
Tangsa	390	21.54	28.97	3.85	45.64	0.136	0.182	0.682	*46.442	
Singpho	267	33.71	25.47	4.12	36.70	0.214	0.163	0.623	*22.156	
Nyishi	242	32.23	25.25	8.61	33.88	0.231	0.186	0.583	*11.652	
Monpa	438	27.85	29.45	8.61	29.00	0.233	0.244	0.524	*9.538	
Apatani	332	41.56	21.98	9.03	27.40	0.299	0.171	0.529	7.565	
Galo	441	31.52	20.86	7.03	40.49	0.215	0.152	0.638	*23.540	
Idu Mishmi	322	26.71	25.60	10.25	45.34	0.203	0.149	0.648	*32.827	
Khampti	293	22.18	25.60	7.51	44.71	0.161	0.181	0.658	*31.736	

*Significant at 5 per cent level.

A comparative observation of the ABO blood group frequency per cent distribution of the tribes of Arunachal Pradesh (Table 8.3) reveals the general trend of O > A > B > AB (except Apatani and the Sherdukpen of the present study) which are found among the Nocte, Wancho, Tangsa, Singpho, Nishi (Nyishi), Galong (Galo), Idu Mishmi, Digaru Mishmi (Goswami and Das, 1990); Digaru Mishmi, (Kotal *et al.,* 2003) and some of the tribes of Manipur like Chothe (Jibonkumar and Vokendro, 2007), Kabui (Singh, 1986), Tangkhul (Kapaiwo, 1995), Chiru (Singh and Shah, 1997), and Koireng (Shah, 2001) and Manipuri Muslims (Shah and Singh, 1986). The higher occurrence of O blood group among the Chothe and Manipuri Muslims may be accounted for their preferential consanguineous types of marriage (Jibonkumar and Vokendro, 2007). The occurrence of comparatively higher O blood group frequency among the above mentioned tribes of Arunachal maybe because of the strict endogamous rules of the marriage of the tribes. The Chi-square value shows that barring Apatani, the Sherdukpens differ statistically significant with all the tribes taken into consideration in respect of this trait.

An attempt has also been made to know the morphological and behavioural traits for both male and female Sherdukpens of Thongre village.

A sample consists of 80 Sherdukpen individuals (40 males and 40 females) selected at random from the aforesaid village.

In arm folding, 18 (45.0 per cent) males have left arm folding and 20 (50.0 per cent) are right arm folder. Only two (5.0 per cent) are reported to have ambiguous folding. In case of females, out of 40, 22 (55.0 per cent) females have left folding and 12 (30.0 per cent) are right arms folded. Only 6 (15.0 per cent) are reported to have ambiguous folding. In hand clasping, 21 (52.5 per cent) males are having left-hand clasping and the remaining 19 (47.5 per cent) are all right-hand clasping; 20 (50.0 per cent) females have left-hand clasping and the remaining 20 (50.0 per cent) are all right hand clasped. Interestingly, out of the 40 males and 40 females so observed, only two (5.0 per cent) are left-handed in each category of genders and the remaining are right handed (95.0 per cent).

For the hyper-extensivity of thumb, equal numbers of the male have left extensivity (50.0 per cent) as well as right extensivity (50.0 per cent) of thumb. In case of females, 28 (70.00 per cent) females have shown the presence of hyper-extensibility of thumb and the remaining 12 (30.0 per cent) females are devoid of the absence of hyper-extensibility of thumb.

Regarding the finger length pattern of males, the numbers of males whose ring finger is longer than the index finger are 25 (62.5 per cent). Only 5 (12.50 per cent) males have longer index finger than the ring finger. The remaining 10 (25.00 per cent) males have equal length of index finger and ring finger. The number of women whose ring finger is longer than the index finger is 22 (55.00 per cent). Only 5 (12.50 per cent) females have a longer index finger. The remaining 13 (32.50 per cent) females have equal length of index finger and ring finger.

Observation of dimple cheek shows that out of 40 males, 18 have dimple cheeks (45.00 per cent) while in case of a female, 20 (50.00 per cent) of females show the trait. In case of leg folding, only 5 (12.5 per cent) males have left leg folding behavioural trait. Only 2 (5.00 per cent) are both types. In case of leg folding of females, 34 females (85.00 per cent) have right leg folding behaviour trait. Only 4 (10.0 per cent) females have left leg folding behavioural trait. Only two females (5.00 per cent) are of both types.

In case of toe formula, 18 males (45.00 per cent) have longer big toe than the second toe. Interestingly equal numbers of males i.e. 11 (27.50 per cent) have equal length of big toe and bigger second toe. In case of females, 18 females (45.00 per cent) have longer big toe than the second toe. Only 13 females (32.50 per cent) have small toe and 9 females (22.50 per cent) have equal length of big toe and second toe.

The presence of hairy ear rims, known as hypertrichosis, which is only found in males are observed in 8 males (20.00 per cent). The higher occurrence of this *holandric* trait may be accounted for a founder effect.

In case of earlobe attachment, 18 males (45.00 per cent) have free earlobe. The remaining 22 (55.00 per cent) have attached earlobes whereas in females 16 (40.0 per cent) have free earlobe. For cerumen type, 33 (82.50 per cent) females and 29 (72.50 per cent) males have dry cerumen type.

For cleft chin, only 5(12.5 per cent) males present the trait out of the 40 males; in case of females, only 3 (7.50 per cent) females have presented the trait and 36 (90.00 per cent) shows the absence of the trait.

Out of 40 males, 12 males (30.00 per cent) can fold their tongues and 21 (52.50 per cent) males can roll their tongue. In case of females, the incidence of tongue folding and tongue rolling ability is exactly equal, the percentage being 50.0 per cent in each trait.

References

Das, PB. and B. Choudhury. 1975. 'Hand clasping, arms folding, earlobe attachment and colour blindness among the Gallong of Arunachal Pradesh'. *Bulletin of the Department of Anthropology.* Gauhati University. 4:65-70.

Duarah, DK., 1979. 'Distribution of ABO, MN, Rh blood groups among the Mishmis (Taraons) of Lohit, Arunachal Pradesh'. *Resarun.* 5(2): 22-28.

Goswami, MC., and PB. Das, 1990. *The People of Arunachal Pradesh: A Physical Survey.* Directorate of Research, Govt. of Arunachal Pradesh, Itanagar.

Kapaiwo, Th. 1995. *ABO and Rh-Blood Group Distribution among the Tangkhuls of Manipur.* Unpublished M.A. Dissertation. Canchipur: Department of Anthropology, Manipur University, Canchipur, Imphal.

Kar, RK., 1975. 'The Rh blood group among the Adi of Pasighat, Arunachal Pradesh'. *Eastern Anthropologists,* 28(2):165-168.

Kotal, Murali, Pinuma Barua, and Sarthak Sengupta, 2003. 'A genetic study among the Digaru Mishmis of Arunachal Pradesh'. *Anthropologist.* 5(3): 193-195.

Mourant, A. Ernest, Ada C. Kopec, and Kazimiera Domaniewska-Sobczak. 1976. *The Distribution of the Human Blood Groups and Other Polymorphisms.* London: Oxford University Press.

Nath, BK., CK. Singh and A. Singh, 2000. 'Distribution of the ABO and Rh blood group in Adi (mixed) tribal populations of Arunachal Pradesh'. *J. Hum. Ecol.* 11:493-494.

Race, RR. and R. Sanger. 1962. *Blood Groups in Man.* Oxford; Blackwell Scientific Publication.

Singh, S. Jibonkumar and H. Vokendro 2007. 'A genetic study on the Purum (Chothe) tribe of Manipur'. *Anthropologist.* 9(2): 161-162.

Singh, LR. 1986. *Physical Variation between the two Sections of Kabuis of Manipur and their Ethnic Position*. Unpublished Ph.D. Thesis. Gauhati: Gauhati University, Assam.

Singh, KS., BN. Mukherjee, H.Walter, P. Lindenberg, K. Gilbert, *et al.* 1986.' Genetic markers among Meiteis and Brahmins of Manipur, India'. *Human Heredity.* 36: 177-187.

Shah, ML, and KS. Singh. 1986. 'ABO blood group frequencies among the Muslims of Manipur'. *Bull. Deptt. Anthrop. Dibrugarh University*, 15: 121-127.

Shah, Latif. 1990. *Bio-anthropology of the Muslims of Manipur*. Unpublished Ph.D. Thesis, Canchipur: Department of Anthropology, Manipur University.

Shah, Md Latif. 2001. 'ABO blood groups among the Koirengs of Manipur'. *Journal of Anthropological Society of Manipur* 3: 47-51.

Yaiphaba S. Meitei, M. Asghar, N. Achoubi Devi, Benrithung Murrey, NK. Saraswathy and MP. Sachdeva, 2010. 'Distribution of ABO and Rh (D) blood groups among four populations in Manipur, North East India. *Anthropological Notebooks.* 16(2): 19-28.

Chapter - 9

Spectrum of Vaishnavite Mask in the Majuli Island of Assam

—*Arifur Zaman*

Introduction

Mask is an integral object of culture complex in a good number of societies in cross-cultural perspective. It is one of the forms of camouflages which conceal one's factual and natural identity and reveal the identity of another being. Masks have a great influence on human society and among some; it is conspicuously related with religious, socio-economic, as well as cultural aspects. The study under consideration was carried out in one of the important Vaishnavite institution, i.e., *satra* (monastery or math) of Majuli, situated at Majuli District of Assam. The concerned *satra* has a praiseworthy tradition of mask making. This pristine skill stands as one of the proud components of the cultural heritage of Assam as well as for the whole of the country. The mask-makers are endowed with dignified appellation like Sangeet Natak Academy Award by Government of India, awarded artist pension by State Government, etc., for their praiseworthy skills. All the mask-makers belong to the Natun Chamaguri Satra which is also known as Majuli Chamaguri Satra. Basic data for the present study was mainly collected from the study of this *satra* and cross-verification was made with other mask-making *satras* of Majuli; those are Alengi Narasimha Satra, Bihimpur Satra, and Chamaguri Satra or Prachin Chamaguri Satra.

Meaning of Mask

The mask is commonly understood to conceal the real identity of a person, but often by wearing a mask, a person unmasked his unexpressed aspirations and desire for a time being. Mask is an integral part of each civilisation. Superstitions and beliefs about masks abound in a good number of communities. The masks also hold deep significance in the socio-cultural study of a community which has a custom of mask making. Mask is an object which exhibits close relation with all three environments– geographical, social, and magicoreligious. Mask has close relations to the norms and values of a society, and in some of the societies, it is the medium through which status and prestige of a person are measured. Through a mask, a society communicates with the supernatural.

Masks are usually used for three purposes. After wearing a mask a person becomes a different creature, the mask hides his identity and reveals him as a different one. When he performs, then he becomes an integral part of a ritual. In such a case mask becomes the medium of a demon or a deity. If a mask changes the wearer's outward features only, then he becomes a part of a drama; a mask then becomes a stylised or symbolic face of a supernatural entity.

The Locale

Majuli is the embodiment of socio-economic and cultural awakens of Assam and is known for the visit of Sankaradeva in the early sixteenth century. Majuli is a riverine island situated in the upper reaches of the river Brahmaputra in upper Assam within the latitude of 26°45' North to 27°12' North and longitude of 93°39' East to 94°35' East, with a mean height of 84.5 meters above maximum sea level. Though due to the relentless erosion the area of Majuli has changed frequently, at present total area of the island is 352 square kilometers. On 26th June 2016, it was declared as 33rd District of Assam, curving out of the northern part of Jorhat district of Assam. Majuli has a population of about 1.6 lakh, the majority being tribal, with tremendous potential for spiritual and eco-tourism. In the sixteenth century, Sankaradeva took shelter in Majuli and spent a couple of years at Dhuvahat Belguri in west Majuli which was a place of historic and auspicious glory. Sankaradeva had established the first *Satra* at Belguri of Majuli. In Majuli, he initiated his principal apostle Madhavadeva. Among the *satras* of Majuli, only four have a glorious tradition of mask making. These are Alengi Narasinha Satra, Bihimpur Satra, Chamaguri Satra and Natun Chamaguri Satra.

The Chamaguri Satra is situated at a distance of around 8 km on the southern direction of Majuli Police Station. This *satra* was established by Chakrapani, the son of Sankaradeva's great-granddaughter Keshavapriya, in the year 1663. Segmentation of the *satra* is a well-known fact. In the year 1923, a section of the bards integral to the Chamaguri Satra bifurcated from the original *satra* and had established the Natun Chamaguri Satra.

Both the *satras*, Chamaguri and Natun Chamaguri, have resourced with the notable skill of mask making.

Objectives

The present discussion confined to the following objectives:

(i) Heritage of mask in Assam;

(ii) Vaishnavism of Assam and the *satra* institution;

(iii) Socio-cultural significance of masks of Majuli;

(iv) The making of the masks and its different types;

(v) The position of the mask-makers in the society.

Methodology

Basic data for the present study has been collected from the Natun Chamaguri Satra of Majuli. Standard anthropological field methods were applied to the collections of the empirical data. Information related with the heritage of mask of Assam in general and Majuli in particular, types of mask, processes of mask making had been gathered from interviewing with stalwart mask-makers of the area as well from other persons who are in under training with their master mask-maker and assist the same person in mask making. The other three mask-making satras were also visited in order to know about the position of the pristine skill there and also for cross verifications. *Satradhikars* (Head of the satra, the Vaishnavite monastery of Assam) from different satras of Majuli, devotees, visitors - both global and local were also interviewed in order to know about the significance of the pristine skill in local, national as well as in the global arena. Data gathered from one mask-maker/*satradhikar* were crossed verified with others who involved in the process of mask making for authentication of the gathered information. Secondary sources were also consulted for background knowledge about the auspicious satra institution in general and heritage of mask in particular.

Masks in Assam

Assam has a rich heritage of mask. Till today masks are used in different folk performing art of Assam. Majuli has a great tradition of mask making. This river island is considered as the land of *satras* and revered as the main Vaishnavite seat of Assam. In the *satras* of Majuli *bhaonas* (Vaishnavite one-act play) are observed to propagate the ideologies of Assam's Vaishnavism where masks are invariably used to depict some of the characters of the scriptures related with Lord Vishnu and his principal incarnation Lord Rama and Lord Krishna. Other than *bhaonas* of Majuli, folk performing arts of different places, as for example, in the *Kusan gan* and *Bhari gan* of undivided Goalpara district of Assam, uses of masks are indispensable. In the *Khulia bhaoria,* another folk performing the art of Darrang district also masks are used. It is pertinent to note that all these three types of performing art are usually based on the stories of the *Ramayana* and the *Mahabharata,* where no written scripts are used; instead, the actors portray a story of the said Hindu scriptures using their spontaneous dialogues. In these art forms only male take part, the female characters are also performed by the male members. In such performances for depicting the characters of demons, deities, serpents, imaginary creatures, etc., the actors generally use to wear a different type of masks. Usually, masks are worn to express ferocity and other feelings which are not possible to express by human beings with bare faces.

In most of the societies, tradition restricts the imagination of a mask-maker, and he is not allowed to make a mask ignoring the pristine code. There are many tales about the harassment by demons and deities of the mask-maker for creating a mask ignoring the traditional strictures. Moreover, such masks create displeasure amongst the fellow members of the society. It should be noted that in almost all the societies, mask-making is a male job. In Assam, although it is not tabooed for the woman, yet all the mask-makers of the state are males only. A mask-maker creates a mask within the traditional framework; the spectators of the society can explain every feature of a mask because they are also acquainted with the norms and values of the society. While wearing a mask, it is believed that the person feels the presence of the demon or deity who lives in the mask, in his body and heart. Some of the masks are greatly revered by the people and only pious and good man is allowed to wear such masks.

Vaishnavism of Assam

Majuli is famous for the great Vaishnavite saint and social reformer Sankaradeva (1449-1568) who visited the island in the early sixteenth century. Sankaradeva propagated a form of Vaishnavism which was simpler and more accessible than the Hinduism indispensably related to many rites and rituals of that time. Sankaradeva stressed in doing the regular duties of people, and along with that, one should pray the only God, Lord Vishnu for the wellbeing of the self and the community. The cult propagated by Sankaradeva was based on the worshipping of Lord Vishnu, along with his principal incarnations- Rama and Krishna. Vishnu is the Supreme Being for the Vaishnavas, his worshippers, and they believe that all things emanate from the deity. Vishnu, the preserver, and the restorer have enormous popularity throughout India, whose appeasement invariably emits splendor and gaiety. The followers of Vaishnavism, who believe only in one God Vishnu, are known as the Vaishnava. Vishnu is the Supreme Being for the Vaishnavas, his worshippers, and they believe all things emanate from the deity.

'The doctrine propounded by Sankaradeva proved to be a great unifying force in Assam and initiated by the concept of oneness among the people irrespective of caste and creed in this part of the land. The caste Hindus, different tribal groups, even the Muslims were brought in the universe of Neo-Vaishnavism and had accelerated the process of integration among the diverse groups of Assam' (Medhi, 2009). In the noteworthy book entitled *The Place of Assam in the History and Civilisation of India,* Chatterjee writes: 'He gave to Assam a new discipline of faith… and helped Assam to break away with a past with its complicated esoteric doctrine and its unmeaning practices and gave to the people something simple and straightforward divested of all questionable associations or implications. He was the greatest builders of Assam bringing in a purer spiritual life, and although circumstances prevented his influence from being spread into another part of India, as a religious leader he is unquestionably one of the greatest India has produced and he deserved to be mentioned with Sankaracharyya, Ramanujacharyya, Basavappa, Ramananda, Kabir, Chaitanya, Mira Bai, Guru Nanak and Tulsidasa. He was truly the medium through whom the spiritual light of medieval India as a whole shown up upon the life of Assam' (cited in Neog, 1988:1).

It should be noted here that Vaishnavism of Assam was moulded in accordance with the social environment of that time, for which the simple and illiterate people of Assam were greatly attracted to that religion. Sarma (1999: 1-2) writes: 'The new cult thus moulded according to the local circumstance was popularly known as the *Mahapurusiya-dharma*. The real name of the cult was *Ekasaranadharma* or the religion of supreme surrender to one God, viz. Visnu-Krasna'. The term Mahapurusiya, generally applied to mean Sankaradeva. He was known to his followers as Mahapurusiya (the great being) and therefore the religion propagated by him came to be known as the *Mahapurusiya-dharma*. To propagate the faith Sankaradeva adopted various means among which mention may be made of two religious institutions: *namghar* (the village level prayer house), and *satra* (the Vaishnavite monastery), which proved to be very effective.

The Satra

'A *satra* is a residential unit where a Guru and some devotees (*bhakat*) occupying different hierarchical positions live. From the structural angle, a *satra* is akin to a *namghar* except for its huge structure. In four sides of the prayer house (*kirtan-ghar, namghar)* of a typical *satra,* the residential houses of the devotees are constructed in straight lines. Such a residential line of the devotees are known as *hati'* (Zaman, 2015:22). The head of a *satra* is known as *satradhikar* (owner of the *satra*, the principal abbot) or *gosain* (god). All the *satras* of Assam are principally headed by persons belonging to two castes - Brahman and Kayastha. In some of the *satras,* the *satradhikars* and the *bhakats* are celibates, while in some others they are allowed to marry. The celibate devotees are known as *kevaliya bhakat.*

Sankaradeva established the first *satra*, the Dhuvahat Belguri, at Majuli to nurture and propagate his philosophy and practice of life. In the heyday of Sankaradeva, there were 65 *satras* in Majuli, each with a good number of devotees or disciples and several thousand followers all over the state. The *satra* is a living tradition of Assam. At present there are around 22 *satras* at Majuli, some of which are still flourishing and others are in a dilapidated condition. It should be mentioned here that four *satras* (*chari satra*) are treated by the Assamese Vaishnava as the epitome of the local Vaishnavism. These *satras* are Auniati, Dakshinpat, Gormur, and Kuruabahi. Among these four, the Kuruabahi is situated at Golaghat district and the remaining three are situated at Majuli, for which the Assamese people in general and the Assamese Vaishnavite in particular, revere Majuli as the supreme sacred place of Vaishnavism.

Socio-cultural Significance of the Mask

In some of the Vaishnavite rituals of Assam in general and Majuli in particular, masks are indispensable. These masks are the part of Bhakti movement without any touch of magical fervour. It should be noted here that *Ankiya bhaona,* i.e., the Vaishnavite one-act play, is integral to Assamese Vaishnavism. In these *bhaonas* different stories of the epics Ramayana, Mahabharata, and early life instances of Lord Krishna are invariably depicted. Principally in the *Ankiya bhaonas* and also in different theatrical performances of the Vaishnavite institution's many mythological characters are integral and to express the features and feelings of such mythological characters masks are worn. It is believed that Sankaradeva had innovated the technique of making a mask from bamboo splits and in *Cihna Yatra* (a dramatic performance with illustrations) performed in 1468 AD by the Vaishnavite saint, had for the first time used a wooden mask of Garuda (the mythological bird; the mount of Lord Vishnu).

In Majuli, the mask is treated as animates. Before performing a Vaishnavite one-act play, masks are taken to the *namghar* or *satra* paying great reverence by lighting earthen lamp (*chaki*), burning incense powder (*dhuna*), and incense sticks (*dhup*), playing the drum (*khol*), and cymbals (*tal*), and singing prayer (*nam*). After the ritual performance masks are kept in the storing place showing the same reverence. The Vaishnavite masks acted as the medium to present the events described in the Vaishnavite scriptures to the people with a great precision, and thus they became instruments of recreation and religious teaching.

The Making of the Mask

The craftsmen of Majuli make masks from bamboo, clay, earthen pot, gourd shell, pith plant, the sheath of areca nut leaf, wood, etc. Though wood and pith plant are also used, nowadays the mask-makers of Assam, particularly of Majuli, make masks with the bamboo spilt from a local variety of bamboo known as *jati banh (Bambusa tulda Roxb)*, covered with cotton cloth, *kumar mati* (a special type of sticky clay), cow-dung of calves and *kuhila* (pith plant). In old days the craftsmen used natural colours for the beautification of a mask. *Hengul* (red colour) and *haital* (the yellow orpiment) are extracted from natural ores, the black colour is prepared from the ashes of the cooking pots or from the smoke of kerosene lamps. Nowadays the craftsmen use colours available in the market. Embellishments like hair, mustache, crown, and required ornaments are finally added to a mask which is prepared from jute fiber, *kuhila* (pith plant).

Types of Mask

There are three types of masks in Majuli: These are *mukh mukha, cho mukha or bar mukha* and *lotokai mukha. Mukh mukha* is worn over the face. *Cho mukha* is very big in size and covers almost the whole body of a person. Sometimes a *cho mukha* is made two to five meter in height above the waist of the wearer. The huge structure of such a mask portrays the aura of the character portrayed. It is worthy to note here that in comparison to the huge structure of such masks, they are very light due to the raw materials used and the intricate manner of mask making. Due to its huge structure, a *cho mukha* is generally tied to the body of the wearer with ropes. *Lotokai mukha* is akin to *cho mukha* except for its small size. Due to its small size, the wearer can easily control it and therefore, *lotokai mukha* is not tied to the body of the wearer. *Lotokai mukha* is also known as *lotokari mukha*. A *cho mukha*, sometimes a *lotokai mukha* also, is a combination of a few easily separable parts.

The Position of the Mask Maker

The Natun Chamaguri Satra is endowed with famous mask making since earlier times. Late *satradhikar* (head of a *satra*, principle abbot) Rudrakanta Dev Goswami was a praiseworthy mask-maker who added new aesthetic dimensions to the tradition of mask making. He was wreath with the artist pension in 1988 by the Government of Assam. All his three sons, Dharmakanta, Hemchandra and Krishnakanta, are stalwart mask-makers. Now Krishnakanta worked as a lecturer of sculpture in the Government Art College of Assam. Dharmakanta's son Khagen Goswami is also a skilled mask-maker and renowned theatrical artist who performs in different *mukha bhaonas* (Vaishnavite one-act play where mask are used extensively) across the state. The mask of the demon king Ravana made by the late *satradhikar* Umakanta Dev Goswami is preserved in the State Museum of Assam. The present *satradhikar*, Koshakanta Dev Goswami and his son Prasanna are also mask-makers of repute. Koshakanta Dev Goswami was adorned with artist pension by the Government of Assam. In the year 2003, he was conferred with the prestigious Sangeet Natak Academy Award by the Government of India.

Hemchandra Goswami trained many groups of youth in and outside the state in the mask making style of Assam. In 1980, Hemchandra had established an institute, viz., Sukumar Kalapeeth, in Chamaguri Village, to train the village youths in the art of mask making. Hem Chandra Goswami plays the pivotal role in the acceleration of the pristine skill from local to the national and universal context. Masks prepared by him are at present installed and displayed at reputed institutions like Dibrugarh University; Tezpur University; Srimanta Sankaradeva Kalakshetra, Guwahati; Vivekananda Institution, Guwahati; Indira Gandhi National Centre for Arts, New Delhi; Indira Gandhi Rashtriya Manav Sangrahalaya, Bhopal, etc., and in the museum of abroad like America, Great Britain, France, Germany, Italy, Israel, etc. He has been conferred with several prestigious awards for his expertise in mask-making, which includes Mezo Da Anand Award: 2012, Damodara Deva National Award: 2014, etc., and felicitated by various organisations and institutions of the country. Recently in the year 2017, in 26th Convocation of Gauhati University, he was conferred upon the *Honoris Causa* for his unstinted and tireless effort to promote and popularised the art of mask making.

Conclusion

The Natun Chamaguri Satra of Majuli, Assam though basically a Vaishnavite religious centre, at contemporary times it becomes a secular nerve centre of culture principally due to the multidimensional activities of the principal mask-maker Hem Chandra Goswami. This *satra* is annually visited by a large number of tourists from different corners of our country and abroad to know about the salient features of the mask made in the satra. Two Israeli tourists recently visit the place and undertook training about mask-making in the aforesaid institution under the able guidance of Hem Chandra Goswami. It is important to note here that following the secular footsteps of great saint Srimanta Sankaradeva, the door of Natun Chamaguri Satra under the guidance of Hem Chandra Goswami is always open for any person who is willing to learn that praiseworthy skill irrespective of caste, creed, and religion. In the Sukumar Kalapeeth also the apprentice is coming from different ethnic and religious identities. In future, if cultural tourism is developed in Majuli, Natun Chamaguri Satra will stand as an archetype of prominent cultural nerve centre to train the interested learner the traditional art of Vaishnavite mask making.

References

Medhi, Birinchi K. 2008. 'Concept of Jagannatha among the Assamese Hindus'. In RN. Dash (Ed.): *Jagannatha in Historical Perspective,* pp. 90-102. Bhopal; Indira Gandhi Rashtriya Manav Sangrahalaya.

Neog, Maheswar. 1998. *The Contribution of Sankaradeva Movement to the Culture and Civilisation of India*. Guwahati; Lawyer's Book Stall.

Sarma, SN. 1999. *The Neo-Vaishnavite Movement and the Satra Institution of Assam.* Guwahati; Lawyer's Book Stall.

Zaman, Arifur. 2015. *The Tradition of Mask in Indian Culture: An Anthropological Study of Majuli, Assam.* Bhopal; Indira Gandhi Rashtriya Manav Sangrahalaya.

Chapter - 10

Traditional Village Institutions of the Karbis of Assam

—R.P. Athparia

Introduction

The Karbis are one of the tribes in North East India. They were earlier known as the Mikirs. Most Karbis reside in Karbi Anglong district of Assam, besides, other areas in the neighbouring districts and states. Along with the Karbis, there are other tribal communities such as Dimasa, Rengma Naga, Kuki, Tai-speaking Man, Khasi, Garo, Bodo and Chakma tribes in the district. With a total area of 10,434 sq. km and a density of 93 persons per sq. km, it is the largest and yet one of the less densely populated districts in Assam. As per the 2011 Census, the total population of Karbi Anglong district is 9,65,280. The Scheduled Tribes communities comprise 56.33 per cent of the total population of which 88.18 per cent population are rural and the rest 11.82 per cent urban. The literacy rate is 73.52 per cent in the district. Sex ratio is 956 per 1000 males. A total number of villages as per 2011 census are 2928. According to the government website of the district, there is a total of 775 revenue villages across four revenue circles, namely, Diphu, Phuloni, Silonijan and Donka in the district (Government of Assam, 2013).

Being predominantly inhabited by tribal communities, traditional village institutions occupy a unique position in the district of Karbi Anglong. The chapter concentrates on the traditional village institution of the Karbis. With the introduction of Sixth Schedule in the district resulting in the constitution of the Autonomous Council in the early 1950s and the devolution of powers and responsibility to village level institutions in the form of Panchayati Raj institutions in other parts of the state and country after the Constitution (Seventy-third Amendment) Act, 1992, an examination of the situation in Karbi Anglong was long overdue. The chapter explores the changes that these traditional institutions have undergone across time and discusses the need to look for new avenues and ideas for them to be relevant and useful for the tribal society in the overall context of developmental activities directed towards them.

Traditional Village Institutions of the Karbis

The traditional institution of village headman is one of the most important institutions in a Karbi village. The headman is known as *Sarthe* or *Rong-a-Sarthe* in Karbi (*rong* = village, *sar* = elder, *the* = senior). An individual is chosen by the villagers as their *Sarthe* for his personal qualities. An individual who is experienced, wise, resourceful, and is just in his conduct is generally selected as the *Sarthe* (Timung, 2003). In normal conditions, the eldest son of the *Sarthe* inherits the *Sarthe*-ship; and in the absence of a son, his brother, cousin, nephew and other relatives from his clan are then considered for the post.

The *Sarthe* organises and administers all the works related to the village through the village council locally known as *Mei*. He initiates all the community-related ceremonies and festivals in the village, such as the *Rongker*, a traditional religious festival held once in a year by every village for the prosperity and well-being of all the villagers. Since indigenous tradition and religion are mostly intertwined in a tribal society, he also performs the religious duties for the village. Moreover, he also assists the community in the time of disaster and personal tragedy. Justice is dispensed by him in cases of disputes and minor crimes. He also acts as a witness to major events in the village like marriages and other social occasions. The villagers in Karbi villages pay house tax known as *Chang Khazana* to the *Bor Gaobura* or *Sarkari Gaonbura*. The *Sarkari Gaonbura* acts as the liaison officer between the village and the district council. The villagers, however, respect the *Sarthe* more than the *Sarkari Gaonbura* and do contribute materially and personally to him in cases of community events or activities. He is the custodian of all the land that belongs to the village. He allocates the land among the villagers for the purpose of building houses and cultivation. The unallocated land remains under his guardianship. He may allocate the unallocated land to villagers from other villages as long as they participate in the village events. Apart from these activities, the *Sarthe* is generally regarded as an expert on the tradition, culture and oral history of the tribe and is approached for his counsel and advice. Besides these traditional roles, his contemporary role also includes as a facilitator between the villagers and the officials from various government departments.

The *Sarthe* is assisted by an assembly comprising of the male heads of all the households of the village. He presides over the meeting of village council or *Mei* and consults with the village functionaries while taking important decisions. Among the noteworthy functionaries of the village, the assembly is the *Pherangke* and the *Risobasa.* The *Pherangke* conveys messages from the *Sarthe* to the rest of the villagers. The *Risobasa* is the head of the youths of the village. He is responsible for gathering the youths whenever they are required for any community purposes.

In the context of the traditional administrative arrangement among the Karbis which is still prevalent in Rongkhang area of Hamren subdivision of Karbi Anglong district, the *Sarthe* is a minor official in comparison to the *Lindokpo* (king), *Pinpos* (king's councilors) and the *Habes* (officials superior to the *Sarthe*). Traditionally, the Karbi chief or Raja knew as *Recho* is the head of the whole Karbi territory. There are three broad Karbi territories in the Karbi land. These are Rongkhang, Chinthong, and Amri. Of the whole, the Karbi *Recho* presides over the Karbi judicial and socio-religious affairs through the *Pinpo Arong.* This village is also known as *Barua Gaon*, located at Hamren subdivision of Karbi Anglong district as mentioned above. However, in an arrangement where powers and duties are clearly delineated, as far as the affairs of the village are concerned, the *Sarthe* is the most powerful and influential person in the village. In areas other than Rongkhang, such as Nilip and Lumbajong, and other Karbi inhabited areas in North East India where traditional kingship (*Lindok*-ship) did not develop, the *Sarthes* function on their own without any interference from anyone. There are altogether nine *Lindoks* in the traditional Karbi territory. Out of these nine *Lindoks*, the Ronghang *Lindok* provides the Karbi *Recho* on hereditary principle. The reason for the inconsistent development of kingship across the Karbi inhabited areas can be attributed to the political turmoil that followed the occupation of Assam by the Burmese army and the establishment of British administration in North East India following the Treaty of Yandaboo in 1826 (personal communication from D. Teron). Karbi society was gradually undergoing a transformation from tribalism and was slowly acquiring feudal characteristics under the influence of other cultures such as the Khasis and the Assamese who were their neighbours. The administrative system of Rongkhang which still survives today has an elaborate system which mirrors feudal system to some extent; however, this process was disrupted and could not develop in other areas due to the reasons discussed earlier.

Traditional Administration of the Karbis

Habai: The ancient Karbi kingdom had twelve administrative units locally known as *Longris* and each *Longris* were governed by the *Longri* headman known as *Habai*. But a king can dismiss him anytime if not loyal to the king and to the *Pinpomar*, found physically unfit, married more than one wife, delays some trials and embraces Christianity. Though the *Habai* is the primary authority in the village, he is assisted by the Regional Council called *Longri- a-Mei*. The council consists of different members; such as- *Habai Kethe* (principal *Habai*), *Habai Riso* (assistant *Habai,* must be a younger age), *Brutemen* (expert in traditional laws), *Mutiar* (organising secretary), *Hemai* (assistant to *Mutiar*), *Basapo* (one who arranges the sittings of the *Longri-a-Mei*), *Pheranke* (messenger) and the *Sarthe* (headmen of the villages under the *Habai*). The *Habai* settles all the local disputes with the help of the council which is sent for the final decision of the *Lindokpo*. Since he is the protector of the traditional laws and social order, he is supposed to be a wise and responsible person. Under its jurisdiction, *Habai* looks after all the matters civil and judicial and can impose fines or punishment. The post of the *Habai* is hereditarily transferred but can be changed if he is dismissed by the *Lingdokpo* or dies without a male issue. In such situation, *Lindokpo* can appoint a suitable male member of the clan the deceased *Habai* belonged to (Sarmah, 2011).

The *Habai* performs functions related to civil and judicial matters. He is the provincial head of the villages. A *Habai* is appointed by the *Lindokpo* and placed as the head of a *Longri*. A *Longri* comprises of several villages, including the village of the *Habai*. Under his jurisdiction, he exercises various powers and functions. One of such important functions is that he can appoint the *Sarthe* or the *Gaonbura* of the village under him. *Habai* also looks after the law and order situation of his *Longri*. Any dispute in his *Longri* referred by the *Sarthe* is decided by him. His decisions are final in such instance but if it fails to provide any decision he can take the help of the *Lindokpo*. Being the head of the *Longri* he can take decisions over the customary laws relating to *Jhum* cultivation and other social practices. It is the responsibility of the *Habai* to look into disputes relating to land and collective cultivation and is also empowered to impose a fine for illegal activity (Sarmah, 2011).

Village Council or *Mei*

The Karbi traditional council is a three-tier one. The *Alongri* council stands at the top. The middle is represented by the *Longri* council and *mei*, and the village council occupies the base. The Karbi state is headed by a chief locally known as *Recho*. In discharging his duties, he depends on three regional centres. Each region is known as *Alongri*. The three *Alongris* are the Ronghang, Chinthong, and Amri. The chief had got a council known a *Rechomei*. The representatives of the *Rechomei* are known as *Lindoks* representing the different clans of the community. The chieftainship and *Lindokship* are hereditary (Sengupta, 2011:377).

The second tier *Longri*, the council is headed by the local chief known as *Habai*. In all, there are twelve such *Longris* in the Karbi society. All the *Habais* are appointed by the chiefs. The jurisdiction of the *Habai* extends over a number of villages of a *Longri*. The administration of each village is run by the village council known as *Mei*. Each council is prescribed over by a headman or *Gaonbura* called *Sarthe*. The *Gaonbura* is chosen for his personal character by the householders. On election, he repairs, with beer and spirits, to the head *Gaonbura* or *Mauzadar*, bringing with him two or three other *Gaonburas* (Lyall, 1972: 22). Beside *Sarthe*, the village level functionaries are the *Bruteman* (acts as an advocate), the *Mutiar* (messenger), the *Feranke* (cashier), *Kurusor* (priest of the village), etc. Nowadays, the District Council appoints the *Sarthe* and the *Sarso* (assistant *Gaonbura*).

In the true sense of the term, the *Sarthe* is the pivotal actor of the whole traditional political system. The democratic vision of the institution can be understood by looking into the powers of the *Sarthe*. It has been observed that a *Sarthe* can never alone make any decision, as it needs prior consent of the members. He can only issue proposals relating to the village affairs in a meeting of the Council for its approval. Under the *Sarthe*, there are some assistants to help him, which are locally known as *Sarso*. The order of command, therefore, is as follows:

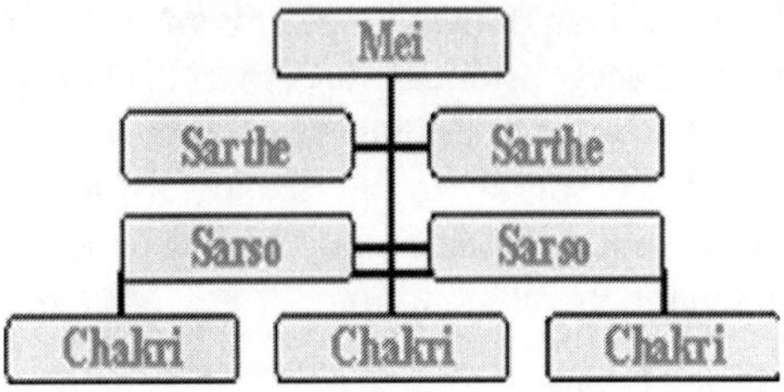

The village councils look into the matters of development of the village as also works as the trial court of the village. Whenever any dispute in relation to ownership of the land, theft, quarrel or adultery, etc., takes place, it is referred to the council which settles it cordially. It can impose a fine on the person found guilty, not exceeding ₹ 50 normally. On the other hand, the unsettled case is sent to the *Habai* or *Lindokpo* or the District Council for final settlement (Sarmah, 2011).

Women can be the members of the traditional council but the patriarchal mindset is still dominant. The people still consider that women are living in the four walls of the house. Therefore, the figure of women members is very minimal in the Karbi community.

Impact of Colonial Rule on the Traditional Village Institutions

With the extension of British administration into the Karbi areas in the early 1830s, the British revenue system was also introduced amongst them. The records show that the British Government collected revenues from Karbi villages as early as the years 1834-35 (Butler, 1855). To facilitate the collection of revenues, various villages were grouped into a *Mauza* in 1835-36 and the post of the *Mauzadar* as the head of the *Mauza* was created. The collection of revenues in kind was subsequently abandoned and a new settlement was effected in 1837-38 (*ibid.*). Although the British Government did not interfere with the traditional institutions of the Karbis and kept them intact, they also introduced new institutions to facilitate revenue collection.

The traditional *Sarthes* were initially not brought within the ambit of any formal laws or regulations by the British administration. It all changed with the introduction of the Chin Hills Regulation, 1896 in Mikir Hills (present Karbi Anglong district) by the government in 1911. Among many things, Chapter 3 of the Regulation formally delineated the powers of the 'headman' and defined his relations with the government officials of the British Empire. The Regulation stated that the headman within the local limits of his jurisdiction in accordance with the local custom will have a general control over the clan or the village or both. There were provisions that allowed him to collect customary dues from the villagers and impose punishments authorised by local customs as long as they were not 'barbarous, excessive or unusual'. He was also allowed to try any person charged with a punishable offense subject to his general control under the Indian Penal Code as specified in the Regulation.

Post-Independence Period

The independence of India in 1947 saw the abolition of the Chin Hills Regulation, 1896. A new framework to administer the tribal areas in the region as now known as North East India was put in place in the form of the Sixth Schedule to the Constitution with the adoption of the Constitution in 1950. The Sixth Schedule provides for the constitution of District Councils that are empowered to make laws with respect to the establishment of village or town committees or councils and their powers; any other matter relating to village and town administration; the appointment of or succession of chiefs and headmen; and social customs; among 10 different subjects enumerated in paragraph 3(1) of the Schedule. Furthermore, with the enactment of the Sixth Schedule to the Constitution (Amendment) Act, 1995 both the District Councils (henceforth known as the Autonomous Councils) of Karbi Anglong and North Cachar Hills (present Dima Hasao) were empowered to make laws on 15 additional subjects.

The Karbi inhabited areas in the form of Mikir Hills Tract of Nowgong and Sibsagar districts and parts of the United Khasi and Jaintia Hills district along with the North Cachar Hills sub-division of Cachar district were constituted as the United Mikir and North Cachar Hills district of Assam in 1951. The North Cachar Hills Autonomous District Council was inaugurated on 19 April 1952 followed by the inauguration of Mikir Hills Autonomous District Council on 23 June 1952 under the provisions of the Sixth Schedule as per Article 244(2). Clause 3 of the Assam United District of Mikir and North Cachar Hills (Administration) Regulation, 1951 provided that the two 'autonomous districts' be united as one 'administrative district' for the administrative purpose (Pakem, 1972:355; Chaube, [1973] 2010: 105). The two autonomous districts were separated into two separate districts in 1970 as Mikir Hills and North Cachar Hills districts. In 1976, Mikir Hills district was subsequently renamed as Karbi Anglong district.

The tribal people of Karbi Anglong and North Cachar Hills District were dissatisfied with the quantum of autonomy available to them under the existing provision of Sixth Schedule and there has been a demand of constituting an autonomous State within the State of Assam comprising the said two districts. A memorandum of understanding was signed on 1st April 1995 between the Government of Assam and some of the representative bodies of the two districts in the presence of the Home Minister, Government of India.

As far as Panchayati Raj institutions are concerned, the autonomous districts under the Sixth Schedule including Karbi Anglong do not have any of these institutions. However, these institutions are endowed with tremendous powers and functions in relation to development-related activities. The Constitution (Seventy-third Amendment) Act, 1992 provides for the inclusion of the Eleventh Schedule into the Constitution. The Eleventh Schedule contains 29 items that are under the domain of the Panchayats. Article 243G lays down the prerequisites for the state government to make laws to empower the Panchayats with powers and authority to function as institutions of self-government and for the further devolution of powers and responsibilities to them.

Traditional Village Institutions and the Autonomous Council

The Sixth Schedule to the Constitution was framed with an understanding that the tribal people of erstwhile Assam, which now comprises the states of North East India, have distinct 'civilisation' and 'culture' compared to the tribal and non-tribal people from other parts of India and so it necessitates a different administrative arrangement for them.

As discussed earlier, the Sixth Schedule envisioned the creation of a separate entity in the form of the District Council which would act as a bridge between the tribal people and the state and the Central Government. Although it is not explicitly mentioned in the Sixth Schedule it is understood that the district council is not only to work for the development of the tribal people but also to support the traditions, cultures, and institutions belonging to them.

The abolition of the Chin Hills Regulation, 1896 led to the withdrawal of the formal recognition of the traditional village institution of headman and the village assembly by the government. Instead, the Autonomous Council is given the power to make law with regards to the establishment of village committee or council and the appointment and the succession of village chief or headman. However, after the constitution of the Autonomous Council in Karbi Anglong in 1952, no legislation has so far been enacted to provide any legal legitimacy to the traditional village institutions. Besides having the post of the *Mauzadar*, the government has also introduced the post of *Sarkari Gaonburah* (SGB) to supervise over a number of villages who function independently of the *Sarthes*.

Panchayati Raj Institutions, the Autonomous Council, and the State Government

In non-Sixth Schedule areas, Panchayati Raj institutions are developed as institutions for local self-government. As discussed previously, these institutions are given enormous powers in relation to development matters. The Eleventh Schedule lists 29 such items which range from agriculture; small-scale industries; roads; rural electrification; poverty alleviation programme; education; including primary and secondary schools; health and sanitation; to the public distribution system. Besides, the provision for the creation of a State Finance Commission by the state government ensures that the Panchayats are financially functional.

In contrast to them, the Autonomous Councils under the Sixth Schedule despite having substantial 'autonomous' powers do not have much say regarding the development activities. For instance, the Sixth Schedule does not confer powers to the autonomous councils with regard to either rural electrification and distribution or poverty alleviation programme or public distribution system. Moreover, the Sixth Schedule does not make provisions for the formation of State Finance Commission to support the Autonomous Councils as is the case with the Panchayats.

However, both these sets of institutions share a commonality which is their dependence on the State Government despite the presence of constitutional provisions. In fact, the allocation of powers enlisted in both the Sixth Schedule and the Eleventh Schedule depends heavily on the political will of the State Government. Kuldeep Mathur (2013) has discussed at length the lack of uniformity in the allocation of the items listed in the Eleventh Schedule to the Panchayats by various State Governments depending on their political objectives. In a similar fashion, a substantial amount of finances meant for the Autonomous Councils are managed by the State Government. This allows the State Government to always exert considerable influence on the 'autonomous' Councils whenever they decide. Baruah (1997) writes that the budget of the Autonomous Council requires being prepared by the State Government in consultation with the Autonomous Council but in practice, it is solely prepared by the Finance Department of the State Government. He further writes that "the District Council has no right even to suggest amendments to its own budget" (p. 144). Both the Panchayati Raj institutions and the Autonomous Councils are, thus, unable to function to their full potential as envisaged by the Constitution.

Conclusion

Presently numerous institutions exist with different objectives and overlapping activities in the districts. The Autonomous Council is yet to constitute village councils or committees. It is also not known whether such councils or committees will be based on the traditional village institution of the *Sarthe* with them being accorded formal status. Nor is there any sign of the introduction of Panchayati Raj institutions in the district by the Autonomous Councils. It also remains to be seen whether Panchayati Raj institutions will be yet another institution in the plethora of institutions in the district or whether the traditional institutions would be modified into Panchayati Raj institutions.

Apart from these primary questions, it also uncertain whether the State Government is ready to grant the fullest level of autonomy as envisaged in the Constitution to the Autonomous Councils and the Panchayati Raj institutions. Moreover, it is also unclear whether the Autonomous Council will be prepared to delegate powers to the traditional institutions. The question also remains as to the status of traditional institutions vis-à-vis the Panchayati Raj institutions if the latter is ever introduced in the district.

The Report of the Expert Committee constituted by the Ministry of Panchayati Raj, India, in their recommendation has urged the Autonomous Council to constitute Village Development Boards along with the traditional Village Councils in the manner of those in Nagaland. The non-implementation of Panchayati Raj institutions nor the formalisation of traditional village committees or councils in Karbi Anglong has meant that developmental work is still carried out by the District Administration and the Autonomous Council despite them being specifically allocated to the village level institutions whether they are known as Panchayats in the rest of the country or as Village Development Boards in Nagaland.

As of now, powers and resources are concentrated with few departments of the government and bureaucrats are the main decision-maker for the various developmental schemes; whereas such decisions should ideally be made by the villagers with their village institutions. The presence of various agencies resulting in overlapping of activities has meant that more bureaucrats and their staff are recruited and maintained. This has created multiple centres of authority and decision-making resulting in the wastage of resources as well as the weakening of democratic traditions at the grassroots level. Most important of all, developmental activities in the district have not produced the results as expected.

The continued relevance of the traditional village institutions such as that of the *Sarthe* will depend upon their utility and effectiveness. Formalising them by introducing legislation by the Autonomous Council would be the first step. However, modernisation of these institutions will also be required to conform to the democratic ethos of the country. Representation of women and minority communities would not only pave the way for the democratisation of these institutions but will also prepare them for the future in a fast-changing world. In addition, the introduction of Panchayati Raj institutions in the district would mean giving the community a greater say in the development of their future and issues close to them. This will also instill in them the feeling of responsibility towards their village and society. The modernisation of these traditional institutions will require that the traditional system is reconciled with modern requirements while modern elements, such as the Village Development Board as in Nagaland, are introduced. The key will essentially lie in the harmonious balance of the old and the new traditions and the wholehearted support of both the Autonomous Council and the State Government to achieve development for the people and the region.

References

Baruah, A. 1997. 'State Government-District Council relationship in Karbi Anglong District'. In LS. Gassah (Ed.), *The Autonomous District Councils*. (pp. 140-148). New Delhi: Omsons Publications.

Butler, J. 1855. *Travels and Adventures in the Province of Assam, During a Residence of Fourteen Years*. London: Smith, Elder, and Co.

Census of India. 2011. Statement 8: Growth of Non-Scheduled Languages-1971, 1981, 1991 and 2001. Retrieved 2013, December 15 from http://www.censusindia.gov.in/Census_Data_2001/Census_Data_Online/Language/Statement8.aspx

Chaube, SK. 2010. *Hill Politics in Northeast India*. New Delhi: Orient Blackswan.

Mathur, K. 2013. *Panchayati Raj: Oxford India Short Introductions*. New Delhi: Oxford University Press.

Pakem, B. 1972. The socio-political system of the Jaintia tribe of Assam: An analysis of continuity and change. In K. Suresh Singh (Ed.) L *Tribal Situation in India:* pp. 352-363. Shimla: Indian Institute of Advanced Studies.

Sarmah, Alaka 2011. The role of traditional institutions in governance-Experience from Karbi Anglong, Assam. *Dialogue*: October-December: 2:2.

The Government of Assam 2013. *Karbi Anglong District Profile*. Retrieved 2013, December 15 from http://karbianglong.nic.in/

The Government of India. 2006. *Planning for the Sixth Schedule Areas (and those areas not covered by Parts IX and IX-A of the Constitution): Report of the Expert Committee*. New Delhi: Ministry of Panchayati Raj.

Timung, L. 2003. *Choti-Choter Lapen Sar Kebat* (Formal Conversations and the Installation of the Headman). Dip hu: Karbi Lammet Amei. (Original in Karbi).

Chapter - 11

Association between Body Mass Index, Blood Pressure, and Age: A Study among Ahoms of North Lakhimpur, Assam

—*M. Gogoi and G Begum*

Introduction

The high prevalence rates of non-communicable diseases (NCDs) in developing countries are gaining much attention. High disease burden in those environs has been consistent with the global projections of the burden of disease from 1990 to 2020 (Murray and Lopez, 1997). Hypertension is believed to be a significant risk factor for adulthood diseases and is getting more prevalent rapidly.

The age-related risk of high blood pressure is a function of lifestyle variables rather than just aging. Different lifestyle behaviours have been shown to be associated with the prevalence of hypertension (Greenlund *et al.*, 2009).Weight gain, the contemporary lifestyle of the people with reduced physical activity, excess in salt, fats and saturated fats, cholesterol and alcohol intakes and low intakes of fresh seasonal fruit and vegetable and increase in the consumption of food are responsible for much of the rise in blood pressure levels seen with age. Hypertension is a major health problem, especially because it has no symptoms. Many people have hypertension without knowing it.

India in a process of rapid economic development and modernisation with changing lifestyle factors has an increasing trend of hypertension especially among urban population (Srikanth *et al.*, 2011). Hypertension is the most prevalent chronic disease, affecting more than 30 per cent of adults aged $\geq$25 years worldwide (WHO, 2013). Hypertension has a multifactorial origin that includes genetic and behavioural factors. Positive association of BMI and blood pressure has also been reported among Asian populations.

Rates of hypertension have been shown to increase in traditional populations undergoing modernisation and also among migrant populations from rural to urban habitats. The traditional rural populations not following the sedentary way of life don't generally show a higher incidence of hypertension.

Body Mass Index (BMI) is positively and independently associated with morbidity and mortality from hypertension, cardiovascular disease, type II diabetes mellitus and other chronic diseases (Pi Sunyer, 1993). The relationship between BMI and BP has been the subject of epidemiological research (Gupta *et al.*, 1995; Kapoor, 2000; Mungriephy *et al.*, 2011). Hypertension is an extremely common comorbid condition in diabetes. Depending on obesity levels and ethnicity, approximately 20–60 per cent of patients with diabetes are affected by hypertension (Folsom *et al.*, 1994).

A strong association has been depicted between BMI and mortality in Caucasians (Hoffmans *et al.*, 1988; Stevens *et al.*, 1998). A similar association has also been demonstrated among Asian populations (Tandon, 2006; Kapoor, 2000; Mungreiphy *et al.*, 2011). Positive associations between obesity and BP, therefore, have been well established in both developed and developing countries (Doll *et al.,* 2002). The significant positive association between BMI and both SBP and DBP has been reported in studies of African-Americans (Croft *et al.*, 1993), Chinese (Folson *et al.,* 1994; He *et al.,* 1994), Africans and Caribbean (Kaufman *et al.,* 1997).

Eva *et al.* (2013) supported a stronger influence of BMI on incident hypertension among Chinese Asians, aged 45-64 years at baseline, over approximately eight years of follow up. Although the BMI associated incidence rate was higher in Chinese Asians, the BMI adjusted prevalence of hypertension was 29.6 per cent in Chinese Asians, 22.5 per cent in American Whites, and substantially higher in American Blacks (44.2 per cent).

Adediran (2008) found that Systolic Blood Pressure and Diastolic Blood Pressure were positively correlated with age while BMI was not or negatively correlated. Thus, BP increases with increasing age, while BMI did not change significantly. A significant correlation between SBP and age was also reported in India (Singh, 1997). Kaur and Talwar (2010) studied the prevalence of hypertension and blood pressure patterns among rural and urban females in Punjab. The mean systolic and diastolic blood pressure was found to increase with age and it was found to be higher among the urban than the rural women.

Very few tribes and caste population of the northeastern region of India have been explored for such studies. Prevalence of hypertension was found to be high (70.0 per cent) among the Deoris of Lakhimpur district (Sarmah and Deuri, 2014). The study has found that the Deori women were unaware of their status of hypertension. The studies in the northeastern states of India reveal a high burden of hypertension in the adult population. Such increase may be related to epidemiological transition involving dietary, lifestyle and behavioural changes added to genetic profile (Hazarika *et al.*, 2000).

The present study, therefore, is an attempt to assess the association between age, nutritional status and blood pressure level of the adult Ahoms of Lakhimpur district, Assam. Ahoms are an Assamese speaking community in Lakhimpur district. Other Assamese speakers are Chutiya, Koch, Mishing and Deori tribe which dominates the district. Assamese and Bengali speaking Muslims also have a sizeable population in the district. Tea tribe community also called Adivasi forms nearly one-tenth of the district's population. Bodo, Tiwa (Lalung) Khamti also forms the fabric of Lakhimpur district.

Material and Methods

The present cross-sectional study was carried out among 411 adults Ahom males and 429 adult Ahom females of North Lakhimpur Assam. Their ages ranged from above 20 years to study the changes from young adults to old adults. The subjects were divided into nine different age groups with five years interval each, to study the trend of change in height, weight, BMI and blood pressure. People using medications for high blood pressure were not included in the study. A correlation between age, nutritional status, and blood pressure at five years age interval is also being studied.

Ahoms are known as the major Tai speaking community in the state of Assam. They are one of the major Mongoloid ethnic groups of Assam. The term "Tai" refers to groups of people and languages spoken over a large area of South East Asia, which are as diverse as the Indo-Aryan languages of India. Under the Indian Constitution, they belong to Other Backward Class. The Ahom population of Assam is mainly concentrated in Upper Assam districts like Golaghat, Sibsagar, Dibrugarh, Dhemaji, Jorhat, Tinsukia and Lakhimpur.

Notwithstanding the formal request to be recognised as a 'Scheduled Tribe', the classification 'Ahom' is no longer used in the modern Indian Census. The official point of view reflects that the Ahom is, for all practical purposes are lowland Hindu Assamese. Such a view has been contested by various Ahom spokesmen.

The Ahoms assimilation with the existing culture of the local people is visible in many aspects. The Ahoms conquered and accepted the culture, religion, and language of the conquered people. The Tai language, the Ahom religion, rituals, dress, food habits and socio-cultural institutions gradually passed into oblivion. The Hindu religion, culture, lifestyle and Assamese language were imbibed replacing the ones of original Tai.

Ahom people worship their ancestors and spirits. There is a section that follows Vaishnavism of Sankardeva and another section who are the follower of *Phura- lung* cult. The ancestors and deities are also worshipped by offering obligation. Traditionally, prior to the assimilation process with the Hindus, the Ahom followed a religious system known as '*Phuralong*'. The system was based on Taoism which consists of the concepts relating to deities and spirits. A very prominent marker among the women folk is the use of vermilion (*sindur*) which signifies the Hindu assimilation. Traditionally, the Ahom women did not use vermilion as the sign of marriage.

Data has been collected from Balijan, Gohaingaon and Charaimoria villages from Kadam circle, Lahongaon, and Bordoloni from North Lakhimpur circle under North Lakhimpur subdivision of the district. Anthropometric measurements like height and weight were taken by using the standardised equipment. Heights of all participants were measured using Martin's anthropometer in standing position without footwear to the nearest 0.1 cm. Body weight was measured with minimum clothes using the weighing machine. BMI was calculated by weight (kg) divided by height (m) squared (kg/m^2). Blood pressure levels i.e. systolic blood pressure (SBP) and diastolic blood pressure (DBP) was measured with the help of Omron Digital Arm Blood Pressure Monitor HEM-7120. The measurement was taken on the right upper arm of the brachial artery in sitting position.

Statistical analyses of the data collected were carried out using SPSS 16.0. Besides descriptive statistics, to test the difference between the age groups, one-way ANOVA was done. Correlation analysis was done to determine the association between BMI, age, systolic and diastolic blood pressure. The value of BMI was calculated and summarised age group-wise, and in order to assess BMI-based nutritional status, recommended cut off for Asians (Barba *et al.*, 2004) were used. The blood pressure was classified based on JNC7 (JNC 7, 2003).

Results and Discussion

The basic data of height, weight, and BMI of Ahom males in nine different age categories are described in Table 11.1. The mean value for height increases among the young adults (20-24.9 years) age group to the next group (25-29.9 years), after that mean height starts decreasing. Mean body weight also increases with age till the age group 30-34.9 years, thereafter the mean body weight decreases but again from 50-54.9 years the body weight has increased. Table 11.1 also shows mean BMI in different age categories. Mean BMI was found to be lowest among 20-24.9 years age category (21.8 kg/m^2) after that it has increased up to 24.2 kg/m^2 (40-44.9 age category) which is the highest. The maximum value for mean BMI was 26.4 kg/m^2, found among 55-59.9 years age group of Ahom males. The mean BMI again has declined in the older age category (60 and above) which is 21.9 $kg/m.^2$

Table 11.1: Age-wise distribution of basic data and BMI among the Ahom males of Lakhimpur district, Assam

Age Groups (in years)	*N*	*Height (cm)*		*Weight (kg)*		*BMI (kg/m^2)*	
		$\bar{X}$±SD	***"t" values***	***$\bar{X}$±SD***	***"t" values***	***$\bar{X}$±SD***	***"t" values***
20-24.9	40	166.7±6.23		58.5±10.3		21.8±3.38	
25-29.9	51	168.5±4.97	1.49	62.8±8.31	2.13	22.1±2.33	0.48
30-34.9	40	167.0±4.36	1.53	65.8±10.3	1.50	23.6±3.61	2.27*
35-39.9	55	166.1±7.02	0.77	64.2±13.5	0.66	23.2±4.38	0.49
40-44.9	45	165.7±6.55	0.29	63.1±9.90	0.47	24.2±9.21	0.67
45-49.9	45	166.1±4.70	0.06	61.8±7.15	0.71	22.4±2.64	1.27
50-54.9	45	166.7±4.16	0.09	63.2±7.30	0.92	22.7±2.29	0.58
55-59.9	45	165.9±4.92	0.84	60.9±7.92	1.43	22.1±2.54	1.18
60 and above	45	164.0±6.87	1.52	59.2±9.80	0.90	21.9±2.78	0.35

* Significant at the level of 0.05.

Table 11.2: Age-wise distribution of basic data and BMI among the Ahom females of Lakhimpur district, Assam

Age Groups (in years)	*N*	*Height (cm)*		*Weight(kg)*		*BMI(kg/m^2)*	
		$\bar{X}$±SD	***"t" values***	***$\bar{X}$±SD***	***"t" values***	***$\bar{X}$±SD***	***"t" values***
20-24.9	53	156.4±5.96		53.9±7.94		22.0±2.81	
25-29.9	45	156.6±5.74	0.17	53.7±7.57	0.13	21.9±3.23	0.26
30-34.9	58	156.2±6.16	0.34	53.8±9.28	0.06	22.0±3.82	0.2
35-39.9	47	155.0±7.34	0.90	57.6±11.0	1.89	23.9±3.81	2.53*
40-44.9	41	156.6±6.73	1.07	60.3±10.81	1.16	23.3±3.66	0.75
45-49.9	45	158.5±7.40	1.4	59.3±11.76	0.42	23.5±4.20	0.24
50-54.9	39	158.1±6.40	0.26	61.5±7.40	1.04	24.6±3.20	1.36
55-59.9	46	157.8±4.28	0.52	65.5±7.54	2.45	26.4±3.39	2.54*
60 and above	55	154.6±6.26	2.60*	54.0±9.54	6.76	22.6±3.51	5.51*

* Significant at the level of 0.05.

Among the Ahom women (Table 11.2) the mean body height is almost similar till the age of 34.9 years. After this, there is a slight fluctuation of increase as well as decrease. In bodyweight, maximum mean body weight could be seen in the age category of 55-59.9 years whereas among the males it is in the 30-34.9 years age categories. The highest mean BMI could also be found in 55-59.9 years. The differences between the ages are statistically insignificant in both the sexes for all the three parameters. BMI among the males decreases with the increase of age whereas among the females it increases till 59.9 years again to get decreased at 60 years and above age category. The mean BMI among the females from 45-49.9 years is higher than the males. The BMI of the males between the age category of 25-29.9 years and 30-34.9 years is significantly different at the probability level of 0.05 whereas among the females it is statistically significant after 55 years.

Das *et al.* (2012) have reported that with the increasing age, the values of height, body weight, and BMI rise significantly but with a subsequent fall, among older rural Bauri women of West Bengal. Das *et al.* (2010) studied the Bishnupriya Manipuri of Cachar and reported that there are also significant age changes in some anthropometric characteristic and body composition characteristics.

As long as men and women are not overweight, BMI values of men are also slightly higher than for women (after age 18 years). In addition, for middle-aged adults, overweight women tend to have higher Body Mass Index values than overweight men. Because BMI uses a person's total body weight and doesn't distinguish lean mass from fatty tissues. Two people with the same BMI can have very different body composition. Women typically have a higher percentage of body fat than men and men tend to have a higher proportion of muscle mass. With the advancement of age, the prevalence of inactivity has also been found to have increased. Sedentary behaviour is a potential threat to the accumulation of the unhealthy amount of adipose tissue without significant weight gain. Females have higher percentages of body fat compared to males of all ages and ethnic groups (Flegat *et al.*, 2009) and for an equivalent BMI, women have the significantly greater amount of total body fat than men throughout the entire lifespan (Romero-Corral *et al.*, 2008).

As body fat or BMI increases, health risks increases. Being overweight or being obese increases the risk of having high blood pressure, heart disease, stroke, diabetes, certain types of cancer, arthritis and breathing problems. In the present study, the prevalence of malnutrition among the Ahom females was evaluated with the help of recently proposed classification BMI classification for Asia–specific population and is presented in Table 11.3. The overall prevalence of undernutrition or CED (BMI≥18.50 kg/m^2) and normal nutritional (BMI 18.50-22.9 kg/m^2) status was found to be 7.54 per cent and 51.82 per cent respectively among the males. The overall prevalence of overweight (BMI≥23.00 kg/m^2) was found to be 22.14 per cent. The prevalence of obesity (BMI- obese I and II) was found to be 16.79 per cent and 1.70 per cent among the Ahoms males.

Table 11.3: Distribution of Grades of Nutritional status as per BMI among the adult Ahom males

Age groups (in years)	*N*	*Underweight <18.5*	*Normal 18.5-22.9*	*Overweight 23.0-24.9*	*Obese -I 25-29.9*	*Obese-II 30*
20-24.9	40	5(12.50%)	21(52.5%)	5(12.50%)	9(22.50%)	-
25-29.9	51	2(3.92%)	33(64.71%)	12(21.53%)	4 (7.84%)	-
30-34.9	40	4(10.00%)	11(27.50%)	13(32.50%)	10(25.00%)	2(5.00%)
35-39.9	55	7(12.73%)	18(32.73%)	13(23.64%)	13(23.64%)	4(7.27%)
40-44.9	45	3(6.67%)	22(48.89%)	6(13.33%)	14(31.11%)	-
45-49.9	45	2(4.44%)	29(64.44%)	7(15.56%)	6(13.33%)	1(2.22%)
50-54.9	45	1(2.22%)	24(53.33%)	13(28.89%)	7(15.56%)	-
55-59.9	45	3(6.67%)	30(66.67%)	7(15.56%)	5(11.11%)	-
60 and above	45	4(8.89%)	25(55.56%)	11(24.44%)	5(11.11%)	-
Total	**411**	**31(7.54%)**	**213(51.82%)**	**91(22.14%)**	**69(16.79%)**	**7(1.70%)**

Table 11.4: Distribution of Grades of Nutritional status as per BMI among the adult Ahom females

Age groups (in years)	*N*	*Underweight <18.5*	*Normal 18.5-22.9*	*Overweight 23.0-24.9*	*Obese -I 25-29.9*	*Obese-II 30*
20-24.9	53	5 (9.43%)	32 (60.38%)	12 (22.64%)	3(5.67%)	1(1.89%)
25-29.9	45	3(6.67%)	31(68.89%)	7 (15.56%)	3(6.67%)	1(2.22%)
30-34.9	58	6(10.34%)	34(58.62%)	8 (13.79%)	7(12.07%)	3(5.17%)
35-39.9	47	4(8.51%)	16(34.04%)	9(19.15%)	14(29.79%)	4(8.51%)
40-44.9	41	2(4.88%)	17(41.46%)	13(31.70%)	8(19.51%)	1(2.44%)
45-49.9	45	5(11.11%)	17(37.78%)	7(15.56%)	12(26.67%)	4(8.89%)
50-54.9	39	2(5.13%)	9(23.08%)	9(23.08%)	17(43.59%)	2(5.13%)
55-59.9	46	-	8(17.39%)	6(13.04%)	25(54.35%)	7(15.22%)
60 and above	55	5(9.09%)	27(49.09%)	8(14.55%)	14(25.45%)	1(1.81%)
Total	**429**	**32(7.46%)**	**191(44.52%)**	**79(18.41%)**	**103(24.01%)**	**24(5.59%)**

The females have a higher prevalence of obesity than their male counterparts (Table 11.4). It is 24.01 per cent as obese-I and 5.59 per cent as obese-II. Declines in physical function are reported in older adults who have gained or lost weight experienced changes in body composition that favour increases in fat mass and decline in muscle mass, have a low or high BMI (Academy of Nutrition and Dietetics, 2012). In the present study also the prevalence of obesity among women is found to be increasing with increasing age. At 55-59.9 years it is 15.22 per cent of obese- II grade. Males have a higher percentage of normal BMI (51.82 per cent) whereas the females have 44.52 per cent of normal BMI. Prevalence of obesity is more among females than males in the upper age categories. The total percentage of occurrence of overweight and obese among the females is 48.01 per cent. Almost half of the adult female population is overweight. Whereas, among the males it is 40.63 per cent. Overweight and obesity is the fifth leading risk of deaths, resulting in around 2.8 million deaths of adults globally every year. The most obvious factors leading to overweight or obesity are an excessive intake of energy-dense food, sedentary lifestyle and lack of physical activity (Sinha and Kapoor, 2010). The fraction of overweight and obesity has been found to be increasing with age, education, and parity of the women (Agrawal and Mishra, 2004; Kain *et al*., 2003). Women with higher parity were found to be overweight or obese in India. This generally implies that women's higher age with declining physical activity helps accumulate more weight. Agrawal and Mishra (2004) have concluded that women media exposure is about two times more at risk of being overweight or obese. Media gives exposure to a good number of energy saving machinery, energy–dense or junk food items, which tend to influence women to adopt. Viewing television for a longer duration can also increase the physical inactiveness and helps in weight gain. This is more common among the non-poor urban India. In the present study, the percentage of overweight is increasing with the increase of age. After 50 years the percentage of occurrence of overweight is very high. The women of the present study are from a rural setting. The women work equally with the men in the agricultural field. But after 50 years of age, their activity level starts getting reduced and they become more confined to the household works. Maybe that is the reason of getting more percentage of overweight among this particular population.

The gender disparity in overweight and obese are exacerbated among women in developing countries as per Kanter and Caballero (2012). Different contextual factors drive gender differences in food consumption and women often report consuming healthier foods, yet may consume more sugar-laden foods than men. Several developing countries are currently undergoing rapid socioeconomic, demographic transition, which leads to the acceleration of several preventable, non-communicable diseases and higher prevalence of overweight-obesity and slightly lower prevalence of under-nutrition in population (Wang *et al.*, 2009; Popkin *et al.*, 2012; Subramanium *et al.*, 2006; Varadharajan *et al.*, 2013; Mondal and Sen, 2014).

Table 11.5: Blood Pressure among the Adult Ahom males of Lakhimpur district, Assam

Age Groups (in years)	*N*	*Blood Pressure (mm/Hg)*							
		Systolic				*Diastolic*			
		$\bar{X}$	± SD	± SE	"t"-values	$\bar{X}$	± SD	± SE	"t" values
20-24.9	40	128.25	7.22	1.14		79.23	6.48	1.03	
25-29.9	51	131.78	9.29	1.30	2.04*	83.7	9.80	1.37	2.50*
30-34.9	40	134.23	18.46	2.92	0.77	85.9	12.77	2.02	0.99
35-39.9	55	134.16	14.83	2.00	0.02	88.53	13.66	1.37	1.01
40-44.9	45	134.4	17.24	2.57	0.07	83.96	10.15	1.51	1.79*
45-49.9	45	135.62	12.55	1.87	0.38	84.6	11.87	1.77	0.27
50-54.9	45	143.06	12.04	1.79	2.38*	91.20	10.67	1.59	2.68*
55-59.9	45	142.87	16.34	2.44	0.06	87.96	12.35	1.84	0.26
60 and above	45	147.8	21.03	3.13	1.26	88.6	15.36	2.29	0.23
Total	**411**	**130.63**	**12.98**	**0.64**		**83.2 1**	**1.51**	**1.67**	

* Significant at the level of 0.05.

In Table 11.5 blood pressures among the adult Ahom males and females are presented in the different age categories. There is an increase in the systolic and diastolic pressure in both the sexes as the age increases. The highest mean values for blood pressure both SBP and DBP were in 60 and above age group. In general blood pressure rises as people get older. Age was positively correlated with BMI and both Systolic and Diastolic BP. Systolic and Diastolic blood pressures increased with age steadily from the youngest to the oldest age group showing the dependence of blood pressure on age. Earlier studies also indicated that high BP is associated with age (Schall *et al.*, 1995; Dressler *et al.,* 1994; Suman *et al.*, 1998). The present study shows a stronger association of age with both SBP and DBP. Age is a known factor for high blood pressure (Gardener *et al.,* 1995; Mungreiphy *et al.*, 2011). The studies of Hazarika *et al.* (2004) states that elevated mean SBP (>146 mmHg) in elderly (> 60 yrs of age) men and women of the native rural population of Assam are a public concern. Uncontrolled hypertension in the elderly group leads to target organ damage, especially stroke. Mungreiphy *et al.* (2011) in her findings also depict similar kind of association. Similar results have also been found by Dua *et al.* (2014) where age has been found to be positively correlated with blood pressure (both SBP and DBP).

Table 11.6: Blood Pressure among the Adult Ahom females of Lakhimpur district, Assam

Age Groups (in years)	*N*	*Blood Pressure (mm/Hg)*							
		Systolic				*Diastolic*			
		X L	*± SD*	*± SE*	*"t"-values*	*X L*	*± SD*	*± SE*	*"t" values*
20-24.9	53	123.4	12.4	1.70		75.9	11.4	1.57	
25-29.9	45	123.3	11.9	1.77	0.04	78.4	9.85	1.47	1.16
30-34.9	58	123.8	9.93	1.30	0.23	80.7	9.70	1.27	1.19
35-39.9	47	129.3	15.84	2.31	2.08*	81.4	10.69	1.56	0.49
40-44.9	41	129.2	12.47	1.95	0.03	82.4	13.02	2.03	0.39
45-49.9	45	134.7	12.55	1.87	2.04*	86.3	10.25	1.53	1.54
50-54.9	39	130.4	9.58	1.54	1.78*	84.3	9.32	1.49	0.93
55-59.9	46	135.6	12.67	1.87	2.15*	89.4	13.08	1.93	2.09*
60 and above	55	146.0	19.50	2.63	3.22*	90.0	16.24	2.19	0.21
Total	**429**	**130.63**	**12.98**	**1.88**		**83.2**	**11.51**	**1.67**	

* Significant at the level of 0.05.

The relationship was found to be stronger and significant in women than in men. A similar result has been observed in the present study also. In Table 11.9 the percentage distribution of BMI, systolic and diastolic BP has been given. It could be seen that only 18.49 per cent of men have a normal systolic BP and it is 30.77 per cent of women who have a normal systolic BP. Most of the adult populations are in the pre-hypertensive category (43.80 per cent males and 44.29 per cent of females). In diastolic BP 29.93 per cent of males and 34.49 per cent of females are in the pre-hypertensive category. Blood pressure rises as people get older. Age is known as the risk factor for high blood pressure (Gardner and Poehlman, 1995).Gender differences in blood pressure are detectable during adolescence and persist into adulthood. In all ethnic groups, men tend to have higher mean SBP and DBP than women through middle age; the prevalence of hypertension is higher among men than women (Stamler *et al.*, 1976).

In Tables 11.7 and 11.8 the distribution of systolic and diastolic blood pressure according to the grades of nutritional status as detected by BMI has been presented for the males and females. As the age increases the percentage occurrence of hypertension has increased not only among the obese (100 per cent in 55-59.9 years) but also among the undernourished (100 per cent in 50-54.9 years category) among the males. It is not the level of nutrition but age which is more correlated to BP because as the age advances even in the undernourished category none among the males are in the normotensive category. Same is the case among the females also.

Undernourished females fall in the pre-hypertensive category (100 per cent in 40-44.9 years and 50-54.9 age category).

Table 11.7: Distribution of Systolic and Diastolic Blood Pressure classification in grades of Nutritional status of Ahom Male

Age Group (in years)	*Nutritional Status*	*n*	*Normo-tensive >90-120, >60-<80*	*Pre-hypertensive 120-139, 80-89*	*Hypertensive >140/90*
20-24.9	Undernourished	5	3 (60.00%)	2 (40.00%)	-
	Normal	21	10 (47.62%)	10 (47.62%)	1 (4.76%)
	Overweight	5	1 (20.00%)	4 (80.00%)	-
	Obese	9	1 (11.11%)	7 (77.78%)	1 (11.11%)
25-29.9	Undernourished	2	-	2 (100%)	-
	Normal	33	6 (18.18%)	23 (69.70%)	4 (12.12%)
	Overweight	12	3 (25.00%)	5 (41.67%)	4 (33.33%)
	Obese	4	-	2 (50.00%)	2 (50.00%)
30-34.9	Undernourished	4	2 (50.00%)	1 (25.00%)	1(25.00%)
	Normal	11	5 (45.45%)	1 (9.09%)	5 (45.45%)
	Overweight	13	3 (23.08%)	4 (30.77%)	6 (46.15%)
	Obese	12	1 (8.33%)	6 (50.00%)	5 (41.67%)
35-39.9	Undernourished	7	2 (28.57%)	3 (42.86%)	2 (28.57%)
	Normal	18	4 (22.22%)	11 (61.11%)	3 (16.67%)
	Overweight	13	2 (15.30%)	8 (61.54%)	3 (23.08%)
	Obese	17	-	12 (70.59%)	5 (29.41%)
40-44.9	Undernourished	3	-	2 (66.67%)	1 (33.33%)
	Normal	22	6 (27.27%)	9 (40.91%)	7 (31.82%)
	Overweight	6	2 (38.33%)	3 (50.00%)	1 (16.67%)
	Obese	14	3 (21.43%)	8 (57.14%)	3 (21.43%)
45-49.9	Undernourished	2	-	1 (50.00%)	1 (50.00%)
	Normal	29	4 (13.79%)	14 (48.28%)	11 (37.93%)
	Overweight	7	1 (14.29%)	4 (57.14%)	2 (28.57%)
	Obese	7	-	3 (42.86%)	4 (57.14%)
50-54.9	Undernourished	1	-	-	1 (100%)
	Normal	24	1 (4.17%)	11 (45.84%)	12 (50.00%)
	Overweight	13	1 (7.69%)	5 (38.46%)	7 (53.85%)
	Obese	7	1 (14.29%)	1 (14.29%)	5 (71.43%)
55-59.9	Undernourished	3	-	1 (33.33%)	2 (66.67%)
	Normal	30	5 (16.67%)	7 (23.33%)	18 (60.00%)
	Overweight	7	1 (14.29%)	2 (28.57%)	4 (57.14%)
	Obese	5	-	-	5 (100%)
60 and above	Undernourished	4	2 (50.00%)	1 (25.00%)	1 (25.00%)
	Normal	25	4 (16.00%)	5 (20.00%)	16 (64.00%)
	Overweight	11	2 (18.18%)	-	9 (81.82%)
	Obese	6	-	3 (50.00%)	3 (50.00%)

Table 11.8: Distribution of Systolic and Diastolic Blood Pressure classification in grades of Nutritional status of Ahom Female

Age Groups (in years)	*Nutritional Status*	*n*	*Normotensive >90-120, >60-<80*	*Pre-hypertensive 120-139, 80-89*	*Hypertensive >140/90*
20-24.9	Undernourished	5	3 (60.00%)	2 (40.00%)	-
	Normal	32	23 (71.88%)	5 (15.63%)	4 (12.50%)
	Overweight	12	6 (50.00%)	5 (41.67%)	1 (8.33%)
	Obese	4	4 (100%)	-	-
25-29.9	Undernourished	3	3 (100%)	-	-
	Normal	31	13 (41.94%)	16 (51.61%)	-
	Overweight	7	3 (42.86%)	2 (28.57%)	2 (28.57%)
	Obese	4	1 (25.00%)	3 (75.00%)	-
30-34.9	Undernourished	6	5 (83.33%)	1(16.67%)	-
	Normal	34	23 (67.65%)	9 (26.47%)	2 (5.88%)
	Overweight	8	6 (75.00%)	2 (25.00%)	-
	Obese	10	3 (30.00%)	4 (40.00%)	3 (30.00%)
35-39.9	Undernourished	4	1 (25%)	3 (75.00%)	-
	Normal	16	2 (12.50%)	11 (68.75%)	3 (18.75%)
	Overweight	9	4 (44.44%)	4 (44.44%)	1(11.11%)
	Obese	18	7 (38.89%)	8 (44.44%)	3 (16.67%)
40-44.9	Undernourished	2	-	2 (100%)	-
	Normal	17	6 (35.29%)	8 ((47.06%)	3 (17.65%)
	Overweight	13	2 (15.38%)	9 (69.23%)	2 (15.38%)
	Obese	9	4 (44.44%)	4 (44.44%)	1 (11.11%)
45-49.9	Undernourished	5	3 (60.00%)	-	2 (40.00%)
	Normal	17	6 (35.29%)	6 (35.29%)	4 (23.53%)
	Overweight	7	-	3 (42.86%)	4 (57.14%)
	Obese	16	4 (24.00%)	7 (43.75%)	5 (31.25%)
50-54.9	Undernourished	2	-	2 (100%)	-
	Normal	9	2 (22.22%)	5 (55.56%)	2 (22.22%)
	Overweight	9	1 (11.11%)	6 (66.67%)	2 (22.22%)
	Obese	19	4 (21.05%)	9 (47.37%)	6 (31.58%)
55-59.9	Undernourished	-	-	-	-
	Normal	8	1 (12.50%)	6 (75.00%)	1 (12.50%)
	Overweight	6	1 (16.67%)	2 (33.33%)	3 (50.00%)
	Obese	32	6 (18.75%)	13 (40.63%)	13 (40.63%)
60 and above	Undernourished	5	-	1(20.00%)	4 (80.00%)
	Normal	27	8 (29.63%)	7 (25.93%)	12 (44.44%)
	Overweight	8	1 (12.50%)	5 (62.50%)	2 (25.00%)
	Obese	15	7 (46.67%)	3 (20.00%)	5 (33.33%)

Table 11.9: Distribution of Ahoms as per BMI and Blood Pressure

BMI and BP classification	*Distribution of subjects in different categories*	
	Males	***Females***
BMI		
Underweight	31 (7.54%)	32 (7.46%)
Normal	213 (51.82%)	191 (44.52%)
Overweight	91 (22.14%)	79 (18.41%)
Pre-obese	69 (16.79%)	103 (24.01%)
Obese	7 (1.70%)	24 (5.59%)
Total	**411 (100%)**	**429 (100%)**
Systolic BP		
Normal	76 (18.49%)	132 (30.77%)
Pre hypertension	180 (43.80%)	190 (44.29%)
Hypertension stage I	111 (27.01%)	81 (18.88%)
Hypertension stage II	44 (10.71%)	26 (6.06%)
Total	**411**	**429 (100%)**
Diastolic BP		
Normal	147 (35.77%)	184 (42.89%)
Pre hypertension	123 (29.93%)	148 (34.49%)
Hypertension stage I	91 (22.14%)	56 (13.05%)
Hypertension stage II	50(12.17%)	41 (9.56%)
Total	**411**	**429**

After 50 years of age, more than 50 per cent men with normal nutritional status are hypertensive. In the age category of 50-54.9 years it is 50 per cent; from 55-59.9 years its 60 per cent and among 60 years and above 64 per cent men are hypertensive even though having a normal nutritional status. But in the case of the females, the occurrence of hypertension among the nutritionally normal category is slightly lesser than men. So men are more affected by their BP status than women and ages are more correlated with BP than their nutritional status. Among the women who are undernourished, 75 per cent in the age category of 35-39.9 years are hypertensive. Similarly, 80 per cent of undernourished women in 60 years and above category are hypertensive. It is more related to the age of the people. Mungreiphy *et al.* (2011) studied the Tangkhul Naga males where the findings also showed that there were maximum numbers of subjects under systolic pre-hypertension than normal. Under diastolic blood pressure, there were maximum numbers of normal than pre-hypertension.

A positive relationship between BMI and blood pressure has also been reported in the study of Srikanth *et al.* (2011) and Dua *et al.* (2014). An increase in BMI and a decrease in BMI were significantly associated with increased and decreased SBP and DBP, respectively, compared to a stable BMI in both genders and all age groups, although the strongest effect was found among those who were 50 years and older. The mean change in both SBP and DBP was higher for those who changed BMI category from first to the second survey than for those who were in the same BMI class at both surveys (Drøyvold, 2005).

Table 11.10: Pearson's Correlation matrix between BMI, Blood pressure and age among the males

Variable	*SBP*	*DBP*	*BMI*	*AGE*
SBP	1	0.644*	0.044	0.414*
DBP	0.644*	1	0.154*	0.345*
BMI	0.044	0.154*	1	0.159*
AGE	0.414*	0.345*	0.159*	1

* Correlation is significant at the 0.01 level.

Table 11.11: Pearson's Correlation matrix between BMI, Blood pressure and age among the females

Variable	*SBP*	*DBP*	*BMI*	*AGE*
SBP	1	0.634*	0.120	0.350*
DBP	0.634*	1	0.172*	0.208*
BMI	0.120	0.172*	1	0.027
AGE	0.35*	0.208*	0.027	1

* Correlation is significant at the 0.01 level.

In Tables 11.10 and 11.11, the correlation of age, nutritional status and blood pressure among the men and women could be studied. The correlation of age with SBP (0.414), DBP (0.345) and BMI (0.159) has been found to be significant at the level of 0.01 among the males. Same is the case among the females also when it is significant with SBP (0.35), DBP (0.208) at 0.01 level. BMI is significantly correlated with DBP among the males (0.154) and also among the females (0.172) at the 0.01 level. So blood pressure is more correlated with age and also influenced by BMI.

A significant positive association between BMI and both SBP and DBP has been reported in studies of, African-American (Croft *et al.,* 1993), Chinese (Folsom *et al.*, 1994; He *et al.*, 1994), Africans and Caribbean's (Kaufman *et al.*, 1997). But Adediran and Jimoh (2008) have found SBP and DBP were positively correlated with age while BMI was not or negatively correlated. Thus, BP increases with increasing age, while BMI did not change significantly. A significant correlation between SBP and age was also reported by Singh *et al.,* (1997).

Conclusion

With the increasing age in both the sexes, the values of height, body weight and BMI rises but with a subsequent fall. The mean BMI among the females from 45-49.9 years is higher than the males. The females have a higher prevalence of obesity than their male counterparts. Males have a higher percentage of normal BMI (51.82 per cent) whereas the females have 44.52 per cent of normal BMI. The females have a higher prevalence of obesity (24.01 per cent as obese-I and 5.59 per cent as obese-II). Among the females, the occurrence of hypertension among the nutritionally normal category is slightly lesser than men. Men are more affected by their BP status than women and age is more correlated with BP than their nutritional status. After 50 years of age, more than 50 per cent men with normal nutritional status are hypertensive.

References

Academy of Nutrition and Dietetics. 2012. 'Food and nutrition for older adults promoting health and wellness recommendations', *Evidence Analysis Library*. website. http://www.and evidence library.com/topic.cfm?cat4879.Accessed Oct 2, 2017.

Adediran, O, A Jimoh, and M Di. 2008. 'Relationship between BMI and blood pressure in rural Nigerian Dwellers'. *The Internet Journal of Nutrition and Wellness*, 7 (1): 1-5.

Agrawal, P, and V. Mishra. 2004. *Covariates of Overweight and Obesity among Women in North India.* Honolulu: East-West Center; pp. 25 (East-West Center Working Papers No. 116, Population and Health Series).

Barba, C, T. Cavalli-Sforza, and J. Cutter *et al*. 2004. 'Appropriate body-mass index for Asian populations and its implications for policy and intervention strategies', *Lancet,* 363 (9403): 157–163.

Croft, JB, DS Strogatz, NL Keenan, SA James, AM Malarcher, and JM Garrett. 1993. 'The independent effects of obesity and body fat distribution on blood pressure in black adults: The Pitt County study'. *Int J Obes Relat Metab Disord*, 17: 391-397.

Das, BM and Subrata K Roy, 2010. 'Age changes in the anthropometric and body composition characteristics of the Bishnupriya Manipuris of Cachar district, Assam', *Advances in Bioscience and Biotechnology*, 1: 122-130.

Das, S, Tamali Chowdhury, and Kaushik Bose. 2012. *Age variations in anthropometric and body composition characteristics among adult Bauri females of Paschim Medinipur, West Bengal, India',* Scholarly J. Sci. Res. and Essay Writing, 1(2): 16-24.

Doll, S, F Paccaud, P Bovet, M Burnier, and V Wietlisbach. 2002. 'Body mass index, abdominal adiposity, and blood pressure: Consistency of their association across developing and developed countries'. *Int J. Obes Relat Metab Disord,* 26: 48-57.

Dressler, WW and JR Bindon. 1994. 'Social status, social context, and arterial blood pressure'. *Am. J.Phys. Anthropol.* 85(18): 82.

Drøyvold, WB, K Midthjell, TI Nilsen, and J Holmen, 2005. 'Change in body mass index and its impact on blood pressure: A prospective population study', *Int J Obes*, 29 (6): 650-655.

Dua, S, M Bhuker, P Sharma, M Dhall and S Kapoor. 2014. 'Body Mass index relates to blood pressure among adults'. *N.Am.J.Med.Sc.*, 6(2):89-95.

Flegal, KM, JA Shepherd, AC Looker *et al.* 2009. 'Comparisons of percentage body fat, body mass index, waist circumference, and waist-stature ratio in adults', *Am J Clin Nutr*, 89(2): 500-508.

Folsom, AR, Y Li, X Rao, R. Cen, K. Zhang, X. Liu, L He, S Irving, and BH Dennis. 1994. 'Body mass, fat distribution and cardiovascular risk factors in a lean population of South China', *J Clin Epidemiol*, 47:173-181.

Gardner, AW, and ET Poehlman. 1995. 'Predictors of age-related increase in blood pressure in men and women'. *J Gerontol A Biol Sci Med Sci.*, 50A: M1-6.

Greenlund, KJ, ML Daviglus, and JB Croft. 2009. 'Differences in healthy lifestyle characteristics between adults with prehypertension and normal blood pressure', *J Hypertens*, 27: 955-962.

Gupta, R, S. Guptha, VP. Gupta, and H. Prakash. 1995. 'Prevalence and determinants of hypertension in the urban population of Jaipur in western India', *J Hypertens*, 13 (10): 1193-1200.

Hazarika, NC, D Biswas, K Narain, RK Phukan, HC Kalita, and J Mahanta. 2000. 'Differences in blood pressure level and hypertension in three ethnic groups of Northeastern India'. *Asia Pac J Public Health*, 12: 71-78.

Hazarika, NC, K Narain, D Biswas, HC Kalita, and J Mahanta. 2004. 'Hypertension in the native rural population of Assam', *Nat. Med. J Ind,* 17: 300-304.

Hazarika, NC., D Biswas, K Narain, HC Kalita, and J. Mahanta, 2002. 'Hypertension and its risk factors in tea garden workers of Assam', *Natl. Med. J. India.* 15(2): 63-68.

He, J, MJ Klag, PK Whelton, JY Chen, MC Quian, GQ He. 1994. 'Body mass and blood pressure in a lean population in Southwestern China'. *Am J Epidemiol*, 139: 380-389.

Hoffman, MD, D Kromhout, and C de Lezenne Coulander. 1988. 'The impact of body mass index of 78,612 18-year-old Dutch men on 32-year mortality from all causes'. *J Clin Epidemiol,* 41: 749-756.

JNC 7. 2003. 'The seventh report of the Joint National Committee on Prevention, Detection, Evaluation, and Treatment of high blood pressure'. *J. Am. Med. Assoc.* 28: 2560-2571.

Kain, J, F Vio, and C Albala. 2003. 'Obesity trends and determinant factors in Latin America'. *Cad Saude Publica*.19 (Suppl 1)): S77-86.

Kanter, Rebecca and Benjamin Caballero. 2012. 'Global gender disparities in obesity: A review American Society for Nutrition'. *Adv. Nutr.*, 3: 491-498.

Kapoor, SS. 2000. 'Blood pressure, waist to hip ratio and body mass index among affluent Punjabi girls of Delhi', *Acta Med Auxol*, 32(3): 153-157.

Katz, Eva G, June Stevens, Kimberly P Truesdale, Jianwen Cai, Kari E North, and Lyn M Steffen. 2013. 'Associations of body mass index with incident hypertension in American white, American black and Chinese Asian adults in early and middle adulthood: The coronary artery risk development in young adults (CARDIA) study, the Atherosclerosis risk in communities (ARIC) study, and the People's Republic of China (PRC) study'. *Asia Pac J Clin Nutr,* 22(4):626-634.

Kaufman, JS, MC Asuzu, J Mufunda, T Forrester, R Wilks, A Luke, AE Long, and RS Cooper. 1997. 'The relationship between blood pressure and body mass index in lean populations'. *Hypertension*. 30:1511-1516.

Kaur, M. and I Talwar, 2010. 'Hypertension and blood pressure patterns in rural and urban females'. In AK Danda and I Talwar (Eds): *On Medical Anthropology: India*, INCAA, Jhargram and IGNCA, New Delhi.

Mondal, N and J Sen. 2014. 'Role of anthropometry in the assessment of excess adiposity and metabolic disorders in Asia Indians'. pp. 71-83. In K Bose and R Chakraborty (Eds): *Public Health in the 21*st *century: Health Consequences of Human Central Obesity*. New York: Nova Biomedical.

Mungreiphy, NK, Satwanti Kapoor, and Rashmi Sinha. 2011. 'Association between BMI, blood pressure, and age: Study among Tangkhul Naga tribal males of Northeast India, *Journal of Anthropology*, Volume 2011, Article ID 748147, 6 pages, 2011. doi:10.1155/2011/748147.

Murray, CJL, and AD Lopez. 1997. 'Mortality by cause for eight regions of the world: Global burden of disease study'. *Lancet*, 349: 1269-1276.

Pi-Sunyer, FX. 1993. 'Medical hazards of obesity'. *Ann Intern Med*, 119: 655-660.

Popkin, BM, LS Adair, W Ngs. 2012. 'Global nutrition transition and the pandemic of obesity in developing countries'. *Nutr. Rev*. 70: 3-21.

Romero-Corralm, A, VK. Somers, J Sierra-Johnson *et al.* 2008. 'Accuracy of body mass index in diagnosing obesity in the adult general population', *Int J Obes*, 32 (6): 959-966.

Sarmah, C and Kamali Deuri. 2014. 'Blood pressure among the adult Deuri women of Lakhimpur District, Assam', *Ind. J. Phys. Anthrop. and Hum. Genet.*, 33 (1) : 99-108.

Schall, JI. 1995. 'Sex differences in the response of blood pressure to modernisation', *American Journal of Human Biology,* 7: 159-172.

Singh, RB, SS Rastogi, V Rastogi, MA Niaz, SV Madhu, M Chen *et al*. 1997. 'Blood pressure trends, plasma insulin levels and risk factors in rural and urban elderly populations of north India'. *Coron Artery Dis*, 8(7): 463-468.

Sinha, R, and AK Kapoor. 2010. 'Cultural practices and nutritional status among premenopausal women of urban setup in India'. *Open Anthropol J*, 3:168-171.

Srikanth, J, K Jayant Kumar, NS Narasimha. 2011. 'Factors influencing obesity among urban high school children Bangalore city'. *Indian J Nutr Dietet*. 48:8-17.

Stamler, J, R Stamler, WF Reidlinger, G Algera, and RH Roberts. 1976. 'Hypertension screening of 1 million Americans'. Community Hypertension Evaluation Clinic (CHEC) Program. *JAMA,* 235:2299-306.

Stevens, J, J Cai, ER Pamuk, DF Williamson, MJ Thun, JL Wood *et al.* 1998. 'The effect of age on the association between body-mass index and mortality'. *N Engl J Med*, 338: 1-7.

Subramanian, SV and GD Smith. 2006. 'Patterns, distribution, and determinants of under- and overnutrition: a population-based study of women in India'. *Am J Clin Nutr*, 84: 633-640.

Tandon, K. 2006. *Obesity, Its Distribution Pattern and Health Implications among Khatri Population*, Unpublished Ph.D. thesis, Department of Anthropology, University of Delhi, Delhi, India.

Varadharajan, KS, T Thomas, and AV Kurpad. 2013. 'Poverty and the state of nutrition in India'. *Asia Pacific Journal Clinical Nutr*. 22: 326-339.

Wang, Y, HU Chen, S Sheikh, and P Mathur. 2009. 'Is obesity becoming a public health problem in India?: Examine the shift from under to over-nutrition problem over time'. *Obesity Revision*, 10:456-474.

World Health Organisation. 2013. *A Global Brief on Hypertension*. WHO/DCO/WHD/ 2013.2 http://apps.who.int/iris/bitstream/10665/79059 (accessed on 25/8/17).

Chapter - 12

Elderly Healthcare: Needs and Strategies for Services

—Chandana Sarmah

Introduction

Ageing of population or increase in the proportion of the elderly population to the total population is a relatively recent phenomenon for developing countries like India. But the rate of growth in our country is quite rapid especially since the last decade of the twentieth century. Presently India has around 8.3 per cent of her population belonging to the elderly category (Census, 2011). Considering the large total population of the country, when this proportion is converted to actual numbers, it adds up to more than ten crores. When we look at the world elderly population in terms of actual numbers, India stands second only to China (UN, 2007) in having a high number of elderly persons. According to the Indian Ageing Report, 2017, the proportion of elderly in India is projected to rise to 19 per cent by 2050.

India is a vast country with diverse cultures, social beliefs, and widespread regional socio-economic disparity. The ecological conditions differ from region to region. These differences have an influence on the life of people specific to the region. Just like growth or any other phase of life, aging of individuals' takes place in a social context. The culture, social organisation, and belief system determine the social status of the elderly. As such the elderly population and their needs throughout the country are not homogenous. Thus, in order to meet the needs of this growing section of the society, a clear understanding of their actual requirements is very important. This is necessary from the point of view of both the policymakers as well as service providers.

The state of Assam is situated in the North Eastern part of India. It is surrounded by hills with two main river valleys in between. The state has a mosaic of different tribes, castes, and communities with independent culture living within its boundaries. Population aging or change in age structure of the people is taking place in the state and as per 2011 census, 6.7 per cent of the state population belong to the elderly category. There are a few characteristic features relating to the aging of the population in the state. The proportion of elderly women is slightly less than men, and proportion of elderly in rural areas (6.5 per cent) is less than urban areas (7.5 per cent). The proportion of elderly among the scheduled tribes of the state is also less. The scheduled tribes of the state are economically poor and are educationally backward. The elderly belonging to the scheduled tribes of Assam have little or no access to healthcare facilities. As such, this paper is an attempt to understand the socio-economic and health condition of the elderly belonging to the scheduled tribes of Tiwa and Karbi living in the Marigaon district of Assam. Considering the socio-economic condition of the elderly, a few strategic policies have been suggested for improving the public healthcare facilities.

Material and methodology

The sample of the study consists of 490 individuals in the age group of 60 years and above. The data were collected from fifteen villages of Garmari, Ghogua and Hatiutha areas of Marigaon district, Assam. Age was mainly the inclusive criterion and all individuals of the said age group were included. Contacts with the villagers were made to the administrative head i.e. the village *gaonbura* and other senior responsible persons of the villages. The objective and methodology were explained to them and an informed verbal consent obtained. After this, the individuals were selected and only when they consented to be part of the study, data were collected. The elderly persons were initially a little apprehensive but once the objective and procedure were explained, they were eager and enthusiastic about being part of the study. The data for the study were collected in the first quarter of 2016 as a part of an ICSSR sponsored research project.

A pretested structured schedule specially designed for the study was used for data collection. It covered demographic characteristics and aspects of health, the prevalence of impairment, nutritional status, and other relevant social aspects. Both quantitative and qualitative data were collected for this cross-sectional study. The qualitative data were collected through group discussion and in-depth interview. Basic frequencies and percentages were used for interpretation of data. The nutritional status was assessed by the Body Mass Index using the formula weight (kgs) divided by height (mts) squared. The WHO standards for Asian population has been used for categorising the elderly population as undernourished (BMI < 18.5), normal (BMI 18.5-23.0) and overweight (BMI > 23.0).

The people

The Tiwa and Karbi are the two constituent communities of the study. The Marigaon district is inhabited by these two numerically predominant scheduled tribes. Both belong to the Mongoloid group and the Tibeto Burman Language family. However, both the tribes in course of migration have lost their language and now speak only Assamese language. The Tiwas were originally matrilineal but when they settled in the plains of Assam, from the adjoining hills of Meghalaya and Karbi Anglong district of Assam, they have adopted patriliny and wet paddy cultivation of the plain dwellers through acculturation. Some matrilineal traits like the tradition of having a resident son-in-law are still being practiced sporadically. However, this practice is slowly eroding. The Karbis, on the other hand, are patrilineal. The clan structure determines kinship relations and behaviour in both the communities. Though both tribes follow tribe endogamy and clan exogamy in marriage relations, yet there is a high prevalence of inter-tribal marriage between the two communities. The Tiwas and Karbis reside close to each other and there is hardly any exclusive single community village in the Marigaon district. Another cultural acculturation seen among the two communities is their conversion to Vaishnavism. Earlier both the tribes were animistic in their religious beliefs but now both Hindu and Vaishnava religious practitioners coexist along with animistic believers.

Socio-economic condition of the elderly

The socio-economic condition of a community influences the health condition and the health seeking behaviour of the people and the subsequent outcomes. The sample consists of 490 individuals in the age group of sixty years and above. The gender component is 47.75 per cent male (234 individuals) and 52.24 per cent females (256 individuals). The sample has been classified into three age groups of 60-69 years (young old), 70-79 years (middle old) and 80+ (very old) age groups. The concentration is highest in the young old age group and thereafter there is a decline. In case of the females, the decline is very sharp. The total sex ratio of elderly is 109 females per hundred males. But if the sex ratio in the broad age groups is looked into, then it can be seen that in the 60-69 years age category there are 128 females per 100 males. But this declines to 55 females per 100 males in the 70-79 years age group. However, the sex ratio in the very old age group becomes 80 females per 100 males. This is an indirect indicator of more females surviving to higher ages. For Assam life expectancy at age 60 years is 15.5 years for male and 17.6 years for female (IAR, 2017).

The Tiwa and Karbi elderly are educationally backward. They are mostly illiterate (69.80 per cent) and there is a high gender difference in educational level among both the communities. Elderly women are found to have hardly attended school. Illiteracy is high even among elderly men (53.42 per cent). 24.79 per cent of the elderly men have studied to the primary level as compared to 10.16 per cent of the elderly women. The remaining 21.79 per cent of the elderly men have studied beyond the primary level. In comparison, only 5.09 per cent of the elderly women have studied beyond the primary level. Thus, educationally it can be said that the elderly of these two scheduled tribes are backward. Educational backwardness in terms of healthcare can be said to be an indicator of their knowledge in terms of medical conditions. Though educational backwardness may not necessarily mean lack of awareness, among them knowledge as well as awareness is found to be lacking.

The Tiwas and Karbis are primarily wet paddy cultivators. Two crops are grown during the year. Those who are not involved in agriculture, have small trades like dealing with poultry, produce from kitchen garden or work as wage earners. Wage-earning is mostly in the form of working in fields or in households. In a few villages among the Karbis, some of the elderly men work as stone crushers. The elderly from both the communities continue to work in fields as long as their physical conditions allow them. Women equally take part in agricultural activities. There is a division of labour between the sexes in agricultural activities. Men plough, till the field and sow the seeds. Women perform transplantation and harvesting activities. Agricultural activities allow the elderly to be involved in some form or the other. The pace and magnitude of work may be reduced, but they continue to be active as long as they remain able. Among the elderly of the study, 28 per cent are no longer able to take part in agriculture or any other economic activities. Women give up being involved in agriculture-related activities earlier than men. But they continue to remain active in household activities or in the kitchen garden or looking after grandchildren. Even men continue to be active even after no longer being able to work for economic gain. They hardly ever remain idle.

Marital status is an important factor in the life of an elderly person as it means having or not having another individual to share everyday happenings as well as joys and sorrows. A gender difference is observed in the marital status of the elderly among the scheduled tribes. Most of the elderly currently have a surviving spouse. But the proportion of elderly males (80.77 per cent) having a surviving spouse is much higher than elderly females (54.30 per cent). Women generally tend to marry men older than themselves which may be one of the reasons for this factor. Among the elderly who no longer have a surviving spouse the proportion of females (44.14 per cent) is much higher than elderly males (17.95 per cent). Not having a surviving spouse also shows an association with age for both male and female elderly. More elderly persons in the higher ages no longer have a surviving spouse as compared to the younger ages. A small proportion of elderly persons are found to have remained unmarried. Such individuals are not found to be living alone and generally live with their married brothers' family in their ancestral homes.

The living arrangement or with whom the elderly persons stay is a significant aspect of the life of an elderly person. It is an indicator of familial care and intergenerational support. Among the Tiwas and Karbis, at least one adult son continues to live with aging parents out of filial piety. Family members provide for their basic needs. Expectation levels of elderly persons from the younger generation are also low and their needs to being frugal. As such joint family is the predominant type of family (82.45 per cent) among households having elderly persons. But a preference for nuclear families is also seen among the next generation. If a family has more than one son, when the second son gets married, he usually sets up of an independent home. Among the Tiwas, there is the practice of having a resident son-in-law in families who do not have a son. This custom also ensures a system of support for aging parents as one of the daughters continue to live in her parent's home after marriage along with her husband. Cases of neglect or abuse are culturally not permitted among both the communities. The social organisation is still very strong and according to village custom if anybody is found to be ill-treating or neglecting their parents the social organisation will reprimand and compel the person to change his behaviour. The elderly can thus be said to occupy a higher status in society. Very few elderly persons were found to live alone (1.43 per cent) or with only their spouse (5.5 per cent). Among those who live alone the number of men is a little higher than women.

The family income of the elderly has been looked into to understand their economic condition. The independent income of elderly persons was examined to understand the level of economic independence among them. Family income has been assessed from the amount of agricultural produce and converted to the current market value. Continuing to be involved in agricultural activities is a contribution to the economy and are considered to have some earning. However, this income is for family consumption and urgent needs of family members compete with needs of elderly persons. Independent monetary income, if any, among elderly, is low and very few have an independent income. 17.95 per cent of the elderly men and 32.81 per cent of elderly women no longer contribute to the economy or are financially dependent. Others contribute in varying degrees and amounts. When the family income is taken into account, 66.24 per cent of the elderly men and 60.16 per cent of the elderly women have an annual income of less than rupees fifty thousand and merely 16.81per cent elderly men and 7.03 per cent elderly women have an earning higher than rupees fifty thousand annually. Thus, we can say that economically the families are backward.

The health condition of the elderly

The increase in life expectancy of people is associated with increased concentration of health problems in old age. Variation in age-related decline in health is modified by social and environmental conditions concomitant with aging. Socio-economic factors determine health conditions in terms of presence or absence of resources to access healthcare facilities, awareness of health conditions, behavioural factors that influence health and most importantly realising the need for intervention in maintaining good functional health. Among tribal population health is defined in terms of functional ability. As long as an individual is able to perform his expected family and social role, he is considered as healthy.

This chapter attempts to look into the health condition of the elderly persons from the prevalence of disease, the type of management procedures they undertake, as well as their nutritional status.

Thirteen per cent of the elderly had suffered from some acute conditions in the last fifteen days recall period of undertaking fieldwork. The most common conditions they reported to are diseases like cold and fever, musculoskeletal pain, general weakness and respiratory problem. 31.43 per cent of the elderly persons were suffering from some chronic condition. The conditions were defined as chronic when they were suffering from a condition intermittently for the last one year at the least. Chronic diseases are generally the result of cumulative effects of years of consumption and activity pattern, in combination with genetic inheritance (Wiley and Allan, 2009). The musculoskeletal pain was reported to be the most prevalent problem followed by high blood pressure, diseases relating to the digestive system and respiratory problems. The prevalence of chronic conditions shows an association with age and more elderly men reported to having chronic conditions than women. This chapter has considered self-reported conditions and as such disease prevalence rate is found to be low. Health screening and consultations are generally absent and actual screening may give a different picture of disease prevalence. Sicknesses are generally maintained with their local knowledge of symptom management.

Consultation with a doctor is mostly done in severe conditions and is determined by the current economic condition of the family.

When the type of treatment followed is looked into, for acute and chronic conditions, medicine from the local drug store or pharmacy is the most common procedure. In case of acute conditions, 57.81 per cent took medicine in consultation with a local pharmacy and in case of chronic conditions, it is 40.91 per cent. Consultation with PHC is slightly higher in chronic conditions (33.12 per cent) than in acute conditions (26.56 per cent). Home remedies or reliance on locally known ethnomedical practices were higher for chronic conditions. Among the elderly who are suffering from chronic conditions, half of the cases have been diagnosed by a doctor at some point. However, they do not follow the prescribed course of medication. The economic condition of the people plays a determining role in this behaviour pattern. But another important aspect that has been understood in the course of the study is that there is the lack of awareness of the need for following prescriptions.

An examination of the prevalence of impairment among the elderly shows that the visual impairment (33.67 per cent) is highest followed by hearing (12.24 per cent) and locomotors (7.14 per cent) impairment. The prevalence of visual and hearing impairment is more or less similar for both men and women, and the prevalence of locomotors impairment is higher among women elderly. However, in the very old age, the gender difference with regard to locomotors impairment no longer exists. Locomotors impairment affects functional ability in activities of daily living which in turn leads to incapacitation of independent living. The prevalence of locomotors impairment is found to be from an earlier age among women indicating the greater need of assistance in them.

Developing countries like India face the problem of age-specific undernutrition. Undernutrition exists at both the lower and the higher age groups along with variation by gender and socio-economic conditions. Studies have shown a U-shaped relationship between body weight and mortality. Both high and low BMI is associated with higher risk of mortality (Willey and Allen, 2009). BMI is not an indicator of ill health but can be used as a screening tool to identify possible health problems. An attempt has been made to understand the nutritional status of the elderly from the scheduled tribes to have an understanding of the nutritional conditions of the rural tribal elderly people. The nutritional status of the elderly people has been assessed from the Body Mass Index. Prevalence of undernutrition is found to be 25.71 per cent, and overweight is found to be 9.39 per cent. Malnutrition prevalence show variation by age and gender. Undernutrition is higher among the higher age groups especially from 70 years onwards and is more among the elderly men. Overweight occurs more in females and in the young old age group. The culturally accepted habits of smoking and drinking of local rice beer may have an impact on their nutritional condition. These could result in the elderly men being more undernourished. In the overweight category, the percentage of women is higher and they belong mostly to the young old age category.

Need for health services

Health conditions in aging are influenced by social and environmental factors concomitant with aging. Increase in years in the life of an individual is accompanied by a fairly progressive deterioration of physical health. Thus, the enhanced years are associated with increased concentration of health problems and consequent disability. This, in turn, gives rise to greater demands on healthcare resources.

In the traditional culture of the Tiwa and Karbi, the elderly or any other weak member of the family is very well integrated into the joint family structure. Caring for them is shared by the members of the family. But under the present changing social norms the family may not continue to be a most important source of care in the near future. In tribal societies, the kinship and community relationship are very strong and dictates social behaviour. The needs of the people are also very frugal and societies are more or less egalitarian. But what has been seen in the present study is that the joint family is slowly disintegrating. Even though joint families are still the predominant type of family, yet there is a growing member of nuclear families. The younger generation prefers to set up nuclear families after marriage even when they reside in the same village. When couples set up independent homes, parents become peripheral relative to the needs of the nuclear families. There is thus a proportion of elderly, who are either living alone or with only their spouse. Though their proportion is small, under the changing socio-economic condition, the picture may soon change.

Another very important factor which is affecting the structure of families is the age-specific migration. The awareness about other sources of income or education opportunities attracts the younger generation outside their place of origin. This cannot be stopped but it has an adverse effect on the life of the elderly. Once separated from home, the frequency and intimacy of contact and most importantly the daily dependence is reduced. As a result, a void in care gives is created.

The traditional occupation of agriculture ensures a higher status for the elderly. But it does not allow making provisions for old age. The immovable property in terms of cultivable land and homestead land is their only assets. Monetary security is more or less not heard of. As long as their physical conditions permit, the elderly continue to work in fields. With increasing age, the pace and involvement level is lowered. These assets, therefore, do not remain useful for sustenance. Moreover, agriculture does not generate income throughout the year and the produce is generally for family's consumption purpose. Monetary earnings are an inadequate and economic transaction of produce is done only for family exigencies. But what has been observed, elderly health, in most cases do not amount to a family exigency. Health and other needs of elderly have to compete with needs of education of children or other such aspects which are considered as priorities.

Moreover, there is very little awareness about health conditions or care among the people in general. Morbidity among elderly remains undetected and causes of mortality are mostly unidentified. In the absence of knowledge about management procedures and how to deal with emergencies, most morbidity leads to an early fatality.

The elderly population is growing at a rapid rate. Very soon the demand for health services will go up. The basic structure of health facilities that is available now is not sufficient to meet the current needs of healthcare to all sections of people. Mother and child health are currently the thrust areas of healthcare at the government level. This is indeed a necessity for a developing country like ours. But at the same time, the needs of a growing section of the population cannot be ignored. With the rapidly growing elderly population, there is no alternative to strengthening the public healthcare facilities. From the public health perspective, the objective is to delay age-related morbidity and ensure successful aging. In achieving this goal, the role of public health service providers will be very important. In planning for public healthcare support the regional differences in availability of health facilities as well as limited affordability of elderly for accessing private healthcare should be kept in mind.

Strategies for strengthening health service

The government has realised the need for strengthening health service for the elderly. The National Programme for Healthcare of the Elderly (NPHCE) and the recently created Rashtriya Varisth Jan Swasthya Yojana (RVJSY) bear testimony to this. The aims and objectives of these policies are very well thought out but the challenge lies in implementing them. While executing these policies the regional differences and local needs have to be looked into. Following are some of the suggestions that could be useful in implementing programmes for scheduled tribes of Assam.

1. The existing healthcare services should incorporate service aimed specifically at elderly. Keeping in mind the needs of local people the targets or policies should be created. Now the stress is mostly on productive and child health which cannot be ignored but health for elderly should also occupy at least 25 per cent of the current expenditure.
2. A devoted group of field service providers like the ANM and ASHA workers should be created for addressing health needs of elderly. The ANM and ASHA workers have succeeded in gaining the trust of the people in rural areas through their service. The creation of a similar workforce can be effective means of providing service towards elderly individuals. They should be trained on the specific needs and care of elderly people. While selecting service providers, individuals from villages who are permanent residents (like daughter-in-law) and who have a stake in the village should be selected. Moreover, this also becomes necessary for addressing emergency health situations that may arise in case of elderly health condition.
3. Mobile healthcare can be an effective means of providing health service in remote areas. The location of the PHC, and uncertainty of meeting doctor act as a deterrent for elderly in seeking health services. In this regards the mobile healthcare units can serve as an economic and effective means of providing healthcare. Visits to villages at a specific gap period can help in identifying needs and providing support in a continuous manner. Mobile health units may be attached to each district, which can visit villages in a rotational manner on a day-to-day basis. The State Health Department of Assam has a mobile Village health outreach programme named Sanjeevani, the implementation of which is the true sense can go a long way.
4. Health promotion and more importantly health literacy should be stressed on. From an earlier age, the health service provides should literate the people about the health outcomes of social practices. The elderly, as well as the family members, need to be sensitised about the fact that some of the age-related morbidity can be prevented and if necessary managed with simple behavioural changes. Most of the age-related morbidity in rural areas is taken to be outcomes of aging and lack of attention. In designing the health literacy programmes the literacy level, social and economic backwardness need to be kept in mind. The approach should be more on a door-to-door policy rather than creating awareness

through mass media. Moreover, the elderly should also be educated about the specific programmes relating to health management and other service provided for them by the government, so that they can demand these services. Such work could be taken up by NGO's working with elderly or be made part of the curriculum like social work, community medicine, rural development, etc. as compulsory fieldwork.

5. Some intervention programmes must be taken up by the government at the regional or local level. This could be in the form of screening for diseases, support through regular medication and vaccination for specific conditions. Screening for early diagnosis, educating about management procedures can help in preventing functional disability and ensuring active healthy aging. Both the NPHCE and RVJSY have provision for the screening of 75+ people but actual implementation at the village level yet to be done.
6. The intervention programmes should have a bottom-up approach and must be designed according to local needs. Most health programmes are formed by the central government where regional or local requirements tend to get diluted. Informing the programmes, the local needs have to address. Given the vast diversity of the country, one umbrella programme will not succeed in combating the regional variation. Accurate knowledge of mortality, morbidity, and disability can help in planning for healthcare facilities. For this community, village and district level knowledge has to be generated. Collaborative work of medical practitioners, health department as well as a social scientist can be useful in this regard.
7. The biggest challenge, however, for implementing various services is the generation of economic resources. Here, considering the magnitude of the services to be provided, government alone would not be able to carry forward the work. Some kind of public, private and government level collaboration may be created. Participation of the beneficiaries at the village level for designing of health service may be effective in identifying the healthcare needs and subsequent care facilities.

Conclusion

In addressing the health needs of the growing section of the elderly population, the objective is to ensure successful and active aging. As far as the social support is concerned the elderly from these two tribes are in an advantageous position. The traditional joint family provide social support in ways of economic support, care in times of illness, physical and emotional security to the elderly. But they face limitation in providing healthcare service. Among the elderly of the scheduled tribes of Assam, morbidity remains undetected and mostly taken to be the outcome of aging. There is a lower level of awareness about management of symptoms of diseases as well as the lack of affordability of healthcare facilities. As a result, health in general and specifically among elderly gets neglected in face of attending to basic needs of survival. Under the circumstances, there is no alternative but to strengthen the public health delivery agencies.

Table 12.1: Distribution of elderly by socio-demographic variables

	Age and Sex				
	60-69 years	*70-79 years*	*80+ years*	*Total*	
Male	168 (71.79)	51 (21.79)	15 (6.14)	234 (47.75)	
Female	216 (84.38)	28 (10.94)	12 (4.69)	256 (52.24)	
	Educational Qualification				
	Illiterate	Primary Level	Beyond Primary	Total	
Male	125 (53.42)	58 (24.79)	51 (21.79)	234 (47.75)	
Female	217 (84.76)	26 (10.16)	13 (5.09)	256 (52.24)	
	Current Occupation				
	Agriculture	Petty Trade/ Wage Earning	Service	No longer working	
Male	167 (71.37)	10 (4.27)	2 (0.85)	55 (23.50)	
Female	159 (62.11)	13 (5.08)	-	84 (32.81)	
	Marital Status				
	Married	Widow/Widower	Never Married	Total	
Male	189 (80.77)	42 (17.95)	3 (1.28)	234	
Female	139 (54.30)	113 (44.14)	4 (1.56)	256	
	Living Arrangement				
	Alone	With the Only Spouse	Nuclear Family	Joint Family	Total
Male	6 (2.56)	15 (6.41)	32 (13.67)	181 (77.35)	234
Female	1 (0.39)	12 (4.69)	20 (7.81)	223 (87.11)	256
	Family income of Elderly				
	No independent income among elderly	Less than Rs. 50,000	More than Rs. 50,000	Total	
Male	42 (17.95)	155 (66.24)	37 (16.81)	234	
Female	84 (32.81)	154 (60.16)	18 (7.03)	256	

(Figures in parentheses indicate percentage)

Table 12.2: Distribution of elderly by prevalence of disease and their management procedures

Prevalence of Acute Disease				
	60-69 years	*70-79 years*	*80+ years*	*Total*
Male	14 (8.33)	14 (27.45)	3 (20)	31 (13.25)
Female	22 (10.19)	7 (25)	4 (33.33)	33 (12.89)
Prevalence of Chronic Disease				
	60-69 years	*70-79 years*	*80+ years*	*Total*
Male	49 (29.17)	28 (54.90)	10 (66.67)	87 (37.18)
Female	47 (21.76)	15 (53.57)	5 (41.67)	67 (26.17)
Management of acute conditions				
	Medicine from pharmacy	*Consulted PHC*	*Home Remedy*	*Total*
Male	20 (64.52)	5 (16.13)	6 (19.35)	31
Female	17 (51.52)	12 (36.36)	4 (12.12)	33
Management of chronic conditions				
Male	42 (48.27)	28 (32.18)	17(19.54)	87
Female	21 (31.34)	23 (34.33)	23 (34.33)	67

(Figures in parentheses indicate percentage).

Table 12.3: Distribution of elderly by their age and prevalence of impairments

Prevalence of Impairment					
	Type of impairment	*60-69 years*	*70-79 years*	*80+ years*	*Total*
Male	Visual	37 (22.02)	35 (68.62)	12 (80)	84 (35.90)
	Hearing	4 (2.38)	15 (29.41)	7 (46.67)	26 (11.11)
	Locomotors	2 (1.19)	2 (3.92)	6 (40)	10 (4.27)
Female	Visual	47 (21.76)	23 (82.14)	11 (91.67)	81 (31.64)
	Hearing	17 (7.87)	10 (35.71)	7 (58.33)	34 (13.28)
	Locomotors	11 (5.09)	9 (75)	5 (41.67)	25 (9.77)

(Figures in parentheses indicate percentage)

Table 12.4: Distributions of elderly by their age and nutritional status

Age	*Sex*	*Underweight*	*Normal*	*Overweight*	*Total*
60-69 years	Male	39 (23.21)	110 (65.48)	13 (7.74)	168
	Female	33 (15.28)	153 (70.83)	30 (13.89)	216
70-79 years	Male	25 (49.02)	25 (49.02)	1 (1.96)	51
	Female	17 (60.71)	11 (39.28)		28
80+ years	Male	6 (40.0)	8 (53.33)	1 (6.67)	15
	Female	6 (50)	5 (41.67)	1 (8.33)	12
Total	**Male**	**70 (29.91)**	**143 (61.11)**	**15 (6.41)**	**234**
	Female	**56 (21.87)**	**169 (66)**	**31 (12.11)**	**256**

(Figures in parentheses indicate percentage)

Acknowledgement

The study is a part of an ICSSR sponsored research project on bio-social aspects of aging among the Tiwa and Karbi communities of Marigaon District, Assam. The author expresses her gratitude to the organisation for the financial support and to research assistant Ms. Priyanka Morang for collecting the data.

References

Caring for our Elderly: *Early Responses, Indian Ageing Report, 2017* United Nations Population Fund (UNFPA), New Delhi.

United Nations, 2007. *World Population Ageing 2007*, Department of Economic and Social Affairs/Population Division, New York: United Nations.

Wiley, AS and JS. Allen, 2009. *Medical Anthropology: A Biocultural Perspective*, Oxford University Press.

Chapter - 13

Maternal Mid Upper Arm Circumference before Delivery and Newborn Birth Weight among Paite of Churachandpur, Manipur

—Evelyn Ngaithianven and R. K. Pathak

Introduction

During a woman's life cycle, pregnancy marks the most vital and unique period. It is a condition of great stress as many anabolic activities take place and fetal growth is accomplished by extensive changes in maternal body composition and metabolism (Sachdeva *et al.*, 2009). The overall development of the fetus and subsequent birth outcomes are highly influenced by maternal nutrition before and during pregnancy. Thus, consumption of a balanced diet during pregnancy is highly recommended as it has an impact on both the mother and the child's health. According to WHO (2015), an estimated 15 million babies are born preterm (gestational age <37 weeks) each year around the world; and about 20 million are born with low birth weight (LBW) (birth weight <2,500 g) (WHO, 2014), with more than 95 per cent of these births occurring in resource-poor countries. The stark reality, however, is that the incidence of (LBW) babies continues to be high in India at about 30 per cent in contrast to 5-7 per cent in developed countries (Kashyap and Dwivedi, 2006). Undernutrition in women, before and during pregnancy is recognised to be a key determinant of poor pregnancy outcomes thus leading to increased infant morbidity and mortality. On the other hand, birth weight is a powerful indicator of the overall growth, development, and survival of an infant and is directly dependent on maternal health and nutrition during pregnancy. Mid-upper arm circumference (MUAC) is recommended as the preferred nutritional index for pregnant women since it does not change significantly during pregnancy. A globally accepted cut-off for low MUAC (<11.5 cm) has been established by the

World Health Organisation for children 6–60 months of age; however, a standardised cut-off for low MUAC for adults does not yet exist.

Sufficient research evidence points out to the fact that maternal nutritional status pre-pregnancy and during pregnancy are associated with neonatal anthropometric characteristics at birth (Black *et al.*, 2008; Muthayya, 2009; Sachdeva *et al.*, 2009; Khoushabi and Saraswathi, 2010; Ramakrishnan *et al.*, 2012). Hence an attempt of its first kind is made among the present study population to find the correlations between maternal nutritional status using the variable MUAC during the third trimester and birth weight of infants, as it influences future life quality and health of the newborns.

Material and Methods

The Paite are the dominant tribe of Churachandpur District of Manipur. Paite is a name of a tribe formed by congeries of clans. Official use of the term came into existence in India since the specification of the term under the provision of Article 342 of the Constitution of India in the modification order of the Constitution, 1956. The Paite belong to the Northern Chin sub-group of Kuki-Chin-Mizo (Grierson, 1967).

For a collection of data, hospitals and maternity clinics in Churachandpur town were approached. Mothers who delivered after completing 37 to 42 weeks of pregnancy were included in the study, and the birth weight of their babies was recorded. However, HIV patients and twin babies were excluded from the present study. The sample comprises 219 mother-infant pairs. After explaining the purpose of the study, permission was obtained from Hospital and Clinic administration and written consent was obtained from the mothers before proceeding with the work. The data were collected for a period of three months (November 2010-February 2011).

The anthropometric variable of the mothers namely MUAC is measured at the third trimester who are admitted to the hospital waiting for their delivery, whereas, newborn babies' weight was recorded within 24 hours of birth. In this setting, MUAC became a useful indicator of protein-energy malnutrition or starvation, as a measurement of weight or height is not feasible in all situations. In the present study, despite various cut-off points being used by different authors, MUAC < 23.0 cm (moderate risk) as recommended in the Sphere standards (Sphere, 2004) was used. The Sphere minimum standards recommend a cut-off point of <21.0 cm for identification of nutritional risk in pregnant women in emergencies. Maternal MUAC was taken with the help of a flexible, non-stretch steel tape calibrated in centimeters and the measurements were recorded to the nearest millimeters. Similarly, the nude body weight of the babies was accurately measured using the aid of spring balance weighing scale designed for infants with a capacity of 20 kilograms. It is recorded in kilogram up to the accuracy of 20 gm. The data were analysed in consultation with a statistical programmer, using computer Microsoft excel for windows and SPSS 16. The results thus obtained are presented in tabular form followed with suitable interpretations.

The limitation of the present study was to measure maternal pre-pregnancy MUAC since among Paite tribe prenatal care is an evolving field and women commonly do not go for regular checkups, and visit hospitals only when they are advanced in pregnancy.

Results

Table 13.1: Mothers' mid-upper arm circumference and Newborns' birth weight

Variables	*Mean (±SD)*	*CV*	*Minimum*	*Maximum*
MUAC (cm) (mothers')	24.47 (2.2)	9.18	19.4	31
Newborn Birth weight (kg)				
Boys	3.24 (0.4)	14.05	2.2	4.5
Girls	3.14 (0.4)	14.32	2	4.5

Table 13.1 shows that mean maternal MUAC before delivery is 24.47 cm (±2.2). The mean birth weight of boys and girls are 3.24 and 3.14 kg respectively. Since there is no significant difference between boys and girls ($t = 0.157$), the sexes were pooled for further analysis.

Table 13.2: Newborn birth weight according to maternal MUAC

MUAC (cm)	*Frequency (Per cent)*	*Birth weight (Kg)*	*LBW (Per cent)*
Severe risk <21.0 cm	11(5.02)	2.7	3 (27.2)
Moderate risk <23.0 cm	46 (21.0)	3.1	2 (4.3)
Normal >23.0 cm	162 (73.9)	3.2	5 (3.1)

It is clear from Table 13.2 that, the majority (73.9 per cent) of the pregnant women are at a level of good nutrition. The birth weights of babies are found higher among mothers who have MUAC >23.0 cm. Prevalence of low birth weight babies was found highest among pregnant women having MUAC < 21.0 cm.

Applying Pearson correlation it becomes clear from Table 13.3 that there are strong positive correlations (r = 0.207) between maternal MUAC before delivery and newborn birth weight.

Table 13.3: Pearson Correlations between maternal Newborn birth weight

Variable	*Mid-upper arm circumference of mothers (cm)*	
	r	*p*
Birth weight (kg)	0.207	<0.001

Discussion

According to Sphere classification, the mean maternal MUAC of 24.47 cm during the third trimester is in the normal range of nutritional status. Further, using Sphere classification, the majority (73.9 per cent) of the mothers are found to have a good nutritional status during their blissful pregnancy journey. On the other hand, only 5.02 per cent mothers are found to be severely malnourished. There is, however, no significant difference between the birth weight of boys and girls. Using WHO cut-off (<2500 g) only 2.74 per cent of babies were found to have low birth weight. This observation is in agreement with the findings of Bharati *et al.,* 2011, wherein they observed that the North-east zone of India shows the lowest prevalence of low birth weight.

The highest newborn birth weight (3.2 kg) is observed among mothers who are well nourished, followed by mothers who are moderately nourished (3.1 kg), and least birth weight (2.7 kg) among severely malnourished mothers. The percentage of low birth weight babies follows a similar pattern; highest (27.2 per cent) among the severely malnourished mothers, followed by moderately nourished mothers (4.3 per cent). A positive correlation (r = 0.207) between maternal MUAC before delivery and newborn birth weight is in accordance with a study conducted by Ricalde *et al.* (1998) among pregnant women of S. Paulo in Brazil.

With a MUAC cut-off ranging between 22-28.9 cm as a predictor of low birth weight babies, findings of present study are corroborated by studies from Bangladesh (Karim and Mascie-Taylor, 1997); India (Mohanty *et al.*, 2006); Zimbabwe (Ogbonna *et al.*, 2007); Nepal (Ojha and Malla, 2007); Bangladesh (Dhar *et al.*, 2008); Sudan (Elshibly and Schmalisch, 2008); Pakistan (Janjua *et al.*, 2009); India (Sen *et al.*, 2010); Ethiopia (Assefa *et al.*, 2012). Further, Shrivastava *et al.* (2016) made an observational case-control study in central India by comparing low birth weight and normal birth weight. They observed a lower MUAC among mothers who gave birth to low birth weight babies.

From the findings of the present study, it is concluded that maternal MUAC during the third trimester had a significant impact on the newborn birth weight. It is further observed that maternal MUAC >21.0 cm is a good predictor in determining low birth weight babies. Thus, MUAC (which is easy to measure) alone can be recommended for use among health workers in an emergency or in field areas where monitoring other nutritional status is not feasible and also for detection of mothers at risk of delivering high or low birth weight babies.

Acknowledgements

Thanks are due to the hospital administrators, staff and the mother-infant pairs who participated in the study.

References

Assefa, N., Y. Berhane, and A. Worku. 2012. 'Wealth status, mid-upper arm circumference (MUAC) and antenatal care (ANC) are determinants of low birth weight in Kersa, Ethiopia'. *PLoS One*. 7(6): e39957.

Bharati, P, M. Pal, M. Bandyopadhyay, A. Bhakta, S. Chakraborty, and S. Bharati. 2011. 'Prevalence and causes of low birth weight in India'. *Malys J Nutr*. 17: 301-313.

Black, RE, LH. Allen, ZA. Bhutta, LE. Caulfield, M. de Onis, M. Ezzati *et al.* 2008. 'Maternal and child undernutrition: Global and regional exposures and health consequences'. *Lancet*. 371 (9608): 243-260.

Dhar, B, and SK. Bhadra. 2008. 'Use of anthropometric indicators for predicting the risk of delivering low birth weight babies'. *Bangladesh Medical Research Council Bulletin*. 34(2): 64-6.

Elshibly, EM, and G. Schmalisc. 2008. 'The effect of maternal anthropometric characteristics and social factors on gestational age and birth weight in Sudanese newborn infants'. *BMC Public Health*. 8:244.

Grierson, GA. 1967. *Linguistic Survey of India*. Delhi: Motilal Banarsidass.

Janjua, NZ, E. Delzell, RR. Larson, S. Meleth, S. Kristensen, E. Kabagambe *et al.* 2009. 'Determinants of low birth weight in urban Pakistan'. *Public Health Nutr*. 12(6): 789-798.

Karim, E, and GCN. Mascie-Taylor.1997. 'The association between birthweight, sociodemographic variables, and maternal anthropometry in an urban sample from Dhaka, Bangladesh'. *Ann Hum Biol*. 24(5): 387-401.

Kashyap, L, and R. Dwivedi. 2006. 'Detection of fetal malnutrition by clinical assessment of nutritional status score (CAN score) at birth and its comparison with other methods of determining intrauterine growth'. *Pediatric Oncall* (Serial online). 3(1).

Khoushabi, F, and G. Saraswathi. 2010. 'Association between maternal nutrition status and birth weight of neonates in selected hospitals in Mysore city, India'. *Pakistan Journal of Nutrition*. 9 (12): 1124-1130.

Mohanty, C, R. Prasad, AS. Reddy, JK. Ghosh, TB. Singh, and BK. Das.2006. 'Maternal anthropometry as predictors of low birth weight'. *J Trop Pediatr*. 52: 24-29.

Muthayya, S. 2009. 'Maternal nutrition and low birth weight—What is really important?'. *Indian Journal of Medical Research,* 130 (5): 600-608.

Ogbonna, C, GB.Woelk, Y. Ning, S. Mudzamiri, K. Mahomed, and MA.Williams. 2007. 'Maternal mid-arm circumference and other anthropometric measures of adiposity in relation to infant birth size among Zimbabwean women'. *Acta Obstetricia et Gynecologica*. 86: 26-32.

Ojha, N, and DS. Malla. 2007. 'Low birth weight at term: Relationship with maternal anthropometry'. *Journal of the Nepal Medical Association*. 46(166): 52-56.

Ramakrishnan, U, F. Grant, T. Goldenberg, A. Zongrone, and R. Martorell. 2012. 'Effect of women's nutrition before and during early pregnancy on maternal and infant outcomes: A systematic review'. *Paediatr Perinat Epidemiol*. 26 (1): 285-301.

Ricalde, AE, G.Velasquez-Melendez, AC. Tanaka, and AAF. De Siqueira.1998. 'Mid-upper arm circumference in pregnant women and its relation to birth weight'. *Revista de Saude Publica*. 32(2): 112-7.

Sachdeva, P, BG. Patel, and BK. Patel. 2009. 'Drug use in pregnancy; A point to ponder!' *Indian J Pharm Sci*. 71 (1): 1-7.

Sen, J, A. Roy, and N. Mondal. 2010. 'Association of maternal nutritional status, body composition and socio-economic variables with low birth weight in India'. *J Trop Pediatr*. 56(4): 254-9.

Shrivastava, J, A. Agrawal, and A. Giri. 2016. 'Maternal anthropometry in relation to the birth weight of newborn: A prospective hospital-based study'. *Indian J Child Health*. 3(1): 59-63.

The Sphere Project. 2011. *Humanitarian Charter and Minimum Standards in Humanitarian Response*, 3rd ed. United Kingdom; Belmont Press Ltd.

World Health Organisation. 2014. *Comprehensive Implementation Plan on Maternal, Infant and Young Child Nutrition*. Geneva: WHO.

World Health Organisation. 2015. *WHO Recommendations on Interventions to Improve Preterm Birth Outcomes*. Geneva: WHO.

Chapter - 14

Revisiting the Status of Tribal Women: Deconstructing Matriliny among the Khasi

—Chandra Jyoti Sonowal

Introduction: The anthropology of tribal women

Anthropology and tribal history are intimately related to each other. The nineteenth-century anthropologists mostly took the pain of exploring tribal world across the globe primarily fulfilling the interest of the colonial rulers. It has quite often been asserted that in conventional anthropological literature, women remain invisible despite the fact that ethnographic accounts have included women through extensive studies on marriage and kinship system of tribal groups. Therefore, the critics of anthropology feel that the problem lies in the process of representing women, not essentially in the availability of data on women. Thus, Moore (1988) observes that in traditional (under the shadow of colonial interest) anthropological field-work and their interpretation, three inherent phenomena have surfaced influencing the representation of women through a gender perspective. These may be asserted as follows:

(i) The anthropologists happened to be outsiders, hailing from non-traditional societies, came to the field with a preoccupied notion that the males of the studied society were more accessible, controlled significant information base and attached to almost all socio-cultural aspects.

(ii) The males of the studied society considered women as a subordinate entity and the same notion was transmitted to the anthropologists.

(iii) Anthropologists hailing from western and non-traditional culture perceived gender system of studied societies similar to the asymmetrical gender system existing in their own society. Thus, they merely failed to understand and interpret the egalitarian or at least differential gender relations present in other traditional societies.

By the year 1971, with the setting up of The Committee on the Status of Women, India (CSWI), there emerged a trend to break the paradigm of "male reporting" and seeing women in "men's perspectives". In any human society, the dominant group designs and controls the *model of expression of social reality* in their own term; and men being the dominant one, dominate the world of expression to outsiders. The females, being a dominated group are expected to express their life experiences in a male-defined model. But the women's life experiences cannot be expressed through such male-dominated model. So, the women do not get any medium to express their views and they get muted (Ardener, 1975). Thus, the anthropology of women tries to analyse the realities of women through female's perspectives re-looking at anthropological and ethnographic data collected through space and time. Deconstruction of conventional myth about the tribal world and tribal women starts here.

Revisiting the status of tribal women

Traditional anthropological and sociological literature assigns a higher status to tribal women compared to women in many non-tribal societies. The general view forwarded for this perception includes tribal women's greater involvement in subsistence and market economy, their ability to possess some landed resources for economic activities, the existence of the system of bride-price (or bride-wealth), ability to chose one's own life partner and relatively free venture in male-dominated domains.

These conventional criteria for assessing tribal women's status have been questioned by present-day anthropologists and social scientist while they find that under the umbrella concept of "higher status", the tribal women's life is not so pleasant. They are dominated by men's dominant paradigm of gender system in various social, economic and political fronts. For instance, women are deprived of the right to inherit valuable resources. If at all they are official heirs; in practice, men control those resources. Despite their greater involvement in work-role performance, the tribal women are mostly lack of power to control the benefits of their labour, production, and reproduction. In terms of health, education, decision-making, and political participation etc the tribal women are mostly found to be lagging behind their male counterparts. Thus, an analysis of the situation of tribal women through gender perspective promises a better and unbiased depiction of the life of tribal women.

The core components of gender differentiation

One can observe a distinct difference in work-role performed by or expected of men and women as social being. It is also true that different levels of importance are assigned to such work-roles and subsequently, the person who performs it receives relative status on that basis. But it is important to understand what makes a society to assign such work-role to a particular gender. Nevertheless, irrespective of work-role performance, males and females have separate domains in each society. They are separated from each other by a complex web of deep-rooted social, cultural and religious beliefs and practices centering around the physiology of women's body. Excretes during menstruation and childbirth remains the major factor to separate men's world from female's in most of the traditional societies. The concept of pollution and perceived danger attached to it plays a major role in denying access to crucial magico-religious domains for women, which holds key to power and authority in society, even beyond this domain.

Determinants of the status of tribal women

Sacks (1979) reveal that among the Australian aborigines, women's position is directly related to the importance of and their control over their economic contribution, their participation in women's rituals valued by both men and women. Leacock (1978), Phyllis Kaberry (1930), Diane Bell (1983) observes that substantially independent worlds of men and women in economic and ritual terms do not imply inferiority or subordination of a particular gender. Moreover, mere involvement in the crucial workforce of production and reproduction and the resource owned do not assure women's higher position in their society. Women may have no *de facto* control over the land due to residence rule and they may have *de jure* control over their children due to the descent rule. Gender ideology plays a crucial role in defining women's social status. For example, women may be perceived as born to serve men. Women may be used or perceived as means to extend a male's status and position in society. They may also be seen as mentally weak enough to hold control over land and other important resources and make social contract etc. All these notions show that the male is the model and measure of perfect human being. In many tribal societies, it was perceived as dangerous to make women aware of the religious, magical and political domain because they take the power they possess with them at the time of marriage to strengthen another group. Besides, the group who receives the new life is afraid of her since she carries power which is derived from another, potentially dangerous group.

The value attached to certain works and control over the skill to do those works possesses crucial importance to determine women's status. Traditional tribal societies were weaving, transplanting, singing folklores, performing traditional dance etc were seen as the special skill of social importance, and women who mastered them were given high regard.

Evidence from across the world shows that income in the hands of tribal women is used to contribute more to household food security and child nutrition compared to their male counterpart due to the fact that women are directly responsible for feeding, clothing, and housing their children. Women's attachment towards their children, their limited extra-domestic work-role opportunity compelled them to involve mostly in subsistence food production in the informal economy resulting women's low productivity compared to that of men. Cambodian situation shows that women's low status can be understood in terms of their undervalued agrarian labour in a rigidly patriarchal society.

Examining women's subordination through violence against women

The issue of violence against women is not unidirectional and is very critical to be defined. John Galtung's (1990) threefold theorisation of violence can be understood as structural, cultural, personal and direct and it opens up the discussion to the issue of inequality and social justice. John Keanes (1996) definition of violence just looks at the physicality of such an action. Violence against women can also be considered as symbolic violence where it is used as a means for social control. Pierre Bourdieu[3] identifies male domination as a paradigmatic form of symbolic violence. Women are always the objects in such situations and are abused because of their second-class status in the society. They are always deprived of various aspects of decision-making in a familial to institutional and political level. And its inception can be seen since the day she is born due to the prevailing stereotypes and the preset mind of the people. This is then directed by the socialisation where processes of violence are practiced and maintained.

Marx's historical materialism and women's subordination

The followers of Marx believe that women's subordination and consequently men's violence against women is related to the issue of women's involvement in production and reproduction and control over valued resources (Maria-Barbara, 1985:1-14). Engels (1972:221) claimed that "the emancipation of women will only be possible when women can take part in production on a large scale, and domestic work no longer claims anything but the insignificant amount of her time." Leacock (1972:34) maintains that women's status in traditional societies with their greater emphasis on communal life will be defined by the women's workload. Contrary to these views, Sanday (1973, 1981) makes it clear that such work involvement is no doubt a necessary prerequisite. But this is not the lone factor in deciding women's greater status in society. There are various other values attached to the social system. Historical materialism model takes into account the function as well as the critical social values of a particular activity within a given system.

The feminist perspectives on women's subordination and violence

Feminist writings and theorising influenced most the conceptualisation of many social scientists about men's violence against women. Rather than putting emphasis on physical strength or biological instinct, the feminist investigators assigned the violence of men against women as an institutionally driven factor in society. Feminist analysis sees violence as a form of social control used to maintain a subordinate social and physical status for women. It also views violence against women as a unitary phenomenon and an outgrowth of male power and privileges. Feminist have emphasised the importance of conceptualising and naming violence in the ways that reflect women's experiences (Marin and Russo, 1999: 18-35). This approach also argues that the social institutions tend to trivialise and/or ignore women's experience of violence.

Patriarchy, women's subordination, and violence: The structural approach

The link between gender and patriarchy has also been a major area of discourse while deliberating the issue of violence against women. Despite the fact that the concept of patriarchy suffers from lack of proper theoretical base in explaining violence against women, the multifaceted meaning of patriarchy was imparted into terms such as "male-dominated society", "sexual inequality" and "feminist perspectives". The core concepts of patriarchy as a system of male domination and female subordination have found their place in the language of the analytical domain of gender study and deliberation of violence against women.

To be precise, patriarchy talks of gender hierarchy and relative dominance of males over females. It also talks about power relation, especially between men and women within the member of a family. Over and above these aspects, patriarchy as a construct relates the gender relations and violence within a social context, extending its underpinning beyond individual aspects. Nevertheless, explaining gender relations and subsequent violence against women only through the lens of the patriarchal concept is not acceptable to a large number of scholars across disciplines. The primary disagreement lies with the simplified explanation of power relation between genders proposed by patriarchy concept.

Patriarchy may be defined as a social arrangement that privilege males, where men as a social group, dominate women as a group, both structurally and ideologically–hierarchical arrangements that manifest in varieties across history and social space. Patriarchal systems can be seen at different levels: at the macro level, these may be seen as bureaucrats, government, law, market, religion etc. At micro level–interaction, families, organisations, patterned behaviour between intimates may be classified. Both macro and the micro patriarchal system exist symbolically. While trying to answer "why do men resort to violence against women" the earlier construct of patriarchy and violence against women views that male's violence against women serves a dual function:

First, violence functions as a tool to exploit men's position of advantage and to maintain patriarchal order. But being powerful does not lead to violence essentially. It is seen that actually, the least powerful men victimise women under social pressure to acquire more power and redeem their "*wounded masculinity*". This means that, in a situation or social arrangement where the male components are given superior status and value, men try to defend these components. In case a man is unable to defend his maleness due to any reason, his masculinity is wounded. In reality, the individual behaviour of men is conditioned and determined by social structure, and violent behaviour is linked to the pathological social arrangement.

This necessitates examining how the masculinity of a person is wounded. Patriarchal arrangement put enormous value on the concept of masculinity. Men try to secure masculine identities through prestige and authority. In a patriarchal arrangement, men get the opportunity to demonstrate that they are better than and different from women. Male's capability and opportunity to demonstrate "better" is endorsed with "prestige" in a society which helps men to separate themselves from femininity. It is asserted that certain structural or individual facts may block such access to opportunity to demonstrate masculinity or opportunity through prestige generation. Devoid of such access to opportunity to demonstrate maleness and thereby inability to secure prestige, such men are likely to resort to violence against women to establish their support and dominance as an alternative and softer means. Thus, to be critical, it is not only gender distance between men and women, rather, it is the distance and difference between men to men that leads to violence.

Apart from the structural condition in patriarchies, there are varied natures of patriarchal ideologies which see the issue of controlling and dominance over women in different perspectives. For instance, if a society put more value on women's reproductive capacity and family care in ideological perspective, then her access to and control over economic resources may not help increase her value in society as a woman. Here, individual women's economic power does not assure non-violence towards her. It does not free her from gendered roles and male-dominated ideology as what else is expected of her as social norms. Even in an abusive situation, many women are socialised to regard their relationships as a core element of their identity and self-worth; some women may strive to preserve relationships at any cost. Thus, it is very important to locate patriarchal gender ideology and contextualise it with structural arrangement of the patriarchal domain to understand gender relationship, women's subordination and causes of violence against women. Domination of women is not simply a matter of structure or achieving economic equality with men. Structural inequality is only a feature of patriarchies. Gender ideologies that favour gender inequalities can diminish the strength of women's structural gains. Scholars opine that patriarchies serve as models of dominance for other hierarchical institutions. For instance, the family is the cultural apparatus that supports other systems of domination. The monopoly of the male head of the family over social control, religious customs etc. have been absorbed by state religion having to underpin with common patriarchal moral norms.

Thus, it necessitates that to explain violence inherent in patriarchy, an assessment of ideological and structural manifestation in patriarch is essential. It would help finding out the contending points between ideology and structure of patriarchies. Finally, it is essential to locate or identify power relations between and among genders—unidirectional and/or multi-directional.

A recent study conducted by the author of this chapter among six tribal societies (Khasi in Meghalaya, Paite in Manipur, Nyishi and Monpa in Arunachal Pradesh and Mishing and Sonowal Kachari in Assam) has opened up several of such hitherto unexplored or less deliberated aspects of gender relations and patriarchal components directly influencing the life of tribal women which are sufficient to deconstruct the popular notion about world of tribal women. A brief but in-depth observation of the world of Matrilineal Khasi women has been extracted from the study for the purpose of the present chapter and placed in the following paragraph.

Part II

Deconstructing Khasi matriliny

Khasi society is one of the few human societies which follow matrilineal descent reckoning. There have been general ideas about Khasi society in terms of power and authority of women, their control over resources and much more. In laymen's view, the Khasi males are put in a very poor light in terms of social status power relations and the status of Khasi women are seen as high. Contrary to such perceptions, the reality is far different from it. Khasi women have never occupied a superior or dominant position in their society. Like many other tribal populations, the Khasi society also has patriarchal components where males are depicted as superior to women in some important social domains. Their mythology, their terminology used to define male etc are very much gender biased. In the following part, it has been tried to examine the world of Khasi women in terms of gender relations and gender subordination and gender dominance etc and the so-called status of Khasi women.

Gender role segregation among the Khasi

The gender role differentiation is symbolically exhibited for the first time in the life of a person during the naming ceremony. In the naming ceremony for a son, in traditional Khasi society, a bow and three arrows are kept close to the baby. For the female, these are substituted by a *dau* (wait), a conical basket and a rain shield (*ka khoh bad ka trap*) and/or a winnowing tray (*u prah*). A male is primarily seen as a warrior who protects and defends the family and community from the enemies and hunters who bring the game home, hence the bow and arrows. The female, on the other hand, is seen not only as a caretaker and nurturer (*ka nongri ka nongbat*) whose duties are to attend to the young and the aged, and the domestic chores of cooking, washing, fetching water fuel, but also a worker in the field. One interesting aspect of the gender division of labour perceived by Khasi is that, while it defines the females as physically and mentally inferior to men, in their domestic role, women are saddled both with reproductive (nurturing) and productive (economic) functions. But such responsibilities do not entitle women to freedom as the Khasi society gives to men.

A man is expected to be brave and emotionally tough, entitled to a high degree of freedom of movement and expression. A man can engage in all kinds of activities, even sexual exploits–so long as they do not violet other men's right. It is found that despite currency of monogamous ethos, families often take pride in the sexual ventures of their sons, calling a man with many wives–*u rang khaddar lama* (a man who bears twelve flags). Contrarily, women are expected to be submissive and subordinate to men. They are to be protected by males and excluded from the important areas of decision-making both within and outside the family. Elected positions within the clan and village, such as *Rangbah Kur* (clan head) and *Rangbah Shnong* (village head) are traditionally reserved for men.

Nevertheless, Khasi women get a symbolic importance in the very concept of family structure. The symbolic expression of Khasi is constituted by three spherical stones representing–*ka lawbei*, the primeval ancestress of the clan, U Thawlong, the first father of the clan, and *U Suidnia*, the first maternal uncle of the clan. This ideally makes the mother, the father, and the mother's brother equal partners in the administration of the family.

Learning to be a woman

In a traditional setting Khasi women's life revolves around the activities primarily related to economic and care to give to the family members. Thus, learning the roles of a woman mainly encompasses how to perform household and economic activities, how to behave with others as a woman, and what activities she should and should not follow etc.

In Khasi society, women are seen as the creator of family and the clan and bearer of the culture. Thus, the behaviour of women in society is perceived to be very important. Women are advised to be obedient and respectful to elders, not to argue with, disobey or talk back to elders, not to laugh too much, say bad words, mingling with boys too much, nor stay out late, treating guests properly, etc. Traditional Khasi domain is full of such instruction through proverbs and folklore. For instance, one of Khasi proverbs says,

> "Lady, when you converse with anyone, does not smile revealing your teeth. As long as you don't know the person, excessive laughter you should suppress, for it will cheapen your womanliness."

Another interesting proverb says that sitting gesture while eating should be respectful. Sitting outstretched or a leg apart is considered as being in bad taste and a misdemeanor. If anyone sits in that way they are compared to laying a trap for the cat.

The Khasi proverbs go on saying about certain model acts as follows:

"Do not take or give anything from behind

Because it is like the ghost's work who had no last rites

Don't take or give anything between your fingers

Or you may get twins" (one boy one girl: this is seen as very bad luck).

In the similar note another proverb says:

> "Whenever you are taking or serving food, don't slide the plate for it is rude, lift it with grace then give, or God will scold, at it is like sending way the bewitched."

Khasis believe that conversations are grounds upon which character is based and judged, and therefore, one must be careful about how one conducts oneself in these situations. A person who laughs too loud without any genuine reason is usually called a "Langshngaiti tiiuhmoh". This proverb is used to caution such a person, especially a woman which says:

"Laugh not in the habit of the vulgar
Like the bald song of the bearded goat."

Another proverb says:

"Shade words of shame concealed them,
Even if they ring true do not pronounce;
Make not a habit of gossip mongering,
For this takes root inauspiciousness
Departs from sulky ways and actions
Lest dignity is weakened."

Another proverb says that whenever elders come visiting, their bags shouldn't be empty while returning. The host should fill them with betel nut and leaves. The host will be blessed and praised and rewarded. Khasis used proverbs while teaching the children on how to welcome their guests or visitors. One should welcome their guests in their house by offering them seats such as the bamboo mat or wooden stool and when the guests are seated offer them betel nut and betel leaves.

Restriction on Khasi women

Contrary to the fact that the Khasi society is a matrilineal one, women have never been in a dominant position in the social arena. In traditional Khasi domain, women encounter a lot of restrictions imposed by patriarchal arrangements. While some of them are related to familial aspects, others are extra-familial in nature. That a woman must be controlled or guided by men and that without a control or guidance, women are like kites with broken threads, is expressed by the proverb "*Ka Phok tkut lot poh* (in Nongtalang dialect). It indicates that like a kite with broken thread, a woman without control or guidance is aimless and cannot perform desired roles.

In traditional Khasi domain, some of the gender roles are very much segregated and the infringement is not expected. The proverb "*Kynih ka 'iarkynthei u shynrang u kha pylleng*" says that "the hen crows while the rooster lays an egg." This is an act against universal truth and nature which cannot be accepted. Likewise, there are certain roles to be performed only by men, and the alternate way is not possible. Khasi verses "*haba kynih ka 'iar kynthei Ia jot ka pyrthei,*" indicates that when the hen starts crowing, the world is heading for disaster. The crowing of the rooster is a very significantly fixed symbol which connotes activities associated exclusively with males. Women are debarred from participating in the highly traditional system of governance such as *Ka Dorbar Hima, Ka Dorbar Raid,* and *Ka Dorbar Shnong.* These are different councils governing the corporate life of the Khasis. In fact, there is a belief that only those with mustache are allowed to participate in the meeting of these councils. In a traditional domain, women are also not encouraged to speak about own qualities or speak too much. Such behaviour of women is seen as an indication of her being actually lack of qualities. The proverb "*U Phiang uba thylli u sawa jam*" says that the empty bronze pot (called *Phiang,* which is kept in Khasi kitchen) sounds the loudest.

Matriliny and authority over valued resources

Khasi matriliny and women's authority over valued resources, material and non-material, are important issues to be delineated while discussing gender relations among them. There is no denying fact that the very basic of Khasi matriliny is reflected in their proverb "*Long jaid na ka kynthei*" which literally means–from women sprung the clan (*jaid/jait* = clan). This indicates that giving birth to children is important to continue the clan. Failure to procreate is a serious concern to the woman as well as to the clan and family. The ancestress is believed to be the great-grandmother bound by the shared sentiment of genealogically connected, joint land ownership etc.

Khasi matriliny is perceived with an unquestionable attachment of daughters with the inheritance of parental property, leading to, along with other advantages, upper hand of women in the economic domain. It is also believed that being authorised to control over property; the Khasi women are in a better position to control the family and her husband. But a critical evaluation of those structural components indicates that everything is not within the comfort zone for the Khasi women.

Matriliny and burden of responsibility on women

Khasi women's right to inheritance of parental property and their responsibility to keep family tradition intact has been seen as a positive indicator towards women's better position and empowerment in laymen's view. But there are several issues to be considered before one can make any such comment.

Among the Khasi, the youngest daughter only inherits the largest part of the parental property. The youngest daughter is called *Khadduh.* She has the responsibility to maintain the parental property, custom, and religion, provide shelter and support to brothers and sisters in distress. She cannot take any decision alone related to the entire family. She is actually the custodian, not the owner of the parental property as such. The mother's brothers are always there as a norm to take noting of her duties to perform. She cannot dispose of the parental property. She has always been dictated by men—as a maternal uncle, a husband etc.

The *khatduh* holds the ancestral property as a custodian but is not supposed to sell it. If she wishes to sell she would require the permission of her siblings and her maternal uncle/s. When a daughter other than khatduh marries, she and her husband move out into a new home built on land given by the community (*Raij*). The couple and their children owned the land as long as they lived and cultivated on it. There was no concept of ownership of land until recent years. In any case, the land was not a commodity, just a space to have a homestead on and grow food. No one amassed so much wealth as to stand out in society.

The *khatduh* must look after her parents as long as they are alive. Her unmarried brothers also live under the same roof. If any of her nieces or nephews are orphaned it is the *khatduh* who must care for them. If her brothers divorce their wives or vice versa they come back to the *'iing khatduh'* or parental home. Along with the inheritance of property, the *khatduh* also carries overwhelming responsibilities including loss of social mobility. If she wishes, she cannot sell or dispose the property at her own decision. Her uncle, brothers and sisters' consent is needed to do it.

Not all Khasi clans or families are wealthy. Not all Khasis own property enough to distribute to all the daughters, with the larger share going to the youngest daughter (*khatduh).* On the flip side, there are many instances when the youngest daughter *(khatduh)* is bereft of any property because her parents did not own property. Some families are too poor to even keep body and soul together.

Status and responsibility of a Khasi mother

In Khasi traditional domain, mother nurtures the child during its incubation. Father provides the structure and form– "*U kpa Uba ai ia ka long rynieng*". The mother contributes flesh and blood to the child– "*ka kmie ka ba ai ia abh ka snam*". Khasis hardly say about the contribution of semen (male's contribution). They say it negatively when a father is unable to fulfill his parental responsibility towards his children– "What can you do? After all, it is only pus" (*sa ia ka ksuit plin leh kumno*). Semen is treated as "pus" which could be drained out of one's body–but, flesh and blood cannot, which is given by the mother. As blood is transmitted from mother to child and it is this blood bond on which the descent principle is based and the clans are formed, women are seen at the centre of family and clan formation. This is because; the father gives only drainable "pus" to his children and retains his blood with him, unlike a woman. Thus, as women are central to reproduction and family life, she is the repository of the family cycle–so, a daughter should be chaste, obedient, polite and virtuous to continue the family honour and family tradition. She should also be the custodian of family rituals. This certainly burdens the daughters to be cautious in selecting their life partner, maintaining the conduct of family and life, curtailing the freedom of a daughter to a great extent.

Men's superiority over women

The gender-segregated nature of responsibility among Khasi leads to an undeniable perception of gender role and status of Khasi people. This is due to the fact that women as the custodian to Khasi clan and society need protection and be guarded by men. While women's contribution to reproduction and her nurture favours her to her children, men's physical and psychological strength give him authority over women. Traditional Khasi proverb says "a man has twelve strengths"- so he is the protector and provider while women are seen as nurturer and holder.

Khasi perceive that the father brings along with him the seed critical for the genesis of life and continuity of the family and the clan. He also brings bread and luck–*ka kamai kajih bad ka lok ka rwiang* – to sustain the family. Khasi saying– "*u kpa u ba ai ia ka long rynieng; u ba kit ia ka khia ka shan*" reveals that the father not only gives structure and form but also bears the heat and burden of the day to provide for the needs of his children.

Khasi believes that such contribution cannot be repaid or returned. Khasi metaphorically expresses the arrival of the father in his conjugal family like accepting rice/ bring rice, because the father is seen as a provider in economic front, as well as a biologically important agent in procreation which is irreversible and cannot be paid back. This notion is reflected in their social action when they disfavour patrilineal cross-cousin marriage of a man to the clan from where his father had come. Khasi refers to a phrase *ai khaw kylliang* (exchange of rice) to indicate the act when a man marries into a family from which his father had come from. For Khasi, this type of relationship is not acceptable.

There are strong social indicators which show that women are held to be inferior to men. The superiority of Khasi men in their perception can be found in the term they use to describe an adult man- *u rangbah*. The term is the combination of two words–*rang* from a complete word *shynrang* meaning man and *bah* which means bear or carry on the back. Thus, the word *rangbah* denotes man as a powerful being infused with high moral integrity and the physical and mental ability to shoulder the multiple responsibilities of society. Women are seen to be physiologically and mentally weaker than man, requiring men's guidance and protection–from mother's brother and brother and husband and father. They are also excluded from important areas of decision-making both within the family and society at large.

There are numbers of gendered terms and phrases in Khasi vocabulary which symbolise the unequal power relations between males and the females. The most widely used phrase talks about the superior male power over female–*u rangbah khaddar bor; ka kynthei snibor*-meaning a man has 12 units of power/ energy; a woman has only one unit. Likewise, to express the superior physiological and intellectual power of men over women they say–*ka kynthei; ka khynnah*, meaning the woman, the children, thus analogically equates women with children.

There are also proverbs that talks of superior position of men in Khasi society. One of such proverbs says

"Rice obtained at the pothead belongs to man, No matter who;
A woman should restrain from a helping, lest the world be confounded."

The above proverb is to teach the manner of respecting male members in the family. The top portion of the rice pot is reserved exclusively for men and it is implied that only when he has eaten, the rest of the family may follow suit. This is a symbolic manner in which respect is shown. Some households still keep aside the first scoop of rice from the pot for men especially in the evening when family members use to eat together.

Men in the Khasi family/society have a respectable position as the father in their wife's house and as uncles in their sister's house. The responsibilities are dual in nature and this trait is intrinsic to the matrilineal system followed by the Khasis. An adage among Khasi says:

"Father the provider,
Maternal uncle, the ceremony keeper."

The factors delineated above work as guiding principles for the formation of gender ideology among the Khasi people and women internalise such ideas through the process of engenderment. Needless to say that the common people see the immediate reasons for male superiority in terms of economic security, social support and social security, social status and such other day-to-day related aspects.

Khasi women as the victim of matriliny

Khasi gender role supports domestication of women and exclusion of women from political domain. A woman who dares to voice her opinion on public affairs is regarded as a "hen that crows"– a freak of nature. There is a story among the Khasi which talks about a roster who could persuade the Sun goddess to cast her light on Earth and he was given the privilege that only he would warn people by crowing about the advent of sunlight to earth every dawn.

It is also perceived that due to the dual duty of a Khasi man (duty in wife's and his sisters' family) a Khasi woman is never fully assured that her husband does not find his sister's home a more congenial place than her own house. Similarly, a sister may suspect her brothers' attraction towards her children as he is also responsible towards his own children and wife. Thus, women in both cases are seen as a negative entity–as a wife for a sister and a sister for a wife who attracts the males and divides the attention this way. The traditional Khasi proverb "*ka nongpah ka nongphon*" says that a woman is "a charmer as well as a schemer" because she attracts a man by offering something interesting (here the relationship) away from their relatives and kin–either using sexuality or charm.

Such role conflict affects women more adversely. If a man fails to meet his conjugal (avuncular) obligation, his wife is held responsible for it. Not the man. There is leniency towards men in Khasi society. This is seen when the only woman is held responsible for a man's inability to fulfill his duty towards matrilineal kin. Also, a polygamous male is often regarded as powerful one–by saying "so what? He is a man of means......", a man with many flags (if he has children from several women). A man can go back to his maternal home and his sister is bound to give him shelter, whereas, when he leaves behind his children and wife–the wife has to take all the responsibility left behind by him. But, if a woman neglects her duty towards maternal home, she loses her share. Thus, a Khasi woman has to accumulate wealth, property and resources to support her children and sometimes her brothers and sisters, in case they come back from their conjugal family. She has to fulfill the duties failed to perform by her brothers and sisters and also by her husband. This shows that Khasi matriliny does not favour women in an actual sense. It is a token authority.

In traditional Khasi domain, marriage generates conflicts between the husband and his wife's brothers. Here, kin loyalties are emphasised at the expense of affinal ties. This is because Khasi makes a sharp distinction between kin and affine. By laying stress on kin solidarity the Khasi even play down the marital tie. Khasi perceives it to be a sign of weakness on the part of a Khasi man to lose his command over his wife in terms of fulfilling his duty towards his natal kin. So, if he has to ignore his affinal duties, he can justify his act by saying– "*sa ia ka kynthei*" meaning "it is only a woman". The traditional arrangement of control of mother's brother has been reduced a lot among present-day Christian Khasi, where the husband/father takes the central position as the controller of the family.

An elder daughter, who does not get the parental property, has to rely on her own resources and her husband's income and resources. This is the case especially for the daughters in between. Compared to youngest daughter, the elder daughters have more autonomy. In the event of the daughter not inheriting the ancestral property, the authority of mother's brother remains limited. But it increases her dependence on her husband. As the children belong to the mother, only a few men consider it necessary to provide for their maintenance once marriage to the woman is terminated. Men's permanent right in their natal *ing* not only infringes upon their conjugal role but also provides ample scope for the callous to neglect their parental duties. Besides, there is no access to free or easy legal aid cell for such divorced women to fight for maintenance from their respective husbands. Men's dual responsibility and advantageous position makes women vulnerable to social and economic risks and deprives her of protection and support of both mother's brother and husband. This necessitates the Khasi women to be active players in the production process. In the event of the dissolution of their marriage, or failure of the brother to extend support, it is the women who have to provide for the family.

Khasi mythology and portrayal of women figure

The Khasi mythology of the origin of Khasi talks about the seven clans or seven huts. According to a mythological story, the supreme God *U Blei* created *Ramew*, a female figure who is the guardian spirit of the Earth and *Basa*, *Remew*'s husband who is seen as the patron god of villages. Both prayed to god for children. By the grace of the god, they gave birth to five children who were bestowed with divine power. *Ka Sngi*, the Sun was their first child, a daughter, followed by only son *U Bnai* as the Moon who was followed by three daughter water, wind and fire. Being the youngest daughter, Fire's duty was to be at home, cook a meal, fulfill daily needs and follow customs of the domain. *Ramew*, the guardian spirit of the earth prayed *U Blei* that there should be someone to give direction and control the powers of her great powerful daughters–wind, fire, and water.

Till this part of the legend indicates that female figures have been assigned with a relentless commitment to serving others and while the elder daughters could go as they wish, the youngest one had to accept the burden of the family and custom. Furthermore, the story also reminds the fact the power and strength of females must be controlled and guided by male figures in one or the other identity. Tradition equates the female with the sun (*ka sngi*) as she is warm and provides light, two things very important for the Khasis. Their theory of creation is full of anecdotes of the terrible darkness that engulfs the earth if *ka sngi* is offended. In Khasi tradition water, air and Fire are believed to be generated from female goddesses. The story of *Ka Ngot* and *Ka Iam* reveals these two goddesses transformed to two water bodies to reach the plains from hills in a competition between them.

Re-marriage (especially widows) is never seen as a good option by many societies. Traditional Khasi domain very often reminds widow, who wants to get married, of the story of–*Ka Likai*. The story talks about a woman *ka Likai* in Rangjir teh village, who had a daughter. She lost her lovable husband. As her daughter was young she remarried to a man for the security of her daughter as well as for herself. The new husband was selfish and was jealous of his stepdaughter as his wife used to pay more attention to her. One day when *Ka Likai* was out of home for some work, the stepfather killed the little girl, cooked her flesh and served her mother when she came back home. *Ka Likai* saw her daughter's chopped hands in the basket of betel nut and realised what had happened. In great distress and sorrow, she jumped down the hill with a loud cry. Falling down deep she turned in to a waterfall with endless cries (sound) of sorrow. People say "*remember Ka-Likai*" if they want to warn any widow attempting remarriage. A recent study by the author of this chapter finds that there is several instances of abusive incidents, even sexual exploitation, perpetrated by the step-fathers on step-daughters. This justifies the legend and worry of Khasi women over widow marriage.

Traditional Khasi society usually does not favour marital relation with unknown or non-Khasi people. They tend to refer to a story to reveal the probable risk of such relation. Symbolically this is a story of a dove–*ka paro* and another bird *U Jylleit*. The beautiful bird *U Jylleit* used to come to the place where the dove *Ka Paro* lived. There were full of juicy barriers all over and *U jylleit* used to come here every day and fell in love with the dove. The dove also got attracted by the beauty and good behaviour of *U jylleit*. As the season changed and the barriers got over, *U jylleit* stopped coming there. Khasi parents thus warn their daughter not to fell in love traps of an outsider whose primary aim is to extract or get benefit from resources the Khasi women have. This very traditional folktale has also found its place in Khasi ethnicity and ethnic awareness and protection of Khasi identity when they restrict Khasi women from getting married to non-Khasis. There has been a state law on descent rule as who should be identified as real Khasi.

Traditional Khasi domain also talks about the consequences a lazy woman has to face. The duty of a woman cannot be substituted by her beauty. The legend of *ka Panshandi* (the Tortoise) talks of a beautiful female tortoise that was lazy. She got married to the brightest star *U Lurmangkhara* of the heaven as she was beautiful. Once her laziness was saturated for her husband, he went back to sky leaving her alone on the earth. Till date, traditional Khasi domain warns lazy women with the ballades of *ka Panshandi*. A forsaken wife who entertains the hope of her husband's return is linked by the Khasi to Ka Panshandi– "*ka Panshandi dem-Lorkhah*".

All these folk narratives have great influence on Khasi tradition. Some of these stories are inseparably attached to the very core of Khasi belief system and cosmology and ethnic beings. Others are invariably used as proverbs and stories to remind people of good and bad consequences of certain acts. These stories mostly seem to be a reference to females as an issue of social sanction, normative guideline and sometimes as reminders of consequences of certain acts.

Khasi ethno-politics and gender aspects

Khasi matriliny and status of Khasi women in terms of power, authority and autonomy have been, to a great extent, influenced by ethnopolitics of the Khasi domain, and also by the movement for establishing a patriarchal tradition in place of matriliny.

In a broader perspective, the Khasi women are also directly and indirectly influenced by the "Khasi custom of lineage Bill, 1997" propagated by the Khasi Hills Autonomous District Council (KHADC), and the "Meghalaya Succession to self-Acquired Property Act, 1984 (Khasi and Jaintia Special Provision). One of the major underpinnings of the Bill was the extension of colonial administration to the Khasi Hills which resulted into the advent of Christianity and education among the Khasi people.

Khasi matriliny tradition makes it possible the entry of non-Khasi elements very easily. While Khasi men marry non-Khasi women, she establishes a new clan as the Khasi husband cannot give his clan name to his children. It makes the Khasi ethnic boundary porous enough. In case, the Khasi woman marries a non-Khasi man, there is no need to search for new identity as the women give their clan name to children and the husband's contribution in reproduction is perceived to be negligible and unaccounted for. Thus, both culturally and biologically the Khasi society has been open for inclusion of non-Khasi elements.

Movement for a separate state Meghalaya gave rise to new ideological and political thinking and a new awareness about the signification of one's cultural identity. Re-organisation of Khasi hills as a separate state, assertion of Khasis as a distinct ethnic group, necessitated the maintaining its identity and purity which lead to the introduction of the Lineage Bill. The Bill was meant to restrict the erosion of Khasi socio-cultural life owing to its matrilineal system. The Bill states that the legislation is meant for the protection of Khasi's interest and to prevent claims of Khasi status by unscrupulous persons for the benefit, concession or privileges conferred on the Khasis. People resented the idea of membership of offspring of Khasi mother to non-Khasi father. Several organisations opined that such an arrangement would make Khasi society vulnerable, a threat to ethnic identity, danger to the economy etc. Such offspring tend to be termed as impure or "half-breed".

As matriliny is closely associated with the institution of *Kur* (clan), and as clans sprung up from women only, thus maintaining clan and controlling the purity of clan becomes an important aspect which ultimately gives rise to the need to control women's reproduction/ sexuality domain. This was reflected in the demand put forwarded by some organisation to dispossess women married to non-Khasi men and their children of Khasi identity and all rights associated with it.

Such demand was catalysed by the Khasi Hills Autonomous District Council (KHADC) adoption of the Khasi customs of Lineage Bill in 1997. This Bill was subsequently transformed into an Act in 2005–Khasi Hills Autonomous District (Khasi custom of Lineage) Act, 1997. The most contentious issue of the Act was regarding the recognition of offspring born out of a union between a Khasi mother and a non-Khasi father. This was not simply a question of intermarriage between Khasi and non-Khasi in that in case of offspring of a Khasi father and a non-Khasi mother, there was hardly any contention of its Khasi origin or purity of blood. Thus, Khasi women are seen as the property of Khasi community. It is believed that recognising children born of a non-Khasi father as Khasi would encourage the proliferation of inter-ethnic marriage and pose grave demographic and economic risks to Khasi society as well. It also endangered their ethnic identity. Such offspring tend to be termed as "Half Breed" or of impure blood.

This controversy also shows the fundamentalist view of male dominance in Khasi society contending the matrilineal system where women are seen as descent producers. It targets only women who marry outside Khasi society but leaves men who marry non-Khasis. In the name of pure blood

(Khasi Pakka) and ethnic purity, the rights of those Khasi women are violated. It also propagates the idea that a woman who marries to non-Khasi men are unpatriotic devoid of any sentiment or attachment to their culture and traditions.

Khasi women's subordinate position may also be attributed to the men's struggle for political domination. Internally, the male domain of Khasi took the opportunity in the process of decolonisation and economic development, the struggle for political autonomy rise of ethnic politics whereby it sharpened the vulnerability of women. Controlling women in the disguise of ethnic identity and custom and tradition became a strategy for the male domain. State politics largely reflect men's interest. Women's marginal position in the political process helped men in this regard. The commissions, councils etc were devoid of women representatives. Also, there was hardly any contention raised by any women against such anti-women reports and Acts.

Meghalaya state Assembly has 60 seats and elections have been held since the year 1972. The record of elected members since the year 1972 thru the year 2013 reveals that there have been only 11 women elected members in the state assembly all through these years as against 409 male elected members. Thus, the average percentage of women MLAs in Meghalaya state assembly is 2.62 only as against 97.38 per cent male MLAs. This is indeed a quite unexpected figure if we look matriliny as a favourable social system for women.

Besides, there is Khasi Hills Autonomous Council in Meghalaya under the Sixth Schedule arrangement of the constitution. Members of this Autonomous Council are elected as well as selected (nominated). If we look at the list of elected and selected members all through the years since its inception in the year 1952, we can find that the representation of women is in this local body is also very poor. There is 10 women representative so far elected to the KHADC since its inception against the total 235 male, representatives over the years. Thus, by percentage share, the male constitute the 96 per cent of the total members of the KHADC till date while women constitute only 4 per cent of it. Owing to the fact that Autonomous district councils are tribal dominated arrangements it becomes very difficult to see lack of adequate representation of Khasi women in it.

Patriarchy and gender sub-ordination among Khasi women: The interlinks

Khasi traditional domain is full of instances of male dominance amidst a matrilineal arrangement. Men represent the family in extra-domestic issues.

Men are viewed as protector and provider (of living and security). The women's importance in the society is limited to childbearing, to continue the clan and family and to take care of the children and family. A woman's life is always guarded and/or guided either through maternal uncle or through the husband, mostly by both. It is important to assert here that link to Khasi gender ideology to their cosmology and myth with a host of oral literature make gender difference deeply embedded in the core of the Khasi society. The practice of matriliny makes them easily visible in the gender division of labour, gender role performance and there is hardly any option for women to defy those gender-specific norms, current in the society. This certainly has created a context of gender stereotype among Khasi. It is well-accepted fact that it is hard or difficult to shed off the stereotyped gender ideology from a society due to the fact that gender aspects are intimately related to almost all spears of social life.

A detailed study was conducted among the Khasi recently locating violence against women within gender system. The issues of gender subordination and subsequent violence against women were analysed using three different perspectives—Historical materialism, Gender ideology and gender division of labour and Patriarchal discourses. For the purpose of the present chapter, a part of the patriarchal discourse in analysing gender subordination among Khasi women has been delineated in the following paragraphs. While some of the components of the following analysis have already been discussed in foregoing paragraphs, some others have been mentioned in brief for the want of the issues to be explained.

Gender role socialisation and masculine mystique

Inculcating maleness by acquiring components or by internalising ideologies present in the society is an important aspect of male's engendered to the masculine mystique. The ideological superiority of masculine identity among Khasi men and submissive and compliance nature of Khasi women takes shape from various traditional components inherent in their culture. Some of such components have been discussed in the foregoing paragraphs.

Power conflicts

Surrounded by patrilineal society, the matrilineal Khasi domain is said to be infested with power conflict between males and females. The conversation between *"Ki Ksiang"* (Marriage spokesman) of both bride and groom parties reveals the traditional arrangement of understanding of the roles and duties of both husband and wife. It indicates that the husband enters wife's house as a temporary person as he knows he has no place in wife's ritualistic events and in the clan. The husband agrees to perform his duty as a husband and it is the duty of the wife and her clan to orient him into their family tradition.

Contrarily, the wife wants him to be good, honest and free from all liabilities, from his natal clan. For the wife, the husband must agree to seek, find and bring in wealth to the wife's family. She also spells out her right to receive, to serve and to own whatever the husband earns. The wife accepts that she is weak, imperfect and incomplete to procreate children alone. So, she looks for help from the husband for begetting children and grandchildren. A Khasi man, by tradition, cannot possess wealth whatever he earns after marriage is normally owned by his wife. He does all hard work, invests his biological content in procreation. But he cannot own anything socially. While his wealth is owned by his wife, children are guided by their maternal uncle in a traditional setting. In case he breaks the marriage tie, children remain with the mother. He goes back empty-handed to his natal family.

A man's higher position in the extra-familial domain is just contrary to his position inside the family domain. In last few decades, there have been lots of changes occurring in Khasi domain. There has been shrinking of traditional resources (Inheritable through the female line) like land and forest ultimately affecting women's traditional resource base. In case of women not inheriting meaningful resources for livelihood, they have to acquire it or depend on husband's earning solely. Introduction of the capitalist market, the monetary economy has shifted the economic pursuits from traditional to the non-traditional base where Khasi women are not equally adept with. Thus, there are several conflicting situations emerging in Khasi society. Especially, couples having no inherited and/or traditional resource base and where the husband is the sole providing, he finds it difficult or contrasting to follow matrilineal arrangement in terms of ownership of his earning, custody of his children and interference of maternal king in his marital family.

Khasi women's socially assigned authority over resources and wealth and Khasi husband's relative exclusion from family and clan-based rituals, etc, creates a feeling of otherness and lack of belonging among some of Khasi husbands. During the studies, several Khasi women expressed their dominant views in terms of running the family, authority over the domestic domain and commented on husband's relative powerlessness. There have been opinions that such mismatch between social system and changing the context of the situation leads to conflict and men resorted to alcohol and drugs ultimately resulting into domestic violence and separation. Divorced and deserted cases have been reported to be relatively high among Khasis.

Distorted gender role scheme

Among the Khasis, gender social definition has been clearly defined in their traditional domain through mythological stories, proverbs, folklore etc. The roles of males and females are well demarcated in between domestic and extra-domestic domain. Thus, there is very little scope for men to inculcate any characters as males' characters beyond already socially defined characters and duties etc. Likewise, there is hardly any scope for men to imbibe any female characters because roles of females are well demarcated and men hardly venture into it. But, there is contention and conflict in positioning males in male's domain, especially while the Khasi domain is infested with patriarchal surroundings. A lot of key informant and respondents in interview reveal that gambling, indulging in alcohol and affair with women other than the wife remains primary reasons for conflict, violence, and separation between Khasi couples.

Based on gender social definition, Khasi men try to rule over women in every sphere of life. But, the matrilineal arrangement gives some upper hand to Khasi women to involve in controlling over valued resources and earning whereby some husbands feel inferior to wife. Women with superior resource power (Material) might tend to involve or behave at par or more with husband. Power of conflict arises here if the husband is relatively resourceless or has lesser resources. There is a conflict between ideological and actual power in managing household and decision-making in the family. In case of a resourceless or feeble husband, the conflict of power emerges more in extent. Further, this power conflict leads to insecurity in the masculine self of the husband because he is unable to perform or exhibit his maleness he is expected to as per social norm. In certain cases, a husband may abuse his power, or sometimes, the wife and her maternal kin may do so, which make the husband further insecure and worthless (as perceived). At this stage, a husband may be abusive verbally and try to defend his wounded masculinity by means of denying, falsifying the situation, etc. Once this defense mechanism of the husband breaks down or he becomes unable to guard his wounded masculinity, he picks up even the smallest or otherwise non-issues as triggering factor and resort to physical violence towards women.

It is quite justified that the wife of such feeble husband protest or blames him for his inability, which might be a case for husband's indulging in drinking. Further, several cases have revealed that abusive husbands also keep extra-marital relations to a certain extent. Men see it as a masculine advantage. But, a wife's protest and interference in husband's joyride challenges males gender superiority and he feels threatened and in case he is unable to cope up, his masculinity is wounded. These are the primary reasons for males' violence against women in the domestic sphere.

Accepting violence as normative incidents or living with violence with protest or resistance by Khasi women indicates their compulsion–sometimes related to women's resourcelessness for survival, for the children's future or for escaping from further violence. Another very important aspect in terms of accepting and living with or being nonresponsive to violence is related to upbringing of Khasi women in the Matrilineal structure of Khasi society. By tradition, Khasi women carry the notion of pride of being a mother and little they are worried about the bringing up of their children and run her family in case her husband fails to perform his duty as a husband and as a father. When she is resourceful she accepts the upbringing of children and running the family as her duty. The cases collected and interviews conducted reveal that Khasi women are least concerned about maintenance to be provided by their deserting husbands. They do not like to look for maintenance like a beggar. Another important aspect related to violence women is that keeping the family in order is seen as the responsibility of a woman. Thus, a failed relationship is indicative of a woman's inability to carry out her assigned duty. Further, for Khasi women, it is also an awkward situation to accept the fact that she has been abused in her own place by a person who comes from outside. It is quite hard for her to digest it. But reporting such incidents, in turn, expresses her poor situation which she never wants to be. Thus, at best she would keep silent about domestic violence to the extent she could tolerate or endure. This explains why cases of domestic violence hardly get reported until it is grave cases of rape and cruelty.

It is quite important to note that advent of education, exposure to the patriarchal social system (especially Christianity), and capital market based monetary economy has affected Khasi matrilineal system to a great extent. While Khasi males encounter with the mismatch between women's authority over resources in the traditional Khasi world and the requirement of male-centric socio-economic arrangement outside world, Khasi women find it difficult to cope-up with new diverse requirements and challenges to survival, the upbringing of children and social security. The male-centric micro-level social domain is to a great extent, hostile and uncongenial to the female-centric matrilineal arrangement. In short, the issue of violence against women among the Khasis has a link between much localised to broader aspects of tradition, gender and political economy rooted in their ethnohistory. In this entire discourse, there has been very limited scope where the Khasi women may be portrait as an entity with higher status in the real sense. The world of Khasi women is the world of subordination and submission and compliance under the hyped umbrella of "Matriliny".

Conclusion

Anthropology of women has a long way to go, especially in northeast India, which is said to be a paradise of Anthropological study. The anthropological tradition in this region is still burdened with the conventional legacy of anthropological traditions. The national level data available with the NFHS, National Sample Survey etc are mostly lack of important components inherent in tribal societies. The structural and contextual components of gender ideologies and gender relations including patriarchal arrangements are essential areas to venture in to. The understanding about the interlinks and interactions of such components are the pre-requisite for policy planning for development and welfare of tribal women in the areas of health, education, income generation and social and political empowerment as well.

Acknowledgements

The author acknowledges the insights taken from writings of Tilput Nongbri, T. Nongsiej, Khynpham Sing Nongkynrih, Esther Syiem and Celine Augustine.

References

Amy J. Marin and J. Nancy F. Russo. 1999. 'Feminist perspective on male violence against women.' In Michele Harway and James M. O'Neil (Eds), *What Causes Men's Violence against Women?* pp. 18-35, London; Sage Publications Inc.

Bell, D. 1980. 'Desert politics: Choices in the marriage market'. In M Etienne and EB. Leacock (Eds.); *Women and Colonisation*. pp. 239-269. New York; Bergin and Garvey.

Engels, Frederick. 1972. [1884] *The Origin of the Family, Private Property, and the State*. New York; International Publishers.

Johan Galtung. 1990. 'Cultural violence'. *Journal of Peace Research*, 27 (3): 291-305.

Kabery, Phyllis. 1939. *Aboriginal Women: Sacred and Profane*. London; Rutledge and Kegan Paul.

Keane, J. 1996. *Reections on Violence*. Verso: London.

Leacock, Eleanor B. 1972. 'Introduction.' In Frederick Engels, *The Origin of the Family, Private Property, and the State*. New York; International Publishers.

Leacock, Eleanor B. 1978. 'Women's status in egalitarian society: implications for social evolution'. *Current Anthropology*, 19 (2): 247-275.

Maria Barbara and Watson Franke. 1985. 'Production and the status of women: An anthropological interpretation of historical materialism.' *Anthropos*, Bd. 80, H. 1(3): 1-14.

Moore, Henrietta L. 1988. *Feminism and Anthropology*. University of Minnesota Press.

Sacks, Karen. 1979. *Sisters and Wives: The Past and Future of Sexual Equality*. Westport, Conn.: Greenwood Press.

Sanday, Peggy R. 1973. 'Toward a theory of the status of women.' *American Anthropologist* 75: 1682-1700.

Sanday, Peggy R. 1981. *Female Power and Male Dominance: On the Origins of Sexual Inequality*. Cambridge; Cambridge University Press.

Shirley Ardener, 1975. *Perceiving Women*. Malaby Press.

Chapter - 15

Life in Melody: The Musical World of the Garo

—Geetika Ranjan and Pynshailang Dohling

Introduction

Music soothes the soul (Bernstein, 2005) and is a powerful medium of expression; expression of hope, despair, love, loss, worldview etc., endless emotions which make up the creature called man. Music can also produce emotion in the listeners. The distinction between perception and production is related to the distinction between cognitivism and emotivism proposed by philosophers in their analysis of emotion in music (Scherer and Zenter, 2001:361).

Music among the tribes

Music has a universal appeal. Each culture is exclusive. Yet what transcends border differences between people is music. Tribal societies are marked by a conspicuous element of shared living. In the same vein, 'music amongst tribals is not conceived as an exclusive property of its individual members, but of the community as a whole. For this very reason, tribal music even if framed by individual composers remains anonymous' (http://www.indianetzone.com/37/indian_tribal_music.htm). However, this statement stands true for the music composed in the remote past. Now, as we shall see in the following pages, the composers are not anonymous, rather, they are known individuals who are carrying forward the legacy of Garo traditional music by composing songs and training their children to take the tradition forward.

Tribal music is context based and reveals the historical, ecological and cultural background of the community. In a very interesting work, 'Three Perspectives on Music and the Idea of Tribe in India', Wolf (2000), discusses three ethno musicological approaches to the idea of tribe in India:

(i) the " popular representational" approach-that is, to study a tribe or tribes from their representations in Indian popular media and academic writing; (ii) the "on the ground" approach-to study the idea of tribe by investigating the concepts and categories used by a present day mixture of people living in a multi-ethnic setting; and (iii) the "synthetic ethno musicological" approach to study tribal music by discovering to what extent the many musical traditions across India that we call tribal share elements of style or structure, and to assess the significance of these common elements (page 5). Such perspectives help in garnering the dynamics in the world of tribal music.

The Garo

Garo is a tribe predominantly living in Meghalaya. They are also found in some parts of Bangladesh. The state of Meghalaya is the abode of three main tribes-Khasi, Jaintia, and Garo. Garo also known as the A'chiks (people of the hills), trace their roots from Tibet and belong to the Tibeto-Burman stock.

The present chapter deals with the musical world of the Garo both primary and secondary sources have been consulted to understand the place of music among the Garo. Music among the Garo informs that music is embedded in practically every aspect of Garo life, mirroring the Garo joy during festivals, pain on death, faith in religion, and as a daily entertainment in leisure.

Colour to songs and dances are added by musical instruments. Despite the technical advancements witnessed in the arena of musical gadgets, there is no beating the melody, the earthy essence and the accompanying nostalgia that accompanies the traditional instruments of a community.

Garo musical instruments

Christianity brought in many changes in the way of life of the Garo and practically every sphere of their lives saw an alteration including music. Western music is a passion among the Garo youth. At the same time, the Garo are firmly rooted in their culture and its heritage. Alva Sangma, the editor of *Achik Songbad*, a Garo weekly, say's "We Garos are tuned into world music and culture. But outsiders do not know how attached we are to our culture. We may not continue to live in traditional wooden houses, but we know our dances and our culture." (The Hindu, November 24, 2012).

Songs in Garo accompanied by their musical instruments continue to enthrall the Garo. Despite the popular usage of the guitar, the Garo continue to enjoy using their traditional musical instruments and their penchant for music leads them to innovate fusion music, a nice blend of the traditional Garo music and the music of thc current times.

The gifts of nature-bamboo, cane, wood, metal and animal skin constitute the material to make the Garo traditional instruments. Cymbals (*kakwa*), gongs (*rangs*), flutes (*bangsi*) such as *Illep, Dakok, Otekra, Olongma* etc., string instruments such as *Sarenda*, *Chigring*, *Dimchrang* or *Kimjim*, *Gonggina*, etc. and instruments made out of the skin of animals, like, drum and its variants, *Dama, Kram, Nagra,* etc. are the most common instruments made and played by the Garo.

Dama (drum)

This is the most indispensable instrument used by the Garos particularly during *Wangala, Ahaia* and *Agalmaka* festivals. It reminds of the days of the *Nokpante* i.e. bachelor's house among the Garo which was also the training ground of the youth in their enculturation into Garo music. *Nokpantes* resounded with Garo music as the youth their practiced the songs and dances.

Dama is hollowed out wood and the cow's skin is stretched out on the frame on its two ends. *Mildang*-it's a long drum with one end wider than the other and made out of hollow tree bark or baked mud (Chand *et al.*, 1999).

Chigring (string instrument)

It is a long instrument made from bamboo. It has three strings each on either side of the bamboo shaft. It is played by rhythmically beating sticks on the strings. It was earlier used as the main instrument during *Wangala* festival but later the *Dama* became more popular out of sheer vigour and enthusiasm which the latter generates. *Chingring* is an instrument accompanying folk songs of merry-making and songs sung during harvest. It has a very wide range which is best manifested when played by one who is skilled in playing it. It is popularly used in *Ajea* and *Doroa*-poetry battles between two people or groups or between a man and a woman. *Ajea* and *Doroa* are poetic rejoinders.

Dimchrang or *Kimjim* (string cum drumming instrument)

It is an instrument made from cane which is used to make the strings as well as the body of the instrument. One side contains five strings and the other side is used for drumming. These are mostly played by the Atongs (a dialect group among the Garo) during funerals and post-funeral and is accompanied by the playing of *Dama*. It is also used as an accompanying instrument to narrate the story about Garo heroes and warriors like the romantic lore of Dikki, Bandi (Dikki's brother) and Giting (Dikki's wife) and another one of Jingjang, the hero, and Ruta, the heroine.

Sarenda (violin-like string instrument)

The body of this instrument is made of wood and its wand is made of bamboo. It is a two-stringed instrument; one string is used for the body and the other for the wand. It is a small sized instrument. In the past, the villagers working in the fields entertained themselves by playing this instrument to break the drudgery of their work.

Chand *et al.* (1999) mention the use of wind instruments such as trumpet or *Adil* and *Bangsi* or flute. *Adil* is made of Buffaloe's horn or any other wild animal's horn. The flute is made out of bamboo.

Bangsi (flute)

During fieldwork, it was observed that flutes are of four types which differ from each other in size and diameter of the tune holes which determine the kind of sound which each type produces. These are as follows:

(i) *Illep*- It is the smallest in size.

(ii) *Dakok*- It is bigger than the *Illep* but smaller than the others.

(iii) *Otekra*- These are of six types and a little bigger than the *Illep* and *Dakok*.

(iv) *Olongma*- This is the largest in the flute family and is of three types.

Gonggina (Oral instrument)

This is a very small instrument made of iron. It is a mouth instrument.

Chand *et al.* (1999) writes in detail about the musical instruments which accompany Garo dances. Among these of very common usage are the gongs and cymbals used by the Garo. *Rang* is a big gong made of brass plate. *Kakwa* or cymbal is also made of brass.

The Garos informed that in the earlier days, drums and flutes were not played while carrying out agricultural activities because the Garos believed that if these were played, the wild beasts would make the farmers their prey. The *Dama, Chigring* and the *Gonggina* are played accompanying songs like *Nomil Dongja Kadingja, Chipe Dongja Sedingja* (No Woman No Smile, No Snakes No Bite).

It's rather interesting to observe the linguistic connection/ borrowing/ in the names of some instruments used by the Garo with those of the non-tribal world. The *mildang* of the Garo is exactly like the *mridang* of Hindustani and Karnatic music. Similarly, the *bangsi* of the Garo is the *bansi* or *bansuri* of the Hindi-speaking belt.

While doing fieldwork among the Garo living in Asanang village, under Rongram block in West Garo Hills, Meghalaya, in January 2016, one of the authors (P.D) elaborates on the profile of some Garo musicians.

Profile of a Garo musician

Ringjeng T. Sangma is a well-known instrumentalist of Garo instruments. He is around 67-70 years of age. Ringjeng can play and make most instruments. He makes the *Dama* (drum), *Dimchrang* (string cum drumming instrument), *Chigring* (stringed instrument), *Kram* (drums used by Nokmas or Headmen), *Bangsi* (all types of flutes), *Sarenda* (violin-like string instrument). He started playing the instruments at a very young age by observing his uncle Siljohn T. Sangma who was a musician-cum manufacturer of musical instruments. As a professional, he started giving performances from 1975-1976. He reminisces about his first performance which was at Shillong in 1975 where he got recognition for his flawless *Sarenda* and flute playing ability. *Sarenda* is his favourite musical instrument and Sangma excels in playing that. On 15th of August 2010 *i.e.*, Independence Day he received a certificate of recognition from Shri Ranjit Mooshahary, the then Governor of Meghalaya. He has travelled widely to different places such as Tura, Shillong, Tripura, Chennai, to give performances. His skill in playing Garo instruments has won him much popularity and appreciation and many music competitions. He was invited by the Don Bosco Museum of Indigenous Cultures at Shillong in 2010 to play the *Dakok* (flute), *Dama* (drum) and *Chigring* (stringed instrument). The museum is well visited by tourists who greatly enjoy Sangma's music video which the museum plays for its visitors. Ringjeng's wife, Sotjak Ch. Sangma is also a musician and accompanies her husband for his performances. She can play the *Chigring* and the *Gonggina*.

Religious music

Impact of Christianity is well evident in the lives of the Garo. The church forms an integral training ground where music and religion blend in harmonious synchrony. The Music Committee of Asanang Baptist Church in Asanang has staffs which are well trained and devoted to church songs. One of them, a former Choir Director from 2009 to 2011 at the mentioned church, Withingstone Ch. Sangma who is about forty years of age, is skilled in playing guitar which he learned following the books while in school. He later learned the tonic-solfa in Shillong. According to Withingstone, the church has a Church Music Committee which is in charge of church music and to teach young individuals of the church to learn church music. The main people involved in the committee are as follows:

(i) Music Convener. (Main person)

(ii) Music Secretary.

(iii) Choir Director.

(iv) Adviser.

(v) Sound System in-charge.

They are devoted to training the youth in church songs who take the music forward by showcasing it during the celebration of festivals and in conferences. Church songs play an instrumental role in imparting hope and conviction to the followers of the church. Withingstone Ch. Sangma is of the opinion that church songs serve as a greater duty towards the Christ as they encourage the adherents to live a 'good' Christian life. For the Garo, Church songs are different from the other songs as the former are divinely ordained. Church teachings are well understood and appreciated when accompanied by music according to Withingstone. Religious music plays a major role in drawing the Church going people more strongly towards the Church and its teachings and this strengthens their faith and conviction to be upright Christian individuals devoted to peace and harmony.

During the period of fieldwork Asanang Church Music Committee organised a Talent Hunt competition on 24th December 2013. The competition was conducted in three zones or groups i.e, Upper Asanang, Middle Asanang and Lower Asanang of the Asanang area. The show drew many young individuals to the event that performed solo as well as group songs. This religious musical event gave a platform to the young to showcase their talents. Beyond the general purpose of the event which was entertainment, lay a deeper goal which was to bring the youth closer to the teachings of the Church.

Withingstone Ch. Sangma during his tenure as a Choir Director had composed two Garo choir songs and these are as follows:

(i) *Kristoni Mondoli*- This translates to 'Church of Christ'. Withingstone arranged the music as well as the lyrics himself.

(ii) *Re·na Hai Ja·kusan*- This translates to 'Walk Together'. For this, he arranged only the music.

Holy Spirit Power Conference

In Garo Hills, church festivals and conferences are quite common. One such conference The Holy Spirit Power Conference was organised at Asanang by the Full Gospel Fellowship Church (FGF) of Garo Hills. The invited speaker of the conference came from Nigeria, Africa. The conference took place from the 8th to 11th of January 2015.

This event showcased the importance of religion and how prayer blending with dance and music, can move the people towards higher spiritual goals. Songs in praise of the almighty were performed by trained bands of Garo youths.

Other genres of music among the Garo

The Garo come across as people who have retained their folk music culture by blending it well with western music and this kind of music is very popular among them. There are many music bands in Garo Hills who incorporate Garo lyrics with rock music. Apart from this form, another form of music is one where the Garo folk songs are performed against the backdrop of rock music. In this kind of music, there is heavy usage of different guitars (rhythm, lead, and bass guitars) and drums. Sometimes keyboards are also included. One of the present exponents of this form of music in Asanang is Dicky N. Sangma. He is about 40 years of age. He informs the decade of the 1980s and early 1990s was a period which can be called a period of revolution and revival of Garo music. The Garo youth, while being drawn towards western and other forms of music, was simultaneously getting awakened to the need to revolutionise the traditional Garo folk music. Many music bands came up who became very popular among the youth. Some of these such as Rip Rap, Rough Road, Hidden Daiden, Olma Walsrip are still very popular. These have composed several albums.

In the late 1980's, Dicky N. Sangma and three of his friends formed a soft rock band while studying in Shillong. Olma Walsrip was the name given to it. The names of the members of the group are as follows:

(i) Eisenhower K. Marak (Vocals/Rhythm)

(ii) Rocky N. Sangma (Vocals/Lead)

(iii) Cherak N. Sangma (Bass)

(iv) Dicky N. Sangma (Drums)

Their songs were based on subjects like love, devotion towards parents, patriotism, and altruism. According to Dicky, Olma Walsrip was the first ever Garo band to record an album in a studio in Guwahati in 1989. This was the only album recorded by them in their stint as a band.

The following songs are composed by Olma Walsrip:

> *Batang Gimin Ua Salrang*: This song highlights the days of childhood, a period when innocence prevailed and there were fewer worries and more joy.

Tingtota Ripa·mchi: It's a romantic song which basically translates to 'Dewdrop Falls'.

Jada Suda: This song conveys the carefree attitude of enjoying and merrymaking, with no worries about the future.

Wai Mechik and *Ka·saoba Sonan* are love songs, the former bringing forth the love of a man for a woman. He wants her to reciprocate his love and take his love for her seriously.

Ang Atchiram: This is a patriotic song which talks about their birthplace and their roots. Dickey Sangma, opines that no matter how much we as a community may change with the passage of time, we should never forget our roots, our identity.

Garo music has been well handed down the generations as is evident by the example of a family. Its lineage shows pure commitment towards the joy and transmission of music.

Custine S. Momin is 67 years of age and resides in Asanang. He is a famous singer in Garo Hills. He and his siblings were influenced by their late father Shri. Millickson Khotnal Marak, whose songs are still popular and relevant even today. Some of his songs were composed in the pre-Independence years while others after Independence. Custine S. Momin's father, Millickson K. Marak was a composer and singer. He was drawn towards singing in his childhood. Those were the days of the British rule. His early education was at Tura and Jorhat. He attended Gauhati's Cotton College in the 1940's. Gauhati's urban, happening culture further inspired him to compose most of his compositions. He got married in 1941. He also took part in the Second World War when he went to Myanmar to look after labourers. In 1956, Christian missionaries in Tura encouraged him to take his pursuit for music further and helped him record two songs, *Rongthalbatna Onbo* (*'To make more pure'*) *and Kasagipa Ripeng Jisu* (Garo version of the Church song *'What a Friend We Have in Jesus'*).

Millickson mostly sang in churches and even performed at Gauhati and Jorhat. He sang in Garo and also in Assamese. In the pre-independence era, he was even invited by the British to perform in Britain in those times. Millickson composed of 22 songs but not all were recorded and many have passed down as oral tradition. Most of Millickson's songs are based on religion, life, and patriotism. His sons Custine S. Momin and Berkline S. Momin have maintained the legacy of their father and recorded his songs. These are highly popular among the masses. The decade of 1940 is well remembered for Mallickson's music. Millickson's most popular song is '*Dimdimdimchong Dachichong*' better known as '*Dimdimdimchong Dadichong*'.

Millickson was truly committed to music. To motivate his children towards the joy of music, he assigned one song each to his seven children. The songs assigned to them were just for them and them alone. Millickson was, thus able to initiate and influence his children in the realm of music and singing. The songs assigned had been previously performed by Millickson on many occasions and in churches and he chose one each for them. The songs assigned by Millickson to his seven children are as follows:

Nulabell S. Momin– Eldest daughter. Song: *Roa Ang Bisa·o*. This song is about remembering the bygone childhood days.

Lodina S. Momin– Daughter. Song: *Ang Turao*. This is a sentimental patriotic song about missing Tura.

Custine S. Momin– Son. Song: *Atchu Ambi Pagitcham Dongram Biapo*. This is a patriotic song which won Custine many prizes and awards in singing competitions while in school.

Berkline S. Momin– Son. Song: *Aiao! Ongja Ua Salde Reangenga Bate Bate* (actual title – *Reangenga Bilsin Salrangi*). This is a sad melancholic song.

Korina S. Momin– Daughter. Song: *De·e Nangna Rasong* Tura High School.

Grecina S. Momin– Daughter. Song: *Ansengipa Dedrangko Ba·na.* This is a happy song signifying hope of a bright future for a newborn child. A less known song for another son Jenkins S. Momin.

Other famous songs composed by Millickson are; *Rongthalbatna Onbo* (To Make More Pure), *Kasagipa Ripeng Jisu* (What a Friend We Have in Jesus), *Oh Ang Atchiram A·songtang Garo Hills* (My Native Village/Place). Millickson's sons Custine S. Momin and Berkline S. Momin are equally talented singers and composers themselves. Millickson passed away on the 8th of July 1985.

Present scenario

The present scenario among the Garo particularly the youth reveals that they are very passionate about music. Impact of Christianity, as well as contact with the music of other cultures, be it Assamese music or music of Hindi films, has led to the creation of rich and diverse forms of music at the hands of the Garo. It is very interesting to observe that Garo youth, while fully enjoying the music of different genres, continues to remain rooted in their culture and one of the ways this is manifested in is their music. While English songs and their different genres are highly popular amongst them, they are conscientious about cherishing, maintaining, enriching their own Garo culture which is very close to their hearts. They reinvent and revive their traditional Garo songs and are careful of not losing these in the midst of newer forms of music which they have been exposed to. L.K. Marak, one of the founders of the Hundred Drums *Wangala*, says, "There is a need to preserve our culture. Christianity turned us away from head-hunting and education taught us to live alongside the rest of humanity. But we began losing our identity gradually. Our culture is rooted in these hills. The rituals are all inspired by nature. We felt that an annual festival would keep our younger generation aware of who we are and where we are from (The Hindu, 24 November 2012).

Relevance towards social science researchers in India

Music of any community is a pertinent subject of deliberation in social sciences. Music conveys the felt emotions and the philosophical thought of a people. It informs about their way of life. The various aspects of the Garo, a matrilineal tribe of Meghalaya have been studied by some scholars (Chand *et al*, 1999; Sangma, 2013; Thomas, 2007; Sharma, 2008). There are publications on their songs, dances and folk theatre. Studies in the music of a community have focused on its formal appearance, its structure. While addressing the understanding of music within the purview of musicology is relevant for the enrichment of the field of music within the purview of musicology, when we attempt to understand music as a cultural expression, we are coming towards anthropology. The vast field of social sciences needs to understand the music of a community as a manifestation of the abstract and material aspects of the culture. Scherer and Zenter (2001) and Juslin (2013) highlight the correlation between music and emotion. Studies such as these can play a contributory role in addressing how the understanding of the music of a people helps in a deeper, closer and more correct study of the mindset of a people, or broadly speaking, of their way of life. Anthropological study of the music of a culture, such as the present study on Garo music, is based on empirical research, on fieldwork and brings to the fore place of music in Garo life. Intensive fieldwork helps in arriving at an authentic picture of music among the Garo. Fieldwork-based researchers do not merely scratch the surface of social reality, rather they delve deeper and abstain from broad generalisations. Having said that we do not undermine studies which are more broad-based or extensive. These too enrich the pool of knowledge on culture albeit at a macro level with the applicable methodology. The example of Barthakur's work (2003) is a valuable contribution where the author smoothly moves from the macro to the micro in analysing the place of music in a population. The wide and complex reality which culture is, it is being understood and explained from a multidisciplinary perspective. What is relevant is to reach out at the finer nuances of the subjective character that is human. It is here that Anthropology, whose cornerstone is intensive fieldwork, can contribute greatly. In today's day and age which is buzzing with researchers on issues such as development, education, employment - parameters which are being explored to understand the quality of life of a people, a study on songs and dances of a community may not appear to be that relevant. However, if this is the case, then it's a highly problematic one. Art, aesthetics, music, dance, folklore - terms which when explored with reference to a people, unearth an array of dimensions of a people in a community and help in the understanding of the latter at a deeper, subtle level. Victor Hugo has rightly said, 'Music expresses that which cannot be said and on which it is impossible to be silent'.

References

Barthakur, Dilip Ranjan, 2003. *The Music and Musical Instruments of North Eastern India*. New Delhi: Mittal Publications.

Bernstein Mathew. 2005. *Music Soothes the Soul*. Texas: Waldorf Publishing.

Chand Susan, Subhas Marak, and Jashia Marak. 1999. 'Dances of the Garo (A'Chik Mande)'. In Robin D Tribhuwan and Preeti R Tribhuwan (Eds): *Tribal Dances of India*. New Delhi: Discovery Publishing House.

Juslin, Patrick, N. 2013. 'What does music express? Basic emotions and beyond'. *Frontiers in Psychology*. Published online 2013 Sep 6. doi: 10.3389/fpsyg.2013.00596.

Sangma, Barbara. 2013. 'From rituals to stage: A journey of A'chik folk theatre'. *The NEHU Journal*, 11 (2): 55-72.

Scherer, Klaus R., and Marcel R. Zenter. 2001. 'Emotional effects of music: Production rules'. In P.N. Justin and J.A. Slobada (Ed.): *Music and Emotion: Theory and Research*. pp.361, Oxford: OUP.

Sharma, Prabal. 2008. *Music Culture of North East India*. New Delhi: Raj Publications.

Thomas, IW.2007. *Music and Musical Instruments of the Garo Tribe of North-east India*. New Delhi: Akanksha Publishing House.

Wolf, Richard Kent. 2000. 'Three perspectives on music and the idea of Tribe in India'. *Asian Music*. 32 (1): 5-34.

Chapter - 16

The Role of Church in the Rise of Political Consciousness: The Mizoram Example

—Rajat Kanti Das

There is a general perception that the introduction of Christianity in North East India has had landmark effects among some tribes. It has brought in changes in the material conditions of living, opened up educational opportunities and has also resulted in attitudinal changes. But there is another side of it. With tribes taking the form of political ethnic groups, deeply engaged in search of political power, the role of the church in changing ideologies and the political implications of it invite particular attention. One may even speak in terms of the political performances of the church using religious activities as political symbols. The church and the ceremonial forms it takes on could provide the necessary ground for social unity at the tribal level. There was a time when political networks were organised around the church. The same trend still continues in some form and in changing situational context. Of course, the church as the seat of symbolic power has come under the critical eyes of individual actors. It sometimes gives rise to ideological antagonism or a desperate bid to challenge the seat of symbolic power. In the contemporary situation attempts to separate church and state would invariably involve national or party-political interests and programmes to undermine or even reduce the influence of the opposing and rival forces.

Doubts have often been expressed from some quarters that the church has a secret political agenda of its own in promoting local interests, especially for strengthening its own base of influence. In some cases, it even identifies with local experience of the community in accommodating the 'invented tradition' (Hobsbawn and Ranger, 1993; quoted from Herzfeld, 1997) of the nation-state. The main problem confronting political anthropologists working in the Contemporary political situation of North East India is to identify the areas of comparability between the states from its own perspective and similar institutions of control of power relations. The church could be one such institution but its involvement in power structure remains hidden and at the times of dubious. Herzfeld (1997) has also recognised the problem of providing ethnographies 'of' the state and other comparable institutional structures, of which the church may be, an important one. It is necessary to look into the whole process, starting with the introduction of the church into the tribal system, the opposition it faced and continuous struggles through which it could establish itself to a position of acceptability, its ultimate rise to a position from where it would exercise control over its followers, and its contribution towards making people politically conscious and at times driven by a spirit of self-ruled.

II

In North East India it took a long time for the state to come on its own and take its independent form. For quite a long period of time, the authoritarian structure was revealed here in various forms like chieftainship, village organisation, and kinship. There were, of course, proto-state formations, but they could hardly be linked from their local, indigenous connections. Taking advantage of the society's blind faith in nature worship and ancestral spirit control, Christianity could make its entry with all seriousness and with a sense of dedication that could transform not only the thought process of tribal people but even their entire social life. Here we deal with Christianity as it is practiced in Mizoram, a state situated in the eastern corner of India, having Bangladesh and Tripura on the west and Myanmar on the east and south. The introduction of Christianity in Mizoram was an important event in the sense that it was considered to be the greatest initiators of reforms in the Mizo society. One simple example may substantiate the point. According to Maccall's records (1949), it was chiefly due to missionary efforts that the rate of literacy in the Lushai hills could reach 12.9 per cent in 1931 and 19.3 in 1941 with a span of nearly three or four decades. The cost incurred by the government on the education of the Lushais never exceeded three halfpence per head of population per year within the first forty years of the British administration. But in the later part of this period, seven hundred pounds sterling were spent yearly on 1, 59,000 persons, which speaks of increasing a governmental involvement.

Incidentally, this was the period when the missionaries were active and deeply involved with the task of implementing their welfare programmes. During the post Independence period, when the State Government is on a firm footing, there has been greater control and participation by it in the field of education, as a result of which the literacy rate could cross 90 per cent mark. Even in this case, the contribution of missionaries is no less significant. Education is probably one area where the interest of the church and state has converged without posing much of a problem. Other than education, the missionaries were initially engaged in medical and philanthropic works, such as caring for orphans and destitute, distributing food at the time of need, which helped their cause and contributed substantially to the spread of Christianity among the Mizos. For instance, there were two hospitals–the Welsh Mission Hospital at Durtlang (Aizawl) and the Baptist Mission Hospital at Serkawn (Lunglei) established by the Welsh and London Missions respectively. Today these hospitals have grown into big establishments with qualified doctors and other trained medical staff. Unfortunately, the same hospitals have been commercialised to the extent that poor villagers could hardly afford to have their treatment there. The state government was rather late in making its entry into the health sector in a significant way and even when it did; it could not match the selfless spirit with which the missionaries set about their task. This sense of dedication could win them an increasing number of followers. In Mizoram, Christianity's progress is almost total, offering a new height, hope, and faith. It, however, carries with it a long history of encountering opposition and waging relentless struggles. Right from the nineteenth century, various denominations of Christianity made their appearance in what is Mizoram today. The first among the denominations of Christianity to have made its appearance in the Mizo society was the Welsh Presbyterian headed by a young Presbyterian missionary, Rev. William, who during his brief stay in Mizo Hills, could receive encouraging response from the Mizos to the teachings of Christianity. At the initial stage, they could not be persuaded to leave Mizo Hills for seeking education in places like Khasi Hills. As Rev. William stated:

"They told me that if I should come to live in their country, they would all come to learn……". He at least succeeded in spreading the name of Christ and gospel among a section of Mizos, which helped the later missionaries in proselytism. Rev. William was followed by Rev. F. W. Saridge, who came to Mizo Hills in 1894. At first, two missionaries made an attempt to enter from the south after having established contact with some persons at Kasalong in the Chittagong Hills Tract in 1892, which did not bear fruit. The next attempt to enter the hills from the north also failed. But, they did not give up. They mastered the Lushai language and were the first to reduce the language into writing in simple Roman scripts with phonetic form of spelling. They were also the first who taught a number of Mizos how to read and write. The Bible and Gospels of Luke were translated by them in Lushai. The book entitled "Grammar and Dictionary of Lushai

Language" was written by them, which was later published by the Government of Assam. Simultaneously, the two missionaries started working for the propagation of Christianity and remained actively engaged in preaching in some villages in North Mizo hills. Rev. D.E. Jones who first came to Aizwal on August 3, 1897, continued the good works initiated by its predecessors. Since then, various denominations of Christianity entered into what is now formally recognised as the state of Mizoram at different periods of time to preach Christianity with a great zeal and a spirit of dedication. In addition to Presbyterian and Baptist, there are at present a number of denominations, such as, the Roman Catholic, Salvation Army, the Seventh Day Adventist Mission, the United Penticolastral church, the church of God working in Mizoram. Of all the churches, the Presbyterian Church has more followers. What actually emerges from the activities of the churches is the fact that the missionaries have contributed substantially towards reforms and development of the Mizo society. They have set in motion a process of popularising education, providing health services, abolishing indigenous customary practices, which have far-reaching consequences. The early missionaries were undoubtedly men of grit and determination showing tremendous crusading zeal to enlighten and proselytize the early Mizos amidst difficulties, unknown hazards and unpredictable situations. They could identify themselves completely with all their values and attitudes, wants and constraints of living. The government also relied on the church as an agency working for the spread of education and other social services. The church was not only the religious and cultural agency which could make its presence felt in the remotest part of the district, it was also a source of employment for the educated section of the population who took the teaching and preaching with renewed interest. In a sense, winning favour and patronage of the Church could mean financial assistance to enable a person to reach the threshold of higher education in the plains. So the popularity of the Church was only expected.

It was only its role in the political field that had drawn a lot of attention and produced a lot of controversies as well. Even during the British period, the Church became a centre of power and patronage in the Hill districts. Referring to the Lushai Hills Maccall (1949) wrote,

> "Local educational practice soon gave rise to the belief that education and Christianity were the passports to 'salaried job', relief from the wearisome toil of cultivating a hard land. Education has constituted a means to a dead end; the salaried post...Black-coated occupations became synonymous with progress. Christianity led towards black-coatism."

An oligarchy, representing the privileged section of the community, was created, who became materially powerful. Maccall put on record that most of them were on the missions' pay-roll, were Church executions or were in the employment of government. In the latter case also, the persons were spiritually loyal to the Church. According to Maccall, Christianity coupled with oligarchy bred individualism that flourished in the headquarters and towns. Such people were naturally imbued with the thrill of seeking independence from the Chief's control and freedom from customary communal discipline, which the British administration had always tried to retain in its own interest. The government's attempt to establish control over the people in line with the traditional mode of control incurred displeasure and even wrath of the people, while, on the other hand, the Church continued to gain acceptability and popularity among the people in its own unique way. That was the first sign of a possible rift between the Church and the government. The Christian Missions preached to the Mizos of the loftiness of individuality and equality before God, whereas, ironically, the British administration denied them the equality of opportunity and status by not clearly defining the rights of the subjects. The missionaries, of course, had their own design and in the power structure, the course of action followed by them was not much different from the administration. They wanted the Mizos to be totally dependent on the help provided to them from missionary sources. A self-reliant Mizo society would not quite serve their purpose. During the British rule, both the administration and Church had one common objective, namely, the consolidation of the British power. The strategy adopted by the administration was the least inference into the internal mode of functioning of the tribe, while the activities of the Church were aimed at understanding the basic foundations of the social order. What the British administration wanted to do for itself, was done by the Church on its behalf. The Church's action created some sort of a social imbalance between the traditional order and the reformist measures undertaken by it. The imbalance continued even after Independence, particularly when the assertion of political rights became the main consideration. When Laldenga and his followers demanded Independence for Mizo Hills, they actually twisted the meaning of the words "Excluded Areas" and made the people understand that Mizo Hills was under the excluded areas during the British time and so it could not be converted into a district by the Constitution makers of India. The British design was to keep a few million inhabitants of the hill areas of Assam outside the purview of the general constitutional reforms. It was not given to understand that the excluded areas were the track where there was no possibility of installing an advanced form of government, nor was there any need to do so. The missionaries did not oppose the concept of excluded areas or partially excluded areas developed by the British rulers because they realised that pursuance of such a policy would provide them greater access to the people. The government also did not enforce any strict restriction on their movement in their movement in those areas.

III

Regarding their participation in politics, all Christian missionaries in North East India were not above question. "The works of missionaries were not clean of politics", announced Pandit Jawaharlal Nehru in Kohima on March 30, 1953. The same view has been expressed at different times from different quarters. When the demand for sovereignty or complete Independence was raised by the underground Mizos and some other underground outfits in some other parts of North East India, it was said to have been instigated by the missionaries and Church leaders. From this one should not automatically conclude that the support of the foreign Christians missionaries behind the underground Mizo demand for a sovereign independent Mizoram outside India was an established fact. So far as Mizoram is concerned, the Church was never directly involved with extremist politics and maintained a safe distance from it. During insurgency, the regular programmes or services of the Churches were badly disturbed. Frankly speaking, the Church had little influence in the political affairs of Mizoram. Side by side, it is equally true that the Christian missionaries rarely advocated emotional integration of the Mizo people with the rest of India. When the seeds of ethnic nationalism were seen by the British administration, the foreign missionaries were no less involved. Both the administration and foreign missionaries fomented such tendencies. In this connection, reference may be made about the activities of Rev. Michael Scott, the most active member of the Naga Peace Mission. As a result of some of his questionable activities, the foreign Christian missionaries were put under the scanner of Government of India. The government took the step to ask the foreign Christian missionaries working in Mizo Hills to leave the place just after the breaking out of Mizo extremist activities in 1966, which seemed to be a foregone conclusion. That was also the time when the management of the Church/Missions was taken over by the educated Mizos themselves. In spite of the problems and disadvantages faced by them after their dissociation with the foreign missionaries, it was a test for the local leadership to prove their worth in Church management and at the same time win more and more local support.

Admittedly, the Church had a role to play in arousing in the political consciousness, putting emphasis on modern political values of self-management, integrity, organisational efficiency. This could be regarded as the beginning of a new political phase. Prior to the formation of District Councils, the village administration was carried out by the Chiefs at a coterie of elders. But the Mizo District Council brought in democratic changes in the village administration by enacting the Lushai Hills District (Village Councils) Act on December 1, 1953. After the abolition of chieftainship, the village administration came under the jurisdiction of "Village Councils", which was a significant step in political administration. But more than political administration, it was the vicissitudes of modern politics which had started growing in importance around that time. Even the Mizo District Council, at one stage, refused to accept the provisions of more authoritative control and instead demanded a separate political status in the form of a full-fledged state of Mizoram. No doubt, the principles of forming and maintaining 'Church Government' gave rise to political awareness and a growing faith in the principle of democracy among the Mizos. A number of Church leaders entered into modern politics, sometimes not without controversy. Late Pachhunga, the first President of the first political party in Mizoram, 'Mizo Union', formed on April 19, 1946, was a prominent Church elder of the Dawspis Presbyterian Church, Aizwal. Many others followed his example. Actually, entry into modern politics and growing political consciousness started taking shape with the enlightenment and faith in Church. All the regional parties, which have so far emerged in Mizoram, have vowed to protect the Church. The Mizo National Front (MNF) was initially much favoured for its stand on Christianity, the preservation of which was one of its declared goals. The 'Declaration of Mizoram Independence', signed by sixty-one MNF leaders on 01.03.1966, states:

> "...to make this Declaration of Independence, we must depend on God, we place our resolution, our lives, our glory and our hope to Him, and we make a promise...The great and vast Russia and China are proud of their being the followers of Karl Marx, and we, the Mizo people, also take much pride in our being the followers of Jesus Christ, the savior of all..."

Brigadier T. Sailo's 'People's Conference' also aimed at preserving Christianity at any cost. From February 1966, the hard-core elements of the MNF unilaterally declared Independence. The declaration, in support of its stand, states:

> "...The Mizos created and moulded into Nation and nurtured as such by nature's God, have been intolerably dominated by the people of India in contravention of the Laws of Nature."

The leaders also accused the Government of India of having colonised the territory, suppressed Christianity and established its military control over the Mizos. Here too, it is clear that they attached utmost importance to Christianity. Almost at the same time, the Mizo Union also asserted its identity, rejected the MNF leader Laldenga's cult of violence, repudiated the course charted out by him to achieve Independence, and worked for the restoration of peace and a satisfactory political settlement. Though the Mizo Union's attempts for achieving statehood for the Mizo's did not meet with immediate success, the party could strengthen the forces of peace and help in the emergence of a liberal group. The Church leaders also started asserting themselves and came out with the proposal to persuade MNF leaders to refrain from resorting to violent means. Not only the average Mizos, but the normal activities of the Church also suffered much in the hands of the hostiles and the armed forces. So the Church leaders wanted an end to this violent phase and favoured a peaceful political settlement of the problem to the satisfaction of all the stakeholders. A Christian Peace Mission was formed to contact the underground leaders and Ministers for Publicity, Finance, and Home, convince them in every possible way to see reason and bring them to the conference table on terms agreeable to both the parties. The Mission included Church leaders Rev. Zairema, Rev. H.S. Luaia, Rev. Lalsasoma and Rev. L. N. Ralte, among others. The members of the Peace Mission tried to persuade MNF leaders to desist from violence and follow the Constitutional means in their struggle. Unfortunately, these contacts and appeals could not make any impact on the underground leaders. They, however, continued with their effort, though with little success. The role of the Church in Mizoram may be compared with that of Nagaland, where it could exercise much influence on tribal politics. A possible reason could be that in Nagaland with many tribes and loyalties the Church is a great binding force, trying to unify tribes for a common political cause. There have been studies to show that the political performances of the Church are particularly manifested in converting religious activities into specific forms of political symbolism that find common expression. In Mizoram, with its predominantly Mizo population, religion has not worked as a cementing force, combining social living and political aspirations into one. The Christian Peace Commission, in a letter dated April 27, 1967, observes,

> "The Mizo Church leadership consists largely of 'liberal' Christians, who do not have much authority as spiritual leaders respected for their spiritual fervour, think their primary responsibility is to preach the Gospel, not to talk about political issues. However, the majority of the Mizos, who have spoken out, are in fact, evangelicals. Further, the Mizo brethren have little idea of the Bible's attitude to the government,

politics or economics. This is what they need most unless there is a Biblical understanding on which the Church bases its appeal to the underground and its sympathisers and unless the appeal comes from leaders who have integrity, one cannot expect to see appeals making any impact on the underground."

Still, it goes to the credit of the Church leaders that ultimately they could influence a group of MNF leaders to realise the reality and compelled them to come out of their hideouts. The Presbyterian Pastor and his colleagues have always been discouraging political violence even at the risk of incurring the displeasure of the MNF rebels. This does not mean that the Church as such is opposed to political activities. There is another side of it. Denial of political intent or significance to political activities that had resorted to armed revolt by the Church made it more suspect. They were, in any case, against the personality cult encouraged by the MNF, which had furthered the trend of centralisation of the power structure, rooted deep in the Mizo society in the form of chieftainship. It hindered the practice of intra-party democracy or democratic function of the party organisation at all levels. The Church leaders could realise that Christianity had a better prospect in a democratic environment which could accommodate not only the moderates and intellectuals but also the extremists buying their loyalty. When the Mizoram problem was internationalised in September 1970 with the visit of MNF supreme Laldenga and his Foreign Minister Lalhmingthanga to China, who assured them of help and assistance, the Church had to review its position. Though the Sino-underground Mizo relationship was not based on any ideology, yet it was a marriage of convenience. The Mizos, being mostly Christians, did not welcome the idea of seeking help from a Communist country. Even the Church leaders saw in it a threat not only to the existence of Mizo people but also to the Mizo way of life.

When Mizoram was at the height of the insurgency, the Churches almost stopped functioning in the territory. The rural Mizos were so terror-stricken that they dared not to visit Churches. The Pastor's visit to different villages for carrying on spiritual and evangelical works was too difficult and was drastically cut down. Insurgency thus affected the regular programmes services of the Churches. When Armed Forces succeeded in restoring normally, the Churches once again began to have regular services and other activities attended by bigger congregations. After all, the Church in Mizoram is rooted to the soil. An air of uncertainty was, however, created regarding what actually constituted the Biblical understanding of the political problem. There were occasions when the Church incurred the displeasure of the MNF rebels as well as the common Mizos. The Church might not be solely responsible for the loss of local support by the MNF. What is clear is that the job of a Church leader used to carry a lot of clouts. Still, there is no denying the fact that Mizo political awareness has considerably been influenced by the Church. The rapid spread of education among the Mizos mainly at the Church's initiative had contributed to the process of political awakening among them. For a long time, the Church did not go against regional politics which had dominated the scene. Today, the Church functions more like a global window to the Mizos. It carries them across the country and even beyond. Some years back, I met a Christian Mizo lady from an interior village of Mizoram at Kuala Lumpur airport, who was waiting for fellow women members from Japan, Australia to arrive to attend a conference of the NGO she was a member of. During our brief conversation, however, she did not hide her allegiance to the Church and project her Christian identity. Apparently, Christianity has become a way of life for the Mizo people. The growing member of Churches, the rapidly increasing cemeteries on almost all roadside vacant spaces in Aizwal and other settlement areas bear testimony to that. On the question of Church's political functions today, opinions may differ as to whether the Church in Mizoram promotes or disregards active politics. The outward show of disregard for politics does not always mean greater allegiance to Church because the Church as such is not opposed to political activities. The Church leaders of today, like their predecessors, draw admiration and respect from others. In a seminar in Aizwal a few years back that I attended, some prominent Church leaders were specially invited and when they spoke on the impact of Christianity on issues like Mizo culture, religion and politics, everybody listened to them with rapt attention. Some people even supported them when they made some critical comments about state activities. One should not get the impression that the Church and state are naturally opposed to each other. There are areas where the two share common concerns. Community-based politics or ethnic politics is one such area where the two merge together. The status enjoyed by the Reang and Hmar in Mizoram vis-à-vis the Mizo, the dominant community, maybe a pointer. Though the Reangs have a fair representation in Mizoram, they have almost been reduced to the status of fringe-dwellers. They are mainly concentrated in the Aizwal district, but also live in some villages of Lunglai and Chimtuipui districts. They were predominantly followers of the traditional faith, but a fair percentage of them have now embraced or have been forced to embrace Christianity. Incidentally, the economic and political demands of the Reangs did not meet with much success because hard conditions were put by the Mizos before any concessionary benefits could be accorded to them.

When the Reangs demanded a political platform to be a part of the ongoing political process, they came in open conflict with the Mizos. The Reangs raised the demand for an Autonomous District Council under the provision of the Sixth Schedule of the Constitution of India, 1997, following the pattern of other non-Mizos like the Chakma, Lai, and Mera Autonomous District Councils. But their demand has not yet been acceded to. A strong political view has now been developed in Mizoram, obviously at the instance of the Mizos, disfavouring any further autonomy to be granted to the smaller ethnic groups on the ground that such concessions may pose a threat to the greater Mizo polity of the state. When the demands of the Reangs were raised through various organisations, they were opposed by the ruling group, namely, the Mizos. Ethnic style between the two tribes erupted and as a result, a large number of Reangs were uprooted from their villages and were forced to take shelter in the adjoining districts of Tripura and Assam. A section of the Reangs tried to regroup them and resorted to armed revolt, which the Mizos considered not only an undesired development but a direct threat to the state's integrity. And what was the role of the Church in this inter-ethnic conflict? The Churches in Mizoram generally impose a cultural behavioural standard with which the non-Christian Reangs could not adjust. A section of them succumbed to the pressure created by the Church and became Christians. In this case, the role of the Church was, if anything, partisan or one-sided because it toed the line of the majority group. In other words, it sided with the state or did not counter the stand taken by the state. The Church's selective approach was probably aimed at avoiding any direct confrontation with the state. Another non-Mizo tribe, Hmar could make more positive strides towards their political objective of creating a political space for themselves. They could even mobilise an underground force to fight their own cause. Though they operated at the inter-state level even across the international boundary, they carried out their underground activities mostly from Mizoram. It may sound ironic, but the initial inspiration for them to take such a course of action might have come from the Mizos. Again, the Mizo attempt to accommodate Poi-Lakher and some Chin group of tribes within their fold on their terms like embracing Christianity and accepting Mizo language and culture could mean identity dilution on the part of non-Mizo tribes. In such cases, there is the risk of a direct clash between identity assertion on the one hand and identity dilution on the other. It may result in internal displacement, in the event of which the Church cannot avoid its responsibility. As the political symbols used by the Church in Mizoram are based essentially on the cultural features and religious performances of the Mizos, any attempt on its part to include other non-Mizo tribes to devise a new set of political symbols will make Church's position a difficult one.

IV

It is understood that all anthropology today is fundamentally political, starting from the most local of social relations to the greater arena of political power. The Church in North East India combines the local social relations operating at the tribal level with political power relations cutting across community, region and assuming a global dimension. The local connection with the national or even global is now increasingly accessible to the ethnographic observation of the kind not particularly dominated by official discourse. From that perspective, there could be scope enough for ethnographic observation on the Church and its community-linked activities displaying a plurality of voices. The abstract moral judgments associated with the Church can be subjected to a critical inquiry from the social contexts it is deeply entangled in and that could be done through intimate investigations of ethnographers from within and outside.

Regarding the status of tribes in North East India, anthropologists have been advocating a policy of anti-assimilation and maintenance of cultural distinctiveness of tribes. In the Bordoloi committee which was set up to work out a scheme of the administrative structure for the Hills district of Assam, B.S. Guha, a noted anthropologist, was inducted to give his advice on the policy of exclusion. He advised the committee that no attempt should be made to assimilate the tribes because it would amount to break up of the existing tribal institutions. The old foundations should be allowed to evolve themselves in the way the tribe wants them to be. At the same time, contact with the outside world should also be maintained. So it was not an isolationist policy. What Guha wanted was that the tribal systems should be allowed to continue in their own way retaining their basic features until the change was initiated by the tribesmen themselves. Further, no attempt should be made to impose any different system on them from outside and there should not be exploited in any form. Whatever adjustment was needed should come from within. The Bardoloi committee accepted the views in principle. It was, however, not clear what would be the status of Church in such a scheme. Today, Church in Mizoram is not regarded as an alien institution, an institution which does not fit well in the tribal system. Tribes are more emotionally linked to the Church than ever before. Verrier Elwin (1963) once spoke of 'the essential harmony' of tribal life, while 'securing their integration without imposition'. It is not simply a question of the formal political organisation but involves a process of emotional integration. The control exercised by the Church on its followers has an emotional content, which may add to the process of emotional integration in the larger context provided the political variables in operation do not prove to be a deterrent. This particularly applies to the Mizoram situation with greater intensity.

References

Das, Rajat Kanti. 2004. *Tribalism and Beyond*. Kolkata; Puthi Pustak.

Elwin, Verrier. 1963. *A New Deal for Tribal India*. New Delhi.

Herzfeld, M. 1997. *Anthropology*. Oxford.

Maccal, AA. 1949. *Lushai Chrysalis*. London; Lizac and Co.Ltd.

Prasad, RN. 1987. *Government and Politics in Mizoram, 1947-1986*. New Delhi; Northern Book Centre.

Chapter - 17

The Deeper Necessity: Folklore and the Lepchas

—Sumitabha Chakraborty and Namgyal Lepcha

Introduction

Folklore names an enormous and deeply significant dimension of culture. It is the traditional art, literature, knowledge, and practice, largely disseminated through oral communication and behavioural example. It is anonymous and follows prescribed formulae. Folklore expresses the ideas and values of a particular group. Every group with a sense of its own identity shares, as a central part of that identity, folk traditions–the things that people traditionally believe, perform activities, make and say experiences of life. The concept of folklore emerged in Europe midway in the nineteenth century. In the past, folklore was generally focused on traditional stories based on oral tradition in the form of folktales, songs etc. and transmitted from one generation to the next. While describing folklore, Sims and Stephens (2005) narrated that folklore exists in cities, suburbs, villages, families, workgroups, and dormitories as an informal communication, whether verbal, customary or material. It involves values traditions, ways of thinking and behaviour. Wilson (1988) mentioned that folklore is more concerned with linking us to the cultural heritage from the past. Folklore has two attributes of traditionality and irrationality, which could only pertain to primitive societies. The folklorist believes that the countryside and the open space of wilderness was folklore's proper breeding ground maintaining a close contact with surrounding nature. Thus, folklore is distinguishable from so-called "high culture" and "pop culture".

In fact, commonality has become a central attribute in the formulation of the concept of folklore and is rivaled only by "tradition". Folklore never allowed any private tales and poems; moreover, any expression has to pass through the sieve of communal approval first before it can be considered folklore (Bhattacharya, 1937). Folklore, in its primary stage, could not have been accessible to modern man. As an attribute folktales and folk songs are told and sung without recourse to any written devices to aid in memorisation and transmission of texts of their ancient predecessors.

The Lepcha society is closely bounded by folklore (Gorer, 1938); believed to be the most important tradition of their culture. To a Lepcha, folklore is not only a means of entertainment but it is an education also. Their myths are connected with the origin of the Lepchas and their country, *Mayel Lyang*, the origin of the first Lepcha couple–*Fodongthing* and *Nuzaongnyoo*; the origin of Lepcha clans; marriage; *'chi'*, the traditional fermented beer etc. Lepcha stories a special motif with folktales and deal with everyday life that makes it more interesting, colourful and fascinating. Many moral stories, especially meant for the children are not only enjoyable and entertaining but also guide the children towards a better path and life. In fact, the Lepchas are living within the close proximity of nature; each landmass, mountains and hills, forest patches, streams, rivers, big stones have own term of reference in their vocabulary. Moreover, since the early days, their folktales and folk songs are very much imbibed with those natural set up in consideration of the values of their life. As time passed, various remarkable incidents happened in the 'Lepcha land' and due to the course of modernisation, the people have to adopt various external customs, which influences their age-old rich tradition. An attempt has been made in the foregoing pages to compile the ancient, colourful and interesting folklore and make it understandable how far it is effective to the society.

The Area

The ancient Lepcha kingdom extended from the Himalayas in the north to Titaliaya (now in Bangladesh) in the south and from Gipmochi Mountain, the tri-junction of Sikkim, Bhutan and Tibet in the east to the Aroon River, Nepal in the west. The vast, old Lepcha kingdom was then known as *Nye Mayel Renjyong Lyang* literally meant 'Holy, hidden, eternal land of the gentlemen', today recognised as *Mayel Lyang* in short. The indigenous Lepchas lived in peace and tranquility with their own lines of Lepcha kings, high priests and priestesses in *Mayel Lyang* until the arrival of '*Khye Bumsa*', the first Tibetan who entered *Mayel Lyang* seeking the blessings of the divine Lepcha high priest and priestess, *Thikoong Tek* and *Nyekoong Ngal*, respectively for a son. The present study was mainly concentrated in an area called Dzongu, because, it is a reserve area for the only inhabitation of the indigenous Lepcha people and this area is believed as a pristine area a out of all infiltration. It consists of beautiful mountains covered with forests, interspersed with villages and a river (*Rongyong chu*) considered to be the very lifeline of the people.

Dzongu is an isolated place separated from the District Headquarter, Mangan of Sikkim state. *Dzongu* is a Tibetan word with two syllables– *Dzon* means hillock and *gu* mean nine, which makes to understand that the place Dzongu is the concentration of nine hillocks. Nowadays, it is one of the important subdivisions of North Sikkim consisting of altogether seven Gram-Panchayat Unit (GPU). Total reserve area of 15,846 hectares is broadly divided into two zones– (i) upper Dzongu and (ii) lower Dzongu and spread on hilly terrain in dense forest. It is triangular in shape, bounded on the south-east by the river Teesta, on the north-east by the Talung river and on the third side of the mountain south of the Khangchendzonga. The geographical position of the reserve area is extending between 27º28′ to 27º38′ North latitude and 88º23′ to 88º38′ East longitude along 700 m to 6000 m amsl altitude. Dzongu is further extended from Sheep-Gyer in the east to Sakyong-Pentong village in the west and Kishong chu lake in the north to Lum village in the south. The area is characterised by a diverse snowy mountainous landscape with steep and narrow valley and gorges with well-drained flanking slopes. The area represents three climatic zones viz. sub-tropical, temperate and alpine. The hill slopes are steep and level pieces of land are rare (Imperial Gazetteer, Sikkim, 1908).

The People

Once the ruling race, the Lepchas are the one and only indigenous settlers of Sikkim. Actually, they call themselves *Mutanchi Rong kup Rum Kup*, meaning the 'beloved children of Mother nature and God' in Lepcha language. The name Lepcha used today is, perhaps, derived from a Lepcha word '*Lapchao*', meaning a resting or waiting place on the wayside where the stones are heaped up as a signpost to direct travellers. When the Nepalese first arrived in the Lepcha land they did not pronounce '*Lapchao*' correctly but uttered 'Lapcha' and later 'Lapche', which was later, anglicized as 'Lepcha' by the Britishers, when they came to this land (Tamsang, 2008). The people never address among themselves as Lepcha rather they address themselves as '*Mutanchi*' or simply '*Rong*' with pride. The people believe that 'God had created them from the untrodden snow of Mt. Khangchendzonga' (Sprigg, 2005). According to the tradition, the ancient Lepcha families were claiming their descent from the ten sons of the creator father and mother, '*Fodongthing* and *Nuzaongnyoo*' and termed as *Rong kup kati*, means ten Lepchas. The population of the Lepcha in Dzongu reserve area is approximately 15000 spread over 38 villages. The Lepcha have their own language known as *Rong-ring*, a Tibeto-Burman family of language and the script is *Mutanchi Rong Aming* with 28 consonants (Mainwarning, 1876). The earliest Lepcha settlers were the believers in Bon and Mun faith, which is basically based on spirits. But nowadays instead of spirit worship, a sizeable population has strong faith in Lamaism. The Lepchas, who have carried their ancient tribal social culture over to present age, have a rich repertoire of romantic folklore. A cozy rendezvous with these ancient tales opens up a door that leads us to the Lepchas' ever simple life fashioned by their unpretentious outlook and uncomplicated philosophies. They love to live with the legion of fabulous folklore.

Divine origin of the Lepcha–The children of Mount Khangchendzonga

According to the *Namthars* (the oldest religious book of the Lepcha), the Lepcha were believed to be created by God (*Rum*), *Itboo-Deboo*, with his own hands out of pure, virgin snow from the pinnacle of the Mt. Khangchendzonga, the 'Guardian Deity'. First God (*Rum*) created a male figure, named *Fodongthing*, means 'most powerful', and infused nine *nongyong* (the life) in it. Perceiving his state of loneliness God (*Rum*) thought of creating his partner in the shape of a female figure, named *Nuzaongnyoo*, means 'ever fortunate' and infused eight *nongyong*. They started their life as brother and sister and forbade entering any physical relations till they attain full maturity. That is why God (*Rum*) separated them from each other; sent *Fodongthing* to live at the top of 'Tungseng Nareng Chu' and put *Nuzaongnyoo* next to 'Naho-Nathar Da' lake at the base of the mountain. As she grew older and beautiful, *Nuzaongnyoo* was unable to control temptation and met *Fodongthing* by climbing up a golden ladder to 'Tungseng Nareng Chu' against the will of God. Both of them disobeyed the God's command and committed a sin on the top of the mountain. In anger, God (*Rum*) punished them and sent to nine steps below down from the Mt. Khangchedzonga to the mundane world, 'Tarvong partam' as husband and wife. There they were blessed with the children, who later spread over the foothills of Mt. Khangchendzonga in course of time. Thus, *Fodongthing* and *Nuzaongnyoo* are called as 'Poomthing', the first ancestors of the Lepchas. Mt. Khangchendzonga is believed as a protector, benefactor, guardian, and life-giver to the Lepchas. There is a great admiration, reverence, love, and respect for Mt. Khangchendzonga in every Lepcha mind and therefore, they offer prayers and supplications to their 'Guardian Deity'[1].

A paradise on earth: *Nye Mayel Kyong*[2]

It is a traditional belief that there was a Lepcha village in the Sikkim Himalayas called *Nye Mayel Kyong*, means a hidden, holy and eternal village, a paradise on earth. Seven Lepcha couples lived in this village in seven traditional huts (*kaden mo lee*). They were immortal. They wore the traditional dresses made of nettle plant threads and hats made of bamboo and cane splits. In the morning they became children, at midday they became youths and in the evening old men and women. Once the road was open to this holy, hidden village but now it is closed forever. In this paradise, village crops grew many times bigger than elsewhere and migratory birds, *Mayel-fo*, sent out to indicate the seasons for commencing various agricultural works. The village was so mysteriously hidden and barred that no one could go there and if by accident anyone reached there, the path and the village disappeared.

One day a Lepcha hunter went tracking a wild boar. Days and nights passed, but he could not reach to it. He lost his way so badly that he could not go back. After several days he came to that paradise village where the wild boar had come and disappeared underneath a house. He marveled that he had been running behind a tamed pig all this time. He put the arrow back in its quiver and went inside the house to ask shelter for the night as the sun was setting by that time. He found an old couple inside the house who enquired about the intention of coming here. The hunter told them the fact and in reply, the old man agreed to be the tamed pig. They allowed him to stay for the night, prepared food and *chi* (traditional beer) and arranged a straw bed for him. Next morning when the hunter woke, he could not find the old couple; rather found two small babies lying on the bed, kicking their two feet and smiling at him. At midday, they turned into a beautiful young couple and prepared food, *chi* and introduced him to the remaining immortal couples. The hunter found that the paradise village was incredibly beautiful and emancipated from hunger, desire, greed or sin; it was the land of eternal beauty, peace, and prosperity; a heaven on the earth. The couple also gave him different types of grains, fruits and vegetable seeds to take home and distribute among the Lepchas. They showed him a staircase to go down and told him that he would find his way at the bottom of the staircase. The Lepcha hunter went down to the ground and turned back to see the staircase and the house that he had come from just a moment ago, but to his surprise, the staircase had disappeared from sight and he could not make out the house where he had stayed. He found himself in the middle of a jungle close to where he had first started the tracking of the boar. The hunter was no other than Thikoong Men Salaong, a famous Boongthing, and great Lepcha litterateur and narrated this story to the Lepchas.

The Lepcha observe 'Sakyoo Rum Fat' every year after harvesting. It is a thanksgiving ceremony and prayers and offerings to those seven immortal Lepcha couples of *Nye Mayel Kyong* who gave them cereals, fruits, vegetable seed to plant in *Mayel Lyang*.

The two Suns

In the creation of the cosmic world, first of all, there were two suns who were sisters; one arose at daybreak, the other at night; thus darkness was never created. As it was always heated, as it was always light the leaves and trees of the forest shriveled up and died; men suffered torments from the heat and could not sleep. So they decided that one day two sisters should be killed, otherwise the world could not be saved. A type of toad, *tun-blo-taluk*, volunteered to kill one of the sisters. He made an arrow from the red cock's comb plant (*kanum*) and shot the younger sister with it. She died at one; her elder sister became very sad and covered herself with a black cloth (*chyalook-dum*). As a result, the whole world became so dark that the wooden pestles (*taling*) turned into snakes, the wooden mortars (*tak-cham*) became tigers and darkness became the cause of most of the evil in the world. Then the fireflies (*tak-pit*) tried to lighten the darkness, but their light was not sufficient. A tree (*num-bum*) turned its leaves over which were of a white colour underneath, but their light was not sufficient either. Half of the human beings and creatures were killed by the snakes and tigers, so they all implored the elder sister to remove the black cloth, but it were to no avail. On seeing the miseries of the world, even the *Rum* (god), creator entered the elder sister to uncover herself but she would not listen.

The bat (*brain*) volunteered to persuade the elder sister to uncover herself armed with a bow and arrow. Going very near to the elder sister the bat said in a nasal tone that if the elder sun remains covered much longer in the intense cold, the entire world will perish. Now the elder sister became very anxious and looked down; she saw the bat was hanging on his bow upside down so that she could not help smiling. As she did so, it became so hot that the bat lost his balance and fell down to the earth; many of her bones were broken down. From that day, the elder sister again appeared in the sky and give shining but there was no warmth. All the creatures met together and decided to cut off the thumb of the toad to pacify the elder sister. After that the elder sister got the power to warm the earth and the younger sister (dead sun) became the moon.

In memory of the younger sister (dead sun) names were given to months. The month of moon is called *lavo*, the name of the period is called *nyom* and the year is called *Nam*, which varies according to the period altered by the addition of an intercalary month (*Nam-cham*).

Origin of Lepcha clans[3]

Under the leadership of Tamsangthing, the Lepcha fought and thrashed Laso Mung Pano, a devil, at the valley of death (*sukver*). When Laso Mung Pano was lying on the ground in defeat, no one was sure if the devil was dead or alive. A brave Lepcha man, holding a sword in his hand approached to Laso Mung Pano and reported that the devil was not completely dead, he was lying unconscious. Fearing the resurrection of Laso Mung, the Lepcha man first broke his both eyes and blinded him; separated the devil's head and legs and crushed the body into many tiny pieces as if the devil could never appear in the earth further. Then the pieces were scattered in the air. When the devil was finally slained, Tamsangthing and the Lepcha man moved to the valley of deliverance (*Tarkaol Tam-E-Tam*).

It is believed that when the Lepchas prayed to the Creator, *Itboo-Deboo*, to save them from the clutches of the devil, Laso Mung Pano, they were given the title of (i) *Munlaommoo*. Those Lepchas who made and prepared weapons like sword, bamfolk etc., to fight against the devil, they were called (ii) *Karvomoo*. Those Lepchas who served Tamsangthing, Nyolik Nyosong Mun, Azaor Boongthing and Lepcha leaders during the battle against the devil were given the title of (iii) *Adenmoo*. Those Lepchas who helped to make bows and arrows to fight Laso Mung Pano were called (iv) *Phyrooong Talimmoo*. Water, rations, and food suppliers were given the title of (v) *Jorimoo*. Those Lepchas who constructed and made bridges, roads, ropes, and bow-string were called (vi) *Brimoo*. The Lepchas who dared to check if Laso Mung Pano's heart was beating and he was breathing, was given the title (vii) *Lutsaommoo*. The Lepcha who broke the eyes and blinded the devil was called (viii) *Seemickmoo*. The Lepcha who separated Laso Mung Pano's head and legs with his bamfolk were called (ix) *Sungngootmoo*. The Lepcha who beat up, crushed the body of Laso Mung Pano into several pieces and spread them in the air from a hilltop was given the title of (x) *Sungdyangmoo*. While conducting the Lepcha rituals, rites, a tradition the priest give offerings to those original ten clans.

Origin of the Lepcha marriage

Thousands of years ago, after performing a long journey, Tarbongthing, a young, robust and powerful Lepcha, at last, explore *Mayel Lyang*. Being tired fatigued and hungry he arrived at a place called *pari pagyen* and looked for a shelter for the night but no village or human settlement was nearby. He saw a fruit tree with hundreds of birds on it. On seeing this he made a plan to set a bamboo trap (*radoo-ramyang*) to catch birds to satisfy his hunger. On the next day, he once again set up the trap and went away. In the afternoon, when he returned to his shelter, he found only a few dry twigs and leaves were hanging instead of birds. Tarbongthing became puzzled, angry as well as curious of thinking that mischievous deeds. On the next day he did the same thing and hid under the bushes; he watched that a young beautiful girl came out from the wood towards the trap and freeing the birds one after another from the trap and putting dry twigs and leaves in it. Meanwhile, Tarbongthing sneaked behind her and caught her firmly. Although surprised the young girl tried to free herself from Tarbongthing but failed. Tarbongthing wanted to know the reason for making free the birds from the trap. In reply, the beautiful girl told that she was the guardian, preserver, and champion of the birds and did not like to cage the birds of *Mayel Lyang* because as like other creatures the birds have equal rights to live freely. During their discussion the beautiful girl told her name as Narip Naom, and place of residence in *Sakyong*; she also gave her willingness to marry Tarbongthing but asked to seek permission first from her mother and uncles and disappeared into the woods.

Tarbongthing returned to his mother, Numkoot Amoo Nyoo, and narrated his stories including his meeting with a young and beautiful girl. He expressed his desire to marry the girl to his mother because he was fall in love with her. Then Numkoot Amoo Nyoo summoned her brothers and sent them to Sakyong to ask for Narip Naom's hands for her son, Tarbongthing. Narip Naom's mother and uncles were also very happy and welcomed the proposal of a marriage between them, however, Narip Naom's mother and uncles said that Tarbongthing and his uncles must adhere to and fulfill the marriage conditions.

A meeting of the Lepchas was convened at Rungjyeng Purtam to finalise the Lepcha marriage customary law and the necessary items to be provided and presented as a bride's price during the wedding to the bride's party. Tarbongthing and his uncles agreed to all the conditions of the Lepcha marriage customary law and the bride price. At the end of the meeting, a bamboo was planted to commemorate the occasion. Thus, the bamboo groove is identified as a sacred grove (*chimoo aeyong moo pobong*) and still sacredly existent in Dzongu Lepcha reserve area. Tarbongthing and his uncles were able to collect the bride price and placed them in front of the bride's mother, uncles, aunts and relatives during the wedding. Thus, the first Lepcha marriage ceremony was solemnised between Narip Naom and Tarbongthing and the first Lepcha Marriage customary law originated in Mayel Lyang. The diehard Lepchas continue to practice their ancient Lepcha Marriage customary law even today. The Lepcha women continue to receive the respect, dignity, and honour from the Lepcha men even today.

During a Lepcha marriage ceremony, *Peeboo* or *Beckboo*, a go between; a boongthing or Mun blessed the newly wedded couple and narrated the story of Tarbongthing and Narip Naom. The Lepcha people believe that marriage is sacred and not only a lasting bond between a Lepcha man and woman, it is a bond between two families, two clans, and two villages. (Chakraborty, 2011)

Origin of traditional beverage: *Chi*

The traditional beverage, the drink is a holy item to the Lepchas popularly termed as *chi*. The figurative speech of *chi* in *Rong* is *Num Feng Moo. Chi* is also known as *chhet syook* or *chhet chhyooko* means power, energy, force, potency, strength, vigour to them. This traditional beverage is extensively used in every phases of life (on the occasion of birth, marriage, and death). During cleansing and naming ceremony (*tungbaong fat*), a newborn baby is fed with a few drops of *chi* by a boongthing (Lepcha priest). After drinking and sharing the *chi* from the same cup during the marriage vows (*sung kyo fat*) a bride and groom become a couple (*nabaom*). As observed in the Lepcha wedding, the immediate relatives of both bride and groom party and the elders' present drink (*chi*) from the same cup and bless the newly married couple. It has also observed during the study that *chi* is also offered to the departed soul at the time of burial and death ceremony with the traditional bamboo cylindrical container (*pathyaot*) and bamboo pipe or straw (*pi-heep*) to mark the observance of rich tradition. It is their belief that the creator Gods and Goddesses (*Itboo-Deboo*); guardian deity (*Kongchen-konglo*) and guardian spirits only accept the *chi* and that is why it is offered to them during several Lepcha ceremonies like *Lee-Rum Fat*, *Chu-Rum Fat*, *Sakyoo-Rum Fat*, *Lyang-Rum Fat*, *Tungrong Hlo-Rum Fat*, *Pik sat*, *Sungkyo Fat* etc. *Chi* is not only an alcoholic beverage but it is also a food to them, therefore, the Lepcha also called it as *chi-zaom*.

According to the Lepcha folklore, when Tamsangthing arrived Dzongu to protect the Lepchas from the wrath of the devil Laso Mung Pano; he found that the morale of Lepcha people was too low and sunken to fight against the devil. To remove fear from the mind of Lepchas, Tamsangthing consecrated a young Mun (*Nyolik-Nyosong*) to rejuvenate the lost morale of the people. Tamsangthing gave supernatural power to the Mun by offering her three young shoots of elephant grass (*pashyaor*). In the beginning Mun found it extremely difficult to communicate and express her thoughts and powers to the horror stricken Lepchas. One day the first Mun (*Nyolik-Nyosong*) heard a humming sound of bumble bee (*tungbum*), got inspired and imitated rhythmically in her prayer. She became successful to communicate the expression of her thoughts to God and got the power to rejuvenate the Lepchas. By using her supernatural power the Mun knew that for the restoration of lost morale of the Lepchas there was a medicine in the form of a fermented object (*bat*), which was only possessed by a sorcerers. The Mun successfully brought the fermented object by a cockroach (*tungdyer palyung*), one of her volunteer. After getting the powerful fermented object (*bat*) Mun cooked millet and then mixed with it to prepare *chi*, fermented beverage and distributed among the Lepcha people to raise their morale for fighting against the devil, Laso Mung Pano. Thus, the fermented beverage was originated and become one of the important food items.

Conclusion

The folklore is a dying tradition to the Lepchas nowadays. Very few Lepcha perhaps know that tradition because of many reasons. Since early period of time, the Lepchas are facing a number of incidents; a blood treaty sealed a friendship between the indigenous Lepchas and immigrant Tibetans, now known as Bhutias. Later on, immigration of the Nepalese as a labourer give a significant impact on the 'Lepcha land' and the timid, shy Lepcha people become lagging behind in education, economy and cornered in every sphere of life; moreover, they have tremendously been exploited by those people. During the course of modernisation their native land is gradually infiltrated with the influx of outsiders other than Bhutias and Nepalese and as a result, the divine ecological settings of Mayel Lyang got disturbed day by day. As more and more cultural contact happens with outsiders in this land, the traditional Lepcha people get the chance to imitate the outside culture leaving their pristine cultural heritage and tradition. Coping with the present situation the Lepchas become educated, modern and have a very limited time to educate themselves with folklore, myths, and legends. It is noticed that with the course of present-day competition a very small boy or girl of the Lepcha society are sent to boarding house away from home to give higher education; naturally he or she get deflected from the essence of such beautiful story of their divine origin, the hidden paradise, the sacred groves and so on. In addition to that day by day with the advent of Lamaism, the importance of traditional priest (boongthing and Mun) become less in their society; the traditional role of boongthing in marriage and death rituals more or less vanished. These significant changes are perhaps major bearings to continue the great tradition of the Lepchas. In spite of that, few Lepchas have already come forward to protect their age-old great tradition as like before, which will indeed be worthy of the society.

Notes

1. As narrated by Sonam Gyatso Lepcha.

2. Collected by Namgyal Lepcha.
3. As narrated by Pempa Tsering Lepcha.

References

Bhattacharya, A. 1937. 'Folk literature of India'. In Suniti Kumar Chatterjee (Eds.): *Cultural Heritage of India*. Calcutta: Ramakrishna Mission Institute of Culture.

Chakraborty, S. 2011. *Myth and Magic of the Lepchas of Sikkim Himalaya.* Unpublished Ph.D. thesis.

Gorer, Geoffrey. 1938. *Himalayan Village: An Account of the Lepchas of Sikkim*. London: M. Joseph Ltd.

Imperial Gazetteer of India. 1908. *Sikkim*, Vol. XXII. Oxford.

Mainwarning, George Byers. 1876. 'A study of plural societies in Sikkim (Lepcha, Bhutia, and Nepalese)'. *Journal of the Japanese Ethnological Society*, 22(182): 15-64.

Sims, C. Martha and Martine Stephen. 2005. *Living Folklore: An Introduction to the Study of People and their Tradition*. pp. 1-2, Logan: Utah State University Press.

Sprigg, R.K. 2005. *Shedding some Light on the History, Language, and Literature of the Lepchas*. Kalimpong. Mani Printing Press.

Tamsang, Lyangsong. 2008. *Lepchas Folklore and Folk Songs*. New Delhi. Sahitya Akademi.

Wilson, A. William. 1988. 'The deeper necessity: Folklore and the humanities'. *Journal of American Folklore*. 101:400.

Chapter - 18

Lifestyle Correlates of Metabolic Syndrome among a Tribal Population Inhabiting Sikkim, India

—*Barun Mukhopadhyay and Sovanjan Sarkar*

Introduction

The Metabolic Syndrome (MS) is characterised by the clustering of several risk factors such as obesity, dyslipidaemia, carbohydrate intolerance and hypertension that influence the development of Non Insulin Dependent Diabetes Mellitus (NIDDM) as well as cardiovascular diseases (CVD) risk factors (Reaven, 1988; Timar *et al.,* 2000). The first official definition of MS was introduced by an expert panel of the World Health Organisation (WHO) in 1998 (Alberti and Zimmet, 1998). Since then continuous attempts to redefine MS were made (NCEP, 2001; Balkau and Charles, 1999). The most recent definition of MS is proposed by the International Diabetes Federation (Alberti *et al.*, 2006), where central obesity as measured by waist circumference (WC) is considered as a core component. The prevalence of MS has drastically risen in parallel with the global obesity and other CVD risk factor epidemic (Zimmet *et al*., 2001; Ford *et al.,* 2002). It is observed that the prevalence estimates of MS among the population living worldwide in non-industrialised societies are sparsely available (Deka *et al.,* 2008).

In the US the prevalence of MS has been estimated to be more than 22 per cent, irrespective of sex (Park *et al.,* 2003). Although MS has been a public health problem of developed countries, it is now increasing notably in the developing nations, including countries of Eastern Mediterranean Region (Alwan, 1993). It has been presumed that the mechanism of MS is based on a complex interaction between genetic, metabolic and behavioural factors (Lidfeldt *et al.,* 2003; Goop, 200). It can be intuitively stated that the transition from a rural traditional lifestyle to an urbanised modern lifestyle leads to a substantial change in socioeconomic and demographic changes. That, in turn, may change education level, occupational status and income level of the population. The changes in these attributes can have an influence on dietary habits, behaviours and physical activity level that in turn affects the MS (Drewmowski and Specter, 2004; Booth *et al*., 2001). The effect of a change in dietary habits and physical activity pattern has been demonstrated in the developing nations, pertaining to CVD and MS (Solomons, 1995). Many studies have reported the association between lifestyle-related factors, including psychosocial factors and MS, along with hypertension, obesity, hypertriglyceridaemia (Everson *et al.,* 2002; Diez Roux *et al*., 2002; Wardle *et al.,* 2002; Wamala, 1999; Brunner *et al.,* 1997). Again, habitual sedentary lifestyle and the lack of physical activity are found to be important factors in the development of MS among the urban population (Erikson *et al*., 1997; Torgensen *et al.,* 1997).

It appears that epidemiological studies showed a high prevalence of MS in urban conglomerate populations (McKeigue *et al*., 1992; Misra and Vikram, 2002; Deepa *et al.,* 2002). The prevalence of MS in an Indian population inhabiting a north Indian city was found to be 22.9 per cent in males, 39.9 per cent in females and 31.6 per cent in total sample considering all ages (Gupta *et al.,* 2004). Among the Indian tribal populations, studies on MS are almost lacking. Furthermore, among the ethnic populations of Northeastern India, many of which are currently exposed to modernising forces study on MS is almost non-existent. However, in a comparative study on the prevalence of MS among the Bhutias of Sikkim was found to be much higher than that of the Totos, another sub-Himalayan tribe inhabiting Terai region of West Bengal (Sarkar *et al*., 2005). The absence of any study in India showing association between a cluster of lifestyle-related variables and MS is only apparent. Such a study is also absent among any of the tribal groups residing in the Northeastern States of the country. The aforesaid facts prompted us to undertake the present study on examining the association of a cluster of lifestyle-related variables on MS among the Bhutias, a tribe residing the eastern Himalayan State of Sikkim.

Research Design and Methods

For the present study, the Bhutias, residing in the town of Gangtok and its neighbourhood, and also those residing in the rural villages of Ralong, Namlung, and Lingding of South District were selected as urban and rural study participants, respectively. The Bhutias posses Mongoloid physical features. Rural Bhutias are mostly agriculturists while the urban Bhutias are predominantly engaged in service and business. After the merger of

Sikkim with the Indian Union in 1975, Bhutias are increasingly taking advantage of expanding developmental programmes in the State. The Sikkimese Bhutias, especially our study participants are exclusively Buddhists. Monogamy is the general norm of marriage among them, but some cases of polygamous marriage are also present. Polyandrous and consanguineous marriages are socially not acceptable among the Bhutias. The Bhutias are mostly non-vegetarians and thrive on carbohydrates, red meat, and milk products. Beef (*langsha*) and pork (*faksha*) are consumed in large amounts. They prepare a traditional edible item from the milk of buffalo named *'churpi'*, which is very rich in saturated fat. Irrespective of sex, consumption of alcohol is very much common among the Bhutias. They drink beer and other alcoholic beverages. Indigenous varieties of beer called *'chhang'* and liquor called *'jaar'* are very popular among them. Further, they regularly consume tea added with salt, but as a result of urbanisation, the use of sugar is now becoming common among the urban Bhutias.

Bhutias of both sexes aged 20 years and above were considered for the study. After an initial household census enumeration in and around Gangtok area, 288 households were systematically selected. From each household, at least one individual (either male or female) or more participated in the study. Thus, 241 males and 266 females constituted the urban sample. Some, who were taking medicine for diabetes, hypertension, dyslipidaemia and other CVDs, were excluded from the study. The overall response rate (>75 per cent for both sexes was satisfactory). All the parameters pertaining to MS, viz. blood pressures, lipid profiles, fasting blood glucose and Waist Circumference was recorded from all the study participants to evaluate the prevalence of MS in the urban sample. Again, 100 males and 100 females were randomly selected from 100 systematically chosen families residing in Gangtok town to collect data on socioeconomic and lifestyle-related variables (socioeconomic status, alcohol consumption, perceived stress, dietary practices, and physical activity pattern).

In the rural area, total enumeration of an entire rural block, considered to be a major Bhutia concentration, was done in selecting study participants. Following the similar inclusion criteria as in the urban area, 228 adults (114 males and 114 females) were selected from 80 families. Correct ages of the study participants, particularly those of older ones, for whom accurate age record was absent, were estimated with the help of a traditional Bhutia calendar which follows a twelve-year cycle.

Data on socioeconomic variables such as education, occupation, monthly household income, media exposure were collected with the help of standard questionnaires (Table 18.1). The education level of each participant was categorised into 'up to primary' (Illiterate to class IV) and 'above primary' (class V and above) groups. Those who are exposed to a minimum of one media (viz. television, newspaper, magazine, and radio) are categorised as 'media exposed'. Data on dietary habits were collected through food frequency questionnaire and 24-hour recall method. A number of servings of each food group per month were used in the inferential statistical analysis. Data on alcohol consumption was recorded as 'drinker' and 'non-drinker'. Smoking status was evaluated by noting whether cigarette smoked regularly or not. However, smoking was excluded from the analysis due to its non-association with hypertension and other CVD risk factors among the study population (Sarkar, 2006). Energy expenditure (in Kcal) was estimated through 24-hour recall method. Perceived activity level was also recorded and used in the statistical analysis. Data on perceived stress was collected through a Likert type pre-tested questionnaire (Levenstein *et al.,* 1993) and perceived stress score index (PSSI) was calculated for each study participant. Waist circumference was measured following standard techniques (Lohman *et al.,* 1988). Blood pressure (BP) measurements of each study participant were recorded for two consecutive times following standard methods i.e., systolic blood pressure (SBP) (Korotkoff phase I) and diastolic blood pressure (DBP) (Korotkoff phase V). A stethoscope and a mercurial sphygmomanometer were used. The blood pressures were taken on the left upper arm with the subject in sitting position after a 10 minutes rest. Both SBP and DBP were taken twice and the average was considered for analyses. Fasting blood glucose level was examined by one drop of whole blood with the help of "Accutrend Alfa" glucometer, made by Roche, Germany. Lipid levels of all the study participants were estimated from 2 ml. of blood in a pathological laboratory in Gangtok following standard techniques using a Reltech-Crony 640 semi-auto analyser and using kits supplied by Human mbH, Germany. While total cholesterol (TC) and triglycerides (TG) were estimated by CHOD-PAP and GPO-PAP methods, respectively, high-density lipoprotein cholesterol (HDL) was estimated by PEG precipitation method. Very low-density lipoprotein cholesterol (VLDL) was calculated as one-fifth of TG and low-density lipoprotein cholesterol (LDL) was derived through a standard formula (LDL = TC – VLDL – HDL). Present study follows the recommended criteria of the International Diabetes Federation (Alberti *et al.,* 2005) for the diagnosis of the MS (WC: >94 cm for males and >80 cm for females; TG: ^{3}150 mg/dL; HDL: <40 mg/dL for males and <50 mg/dL for females; SBP^{3}130 mm Hg and/or DBP^{3} 85 mm Hg; Fasting blood glucose^{3} 100 mg/dL). Individuals, who satisfied WC cut-off and any two other conditions from the rest four criteria, were considered as having MS. Blood pressure and waist circumference was measured by a single measurer (SS). Informed consent was obtained from all the study participants prior to the study. The project was approved by the Institutional Review Board of the Indian Statistical Institute, Kolkata.

Statistical analyses

All statistical analyses have been done with the help of SPSS 11.0 for Windows software. Test of equality of proportion and t-tests were performed to test the significance of the difference between qualitative and quantitative lifestyle-related variables, respectively. Before the inferential statistical analyses, the stepwise discriminant analysis was carried out to identify the set of food groups and socioeconomic variables that significantly discriminate between habitat (i.e. urban and rural) groups. Another set of socioeconomic variables were identified that discriminate between males and females of each habitat group. The identified sets of variables were used in inferential statistical analyses. Test of equality of proportion was separately used to examine the significance of the difference in prevalence of MS between habitat groups and between sexes of each habitat (value not as shown). A t-test was performed to examine the urban-rural difference in mean values of age-adjusted components of MS (table not shown). Logistic regression analysis was used to evaluate the maximum odds ratios (ORs) of the prevalence of MS. Multiple logistic regression analyses were performed to estimate the age-adjusted ORs using lifestyle-related variables as covariates. The analysis was done separately for urban and rural groups, as well as, males and females of each habitat. Wald statistic was used to test the statistical significance.

Results

Urban males (8.7 per cent) and females (54.0 per cent) showed significantly higher ($p<0.05$ and $p<0.001$ for males and females, respectively) prevalence of MS than that of rural males (3.5 per cent) and females (22.8 per cent) (Data not shown).

The descriptive statistics of almost all the quantitative and qualitative lifestyle-related variables showed the significant urban-rural difference, irrespective of sex (Table 18.1). Numbers of servings of different food groups per month were found to be significantly higher for the urban participants, irrespective of sex. Among all the food groups, consumption of vegetables, red meats, and milk products are found to be most prevalent among the study population. Irrespective of sex, PSSI was found to be significantly ($p<0.0001$) higher among the urban participants. The perceived

Table 18.1: Lifestyle related variables, by habitat and sex.

Lifestyle-related variable	Male			Female		
	Urban (100)	*Rural (114)*	*P*	*Urban (100)*	*Rural 114)*	*P*
Cereals	67.28 ± 13.65	66.26 ± 12.54	> 0.05	67.85 ± 13.73	68.19 ± 13.80	> 0.05
Pulses	28.42 ± 22.69	90.82 ± 10.77	< 0.0001	25.65 ± 23.40	90.58 ± 9.17	< 0.001
Tubers	39.83 ± 24.36	13.19 ± 19.04	< 0.0001	45.75 ± 20.59	80.99 ± 14.33	< 0.0001
Vegetables	95.22 ± 32.38	60.49 ± 13.16	< 0.0001	92.35 ± 23.76	58.09 ± 14.46	< 0.0001
Red meats	37.95 ± 22.48	29.01 ± 20.58	< 0.01	34.26 ± 21.90	26.61 ± 21.62	< 0.05
Lean meat	30.46 ± 4.93	10.47 ± 2.01	< 0.001	30.37 ± 4.28	10.49 ± 3.51	< 0.001
Eggs	10.23 ± 12.87	50.03 ± 6.07	< 0.001	10.53 ± 13.80	50.05 ± 6.65	< 0.001
Fish	20.59 ± 3.06	10.15 ± 1.96	< 0.001	20.42 ± 2.87	10.13 ± 2.16	< 0.001
Milk products	75.55 ± 30.32	24.03 ± 20.45	< 0.0001	80.05 ± 30.52	21.01 ± 16.97	< 0.0001
Fruits	16.80 ± 18.67	10.10 ± 6.44	< 0.0001	18.85 ± 22.22	10.02 ± 6.50	< 0.0001
PSSI	00.48 ± 0.06	00.22 ± 0.07	< 0.0001	00.48 ± 0.07	00.20 ± 0.05	< 0.0001
Energy Expenditure (Kcal)	2416.87 554.25	3559.96 1219.05	< 0.0001	2142.18 419.69	236.64 409.93	< 0.05
Activity level More active Less active	20 80	73.68 26.32	< 0.0001	33.00 67.00	80.70 19.30	< 0.0001
Education level Up to primary Above primary	20 80	64.91 35.09	< 0.0001	45.00 55.00	79.82 21.18	< 0.001
Occupation Non-sedentary Sedentary	20 80	73.68 26.32	< 0.0001	12.00 88.00	19.30 80.70	> 0.05
Household income < INR 10,000/m ≥ INR 10,000/m	28.00 72.00	82.45 17.55	< 0.0001	25.00 75.00	80.70 19.30	< 0.0001
Media exposure Non-exposed Exposed	17.00 83.00	78.10 21.90	< 0.0001	18.00 82.00	91.60 80.40	< 0.0001
Alcohol intake Non-drinker Drinker	75.00 25.00	53.43 47.57	< 0.01	90 10	61.06 38.94	< 0.001

Data are n, mean ± sd. and percent. Independent sample t-tests (df = 226) and tests of equality of proportion were performed to ascertain the significance of difference for continuous and per cent values, respectively, between urban and rural participants.

activity level (prevalence of more active) was significantly ($p<0.0001$) higher among the rural participants than their urban counterparts. Among the SES variables, as expected, the education level and household income were significantly ($p<0.001$ to $p<0.0001$) higher among the urban participants. The overwhelming majority of the urban participants, irrespective of sex, is found to be engaged in the sedentary occupation. Significantly ($p<0.0001$) higher prevalence of media exposure was found among the urban participants. Irrespective of sex, consumption of alcoholic beverages is found to be significantly higher among the urban participants.

Stepwise discriminant analysis showed that milk products (Wilks'l=0.417) and media exposure (Wilks'l=0.583) are the most important food group and SES variable, respectively, that discriminate between the habitat groups (Table 18.2). As expected, no food group was selected as significantly discriminating variables between sexes of each habitat group. Among the SES variable, occupation and education were found to be common in the list of variables that significantly discriminate between males and females of both the habitat groups. Additionally, Income (Wilks'l=0.760) and media exposure (Wilks'l=0.642) are found to be significant discriminating variables in urban and rural, respectively.

Table 18.2: Dietary variables and SES traits that significantly discriminate between habitat groups

Urban vs Rural					
Food group	Wilks'	Per cent*	SES trait	Wilks'	Per cent
Milk products	0.417		Media exposure	0.583	
Vegetables	0.334	93.8	Income0.441	86.4	
Tubers	0.309		Occupation	0.437	
Fruits	0.289		Education	0.396	
Eggs	0.282				
Meat groups	0.278				
Male vs Female#					
Urban	Wilks'	%*	RuralWilks'	%	
Occupation	0.859	76.5	Occupation	0.913	89.0
Education	0.782		Media exposure	0.643	
Income	0.760		Education	0.642	

Wilks' is identified by stepwise discriminant analysis which arranges the traits in decreasing order of importance. * Percentage of cases correctly classified by the identified variables. #Only SES traits were considered as no food group was found to be selected as discriminating variable between males and females, irrespective of study area.

Logistic regression analysis revealed significantly higher chance of developing MS among the participants of urban habitat group (OR=0.197, 95 per cent CI=0.118-0.328) when rural habitat was used as a reference (Table 18.3). Females, irrespective of habitat, showed significantly (OR=0.108 and 0.123, 95 per cent CI=0.055-0.214 and 0.041-0.366, respectively for urban and rural) higher chance of developing MS than that of males.

Table 18.3: Maximum likelihood of MetS pertaining to habitat and sex

Factor	*Wald*	*Odds ratio*	*5 per cent CI*	*P*
Habitat Rural Urban	Reference 38.92	0.197	0.118 – 0.328	0.000
Sex Urban male Urban female	Reference 40.92	0.108	0.055 – 0.214	0.000
Rural male Rural female	Reference 14.21	0.123	0.041 - 0.366	0.000

Odds ratio and CI (95 per cent) were derived from logistic regression analysis. Wald statistics were used to test the statistical significance.

Table 18.4: Maximum likelihood of metabolic syndrome pertaining to categorical lifestyle-related variables, by habitat group

Variable	*Sub-category*	*Urban (n=200)*				*Rural (n=228)*			
		Wald	*OR*	*CI (95%)*	*P*	*Wald*	*OR*	*CI (95%)*	*P*
	Lower	Ref.	-	-		Ref.	-	-	
Income	Higher	1.141	0.6	0.234-1.533	> 0.05	2.481	0.193	0.025-1.495	>0.05
	Non-sedentary	Ref.	-	-		Ref.	-	-	
Occupation	Sedentary	24.04	3.952	1.164-13.416	< 0.001	8.767	1.92	0.974-3.365	< 0.05
	Lower	Ref.	-	-		Ref.	-	-	
Education	Higher	1.687	2	0.705-5.619	>0.05	0.631	2.259	0.302-16.863	>0.05
Media	Non-exposed	Ref.	-	-		Ref.	-	-	
	Exposed	0.41	0.72	0.263-1.971	>0.05	1.597	6.396	0.360-113.672	>0.05
Alcohol	Non-drinker	Ref.	-	-		Ref.	-	-	
	Drinker	0.142	0.877	0.443-1.737	>0.05	1.184	0.466	0.118-1.844	>0.05
Energy expenditure		6.027	1.01	0.998-1.100	< 0.01	1.818	1	0.988-1.031	>0.05
Stress		2.658	0.103	0.053-18.844	>0.05	0.378	0.027	0.005-6.819	>0.05
Milk products		0.279	1	0.981-1.111	>0.05	0.896	0.982	0.946-1.020	>0.05
Meat group		4.098	1.02	1.001-1.040	< 0.01	3.39	1.061	0.996-1.131	>0.05
Tubers		0.425	0.994	0.978-1.011	>0.05	0.123	1	0.953-1.049	>0.05
Egg		1.12	0.984	0.954-1.014	>0.05	0.282	0.971	0.869-1.084	>0.05

Multiple logistic regression analyses were performed using dietary, stress, calorie expenditure, alcohol consumption and SES related variables and age as covariates; Wald statistics was used to test the statistical significance; age-adjusted OR and CI (95 per cent) was estimated to evaluate the risk

To compare the impact of lifestyle-related variables on MS, logistic regression analysis was performed separately for urban and rural habitats (Table 18.4). Dietary and SES variables, those significantly discriminate between urban and rural habitats, were used in addition to the other lifestyle-

Table 18.5: Result of logistic regression analysis showing the maximum likelihood of metabolic syndrome pertaining to categorical lifestyle-related variables, by habitat group and sex

Habitat	*Variable*	*Sub-category*	*Male (n=100)*				*Female (n=100)*			
			Wald	*OR*	*CI (95%)*	*P*	*Wald*	*OR*	*CI (95%)*	*P*
Urban	Income	Lower	Ref.	-	-		Ref.	-	-	
		Higher	1.959	0.295	0.053-1.631	>0.05	0.614	1.567	0.509-4.822	>0.05
	Occupation	Non-sedentary	Ref.	-	-		Ref.	-	-	
		Sedentary	0.794	1.591	0.336-7.542	>0.05	0.786	1.264	0.303-5.268	>0.05
	Education	Lower	Ref.	-	-		Ref.	-	-	
		Higher	1.047	1.489	0.191-11.581	>0.05	0.600	1.032	0.318-3.345	>0.05
	Energy expenditure		0.982	1.000	0.978-1.071	>0.05	4.936	1.300	0.988-1.401	< 0.01
	Stress		2.446	0.956	0.914-0.999	>0.05	0.554	0.098	0.020-44.123	>0.05
			Male (n=114)				*Female (n=114)*			
Rural	Occupation	Non-sedentary	Ref.	-	-		Ref.	-	-	
		Sedentary	0.991	5.327	1.133-8.717	>0.05	0.108	0.186	0.036-1.237	>0.05
	Education	Lower	Ref.	-	-		Ref.	-	-	
		Higher	0.015	0.829	0.040-17.380	>0.05	1.647	0.258	0.033-2.042	>0.05
	Media	Non-exposed	Ref.	-	-		Ref.	-	-	
		Exposed	0.015	1.395	0.845-3.791	>0.05	0.545	0.370	0.027-5.179	>0.05
	Energy expenditure		1.401	1.000	0.988-1.300	>0.05	0.167	1.152	0.899-1.500	>0.05
	Stress		3.430	0.998	0.421-2.936	>0.05	0.706	2.906	0.566-14.485	>0.05

Multiple logistic regression analyses were performed using stress, calorie expenditure, and SES related variables and age as covariates; Wald statistics was used to test the statistical significance; age-adjusted OR and CI (95 per cent) was estimated to evaluate the risk.

related variables, as the covariates in the analysis. Individuals engaged in sedentary occupation showed significantly higher age-adjusted odds of having the MS in comparison with their counterparts engaged in a non-sedentary occupation in urban ($p<0.001$) as well as in rural locales ($p<0.05$). Likewise while the group having higher income and education shows higher age-adjusted odds of having MS than those having lower income and education, respectively, media exposure and alcohol drinkers showed higher odds of MS compared to their non-exposed and non-drinker counterparts. Urban participants showed significantly higher age-adjusted ORs, pertaining to energy expenditure (OR=1.010 95 per cent CI=0.998-1.100) and consumption of red meat (OR=1.020 95 per cent CI=1.001-1.040). Dietary variables and energy expenditure do not have any significant impact on the prevalence of MS in the rural habitat, however.

To gain further sex-specific insights on the impact of lifestyle-related variables on MS, age-adjusted odds ratio were estimated through logistic regression analysis, separately for sexes of each habitat (Table 18.5). Perceived stress and energy expenditure were taken as the covariates along with the subset of SES variables that significantly discriminate between the sexes in each habitat. It is observed that higher income, sedentary occupation, and higher education groups showed higher odds of developing MS than lower income, non-sedentary occupation, and lower education groups, respectively. This trend remains similar even separately for both sexes in each habitat. Energy expenditure showed significant impact on the prevalence of MS among the urban females only (OR=1.300 95 per cent CI=0.988-1.401; $p<0.01$) and not among urban males or rural participants, of both sexes.

Conclusions

Increasing modernisation of many developing countries, including India, has a manifold effect on the lifestyles of their populations in general and urban populations in particular. It is generally observed that the process of modernisation creates an environment for the traditional populations to less physical activity and indulge in the high fat-rich diet. This, in turn, influences in increasing the prevalence of CVD risk factors viz. obesity, dyslipidaemia and hypertension, as well as NIDDM.

The present study, which to our understanding, is probably the first of its kind conducted in India, especially, in her Northeastern region, depicted a very high probability of MS among the urban individuals compared to their rural counterparts as has also been shown elsewhere (Solomons, 1995). Females, irrespective of habitat, have also shown higher odds of MS in comparison with males which corroborates the study among the US (Freiberg *et al.*, 2004). The prevalence of MS is found to be significantly higher among the females than that of the males, irrespective of habitat (data not shown). Our findings are opposite to the trend reported among the French (Dallonggeville *et al.*, 2005) and the Mexicans (Ramirez-Vargas *et al.*, 2007).

Urban Bhutias are engaged in the white-collar jobs which need minimum work related energy expenditure. Those who are engaged in business, mostly traders, are also not needed to spend high energy during the working hours. On the contrary, in the rural setting, the study participants are overwhelmingly agriculturists, and therefore need substantial energy expenditure for their agricultural work. The females of either habitat are mostly housewives and usually spend most of their times in household chores. Again, the urban participants are fond of fat-rich snacks available in the market, which are very infrequent in the rural area. It is also observed that the perceived psychosocial stress level is also found to be higher among the urban individuals and affects blood pressure, blood lipid and obesity independently (Sarkar and Mukhopadhaya, 2008). It is therefore clear that all these lifestyle-related variables have influenced the adverse profile of MS in the study population. It will be necessary to formulate an appropriate cardiovascular health education strategy to reduce the prevalence of MS in the study population, especially among the adolescents and young adults.

Acknowledgements

Authors are indebted to all the study participants for their cooperation to conduct the study. Indian Statistical Institute is gratefully acknowledged for financial and other logistic supports.

References

Alberti, KG, PJ. Zimmet and J. Shaw, 2005. 'The metabolic syndrome-A new worldwide definition'. *Lancet* 366: 1059-1062.

Alberti, KG and PJ. Zimmet, 1998. 'Definition, diagnosis, and classification of diabetes mellitus, provisional report of a WHO consultation'. *Diabet Med* 15: 539-553.

Alwan, A. 1993.'Cardiovascular disease in the Eastern Mediterranean region'. *World Health Stat Q* 46: 97-100.

Balkau, B, and MA. Charles, 1999. 'Comment on the provisional report from the WHO consultation. European group for the study of insulin resistance'. *Diabet Med* 16: 442-443.

Booth, SL, JF. Sallis, C. Ritenbaugh, HO. Hill, LL. Birch, LD. Frank, K. Glanz, DA. Himmel-green, M. Mudd, BM. Popkin, KA. Rickard, S. St Jeor, and NP. Hays, 2001. 'Environmental and societal factors affect food choice and physical activity: rationale, influences, and leverage points'. *Nutr Rev* 59:S21-S39.

Brunner, EJ, MG Marmot, K Nanchahal, MJ Shipley, SA Stansfeld, M Juneja, and KG Alberti, 1997. 'Social inequality in coronary risk: central obesity and the metabolic syndrome: evidence from the Whitehall II Study'. *Diabetologia* 40:1341-1349.

Dallongeville, J, D Cottel, J Ferrieres, D Arveiler, A Bingham, JB Ruidavets, B Haas, P Ducimetiere, and P Amouyel, 2005. 'Household income is associated with the risk of metabolic syndrome in a sex-specific manner'. *Diabetes Care* 28: 409-415.

Deepa, R, CS Shanthirani, G Premalatha, NG Sastry, and V Mohan. 2002. 'Prevalence of insulin resistance syndrome in a selected south Indian population–The Chennai urban population study-7 (CUPS-7)'. *Ind J Med Res* 115: 118-127.

Deka, R, NS Narancic, H Xi, S Turek, M Cubrilo-Turek, D Vrhovski-Hebrang, B Janicijevic, A Tomljenovic, L Szirovicza, L Jin, R Chakraborty, and P Rudan, 2008. 'Metabolic syndrome in an island population of the eastern Adriatic coast of Croatia'. *Coll Anthropol* 32: 85-91.

Diez Roux, AV, DR Jacobs, and CI Kiefe, 2002. 'Neighbourhood characteristics and components of the insulin resistance syndrome in young adults: The Coronary Artery Risk Development in Young Adults (CARDIA) Study'. *Diabetes Care* 25:1976-1982.

Drewnowski, A, and SE Specter, 2004. 'Poverty and obesity: The role of energy density and energy costs'. *Am J Clin Nutr* 79: 6-16.

Eriksson, J, S Taimela, and VA Koivisto, 1997. 'Exercise and the metabolic syndrome'. *Diabetologia* 40:125-135.

Everson, SA, SC Maty, JW Lynch, and GA Kaplan. 2002. 'Epidemiologic evidence for the relation between socioeconomic status and depression, obesity, and diabetes'. *J Psychosom res* 53: 891-895.

Executive summary of the Third Report of the National Cholesterol Education Program (NCEP) expert panel on detection, evaluation, and treatment of high blood cholesterol in adults (adult treatment panel III). 2001. *JAMA* 285: 2486-2497.

Ford, ES, WH Giles, and WH Dietz. 2002. 'Prevalence of the metabolic syndrome among US adults: Findings from the third National Health and Nutritional Examination Survey'. *JAMA* 287: 356-369.

Freiberg, MS, HJ Cabral, TC Heeren, RS Vasan, and RC Ellison. 2004. 'Alcohol consumption and the prevalence of the metabolic syndrome in the U.S'. *Diabetes* Care 27: 2954-2959.

Groop, L. 2000. 'Genetics of the metabolic syndrome'. *Br J Nutr* 83 Suppl 1: S39-S48.

Gupta, R, PC Deedwania, A Gupta, S Rastogi, RB Panwar, and K Kothari. 2004. 'Prevalence of metabolic syndrome in Indian urban population'. *Int J Cardiol* 97: 257-261.

Levenstein, S, C Prantera, V Varvo, ML Scribano, E Berto, C Luzi, and A Andreoli.1993. 'Development of the perceived stress questionnaire: A new tool for psychosomatic research'. *Journal of Psychosomatic Research* 37:19-32.

Lidfeldt, J, P Nyberg, C Nerbrand, G Samsioe, B Schersten, and CD Agardh. 2003. 'Socio-demographic and psychosocial factors are associated with features of the metabolic syndrome: the Women's health in the Lund Area (WHILA) study'. *Diabetes Obes Metab* 5:106-112.

Lohman, TG, AF Roche, and R Martorell.1988. *Anthropometric Standardisation Reference Manual*, Champaign, Illinois: Human Kinetics Books.

McKeigue, PM, T Pierpoint, JE Ferrie, and MG Marmot.1992. 'Relationship of glucose intolerance and hyperinsulinaemia to body fat pattern in south Asians and Europeans'. *Diabetologia* 35 : 785-791.

Misra, A, and NK Vikram. 2002. 'Insulin resistance syndrome (metabolic syndrome) and Asian Indians'. *Curr Sci* 83: 1483-1487.

Park, YW, S Zhu, L Palaniappan, S Heshka, MR Carnethon, and SB Heymsfield.2003. 'The metabolic syndrome: Prevalence and association risk factor findings in the US population from the Third National Health and Nutrition Examination Survey, 1988-1994'. *Arch Intern Med* 163: 427-436.

Ramirez-Vargas, E, MR Arnaud-Vinas, and H Delisle. 2007. 'Prevalence of the metabolic syndrome and associated lifestyles in adult males from Oaxaca, Mexico'. *Salud Publica Mex* 49: 94-102.

Reaven, GM (Banting Lecture). 1988 'Role of insulin resistance in human disease'. *Diabetes* 37:1595-1607.

Sarkar, S, M Das, B Mukhopadhyay, CS Chakraborty, and PP Majumder. 2005. 'Prevalence of metabolic syndrome in two tribal populations of the sub-Himalayan region of India: Ethnic and rural-urban difference'. *Am J Hum Biol* 17:814-817.

Sarkar, S, and B Mukhopadhyay. 2008. 'Perceived psychosocial stress and cardiovascular risk: observations among the Bhutias of Sikkim, India'. *Stress and Health* 24: 23-34.

Sarkar, S. 2006. *Risk of Cardiovascular Disease in Relation to Contrasting Lifestyles among the Bhutias of Sikkim*. Unpublished Ph.D. thesis. University of Calcutta, Kolkata, India.

Solomons, NW, and R Gross. 1995. 'Urban nutrition in developing countries'. *Nutr Rev*. 53:90-95.

Timar, O, F Sestier, and E Levy. 2000. 'Metabolic syndrome X: A review'. *Can J Cardiol* 16: 779-789.

Torjensen, PA, KI Birkeland, SA Anderssen, I Hjermann, I Holme, and P Urdal. 1997. 'Lifestyle changes may reverse the development of the insulin resistance syndrome. The Oslo Diet and Exercise Study: A randomized trial'. *Diabetes Care* 20:26-31.

Wamala, SP, J Lynch, M Horsten, MA Mittleman, K Schenck-Gustafsson, and K Orthgomer. 1999. 'Education and the metabolic syndrome in women'. *Diabetes Care* 22:1999-2003.

Wardle, J, J Waller, and MJ Jarvis. 2002. 'Sex differences in the association of socioeconomic status with obesity'. *Am J Pub Health* 92: 1299-1304.

Zimmet, P, KG Alberti, and J Shaw. 2001. Global and societal implications of the diabetes epidemic. *Nature* 414: 782-787.

Index

H

I